D0421634

Book No. **03007125**

30121 0 03007125

National Styles
of
Humor

Recent Titles in
Contributions to the Study of Popular Culture

Behold the Mighty Wurlitzer: The History of the Theatre Pipe Organ
John W. Landon

Mighty Casey: All-American
Eugene C. Murdock

The Baker Street Reader: Cornerstone Writings about Sherlock Holmes
Philip A. Shreffler, editor

Dark Cinema: American *Film Noir* in Cultural Perspective
Jon Tuska

Seven Pillars of Popular Culture
Marshall W. Fishwick

The American West in Film: Critical Approaches to the Western
Jon Tuska

Sport in America: New Historical Perspectives
Donald Spivey, editor

Screwball Comedy: A Genre of Madcap Romance
Wes D. Gehring

Buckskins, Bullets, and Business: A History of Buffalo Bill's Wild West
Sarah J. Blackstone

S. J. Perelman: A Critical Study
Steven H. Gale

The Rhetorics of Popular Culture: Advertising, Advocacy, and Entertainment
Robert L. Root, Jr.

In Manors and Alleys: A Casebook on the American Detective Film
Jon Tuska

National Styles of Humor

Edited by
Avner Ziv

Contributions to the Study of Popular Culture
Number 18

GREENWOOD PRESS

New York • Westport, Connecticut • London

STAFFORDSHIRE
POLYTECHNIC
LIBRARY

STAFFORDSHIRE
POLYTECHNIC

11 APR 1991

CLASS No.
809.7

Library of Congress Cataloging-in-Publication Data

National styles of humor.

(Contributions to the study of popular culture, ISSN
0198–9871 ; no. 18)
Bibliography: p.
Includes index.
1. Wit and humor—History and criticism. I. Ziv,
Avner. II. Series.
PN6147.N34   1988   809.7   87–23635
ISBN 0–313–24992–X (lib. bdg. : alk. paper)

British Library Cataloguing in Publication Data is available.

Copyright © 1988 by Avner Ziv

All rights reserved. No portion of this book may be
reproduced, by any process or technique, without the
express written consent of the publisher.

Library of Congress Catalog Card Number: 87–23635
ISBN: 0–313–24992–X
ISSN: 0198–9871

First published in 1988

Greenwood Press, Inc.
88 Post Road West, Westport, Connecticut 06881

Printed in the United States of America

∞

The paper used in this book complies with the
Permanent Paper Standard issued by the National
Information Standards Organization (Z39.48–1984).

10 9 8 7 6 5 4 3 2 1

Contents

Introduction

Humor and laughter make life more bearable, sometimes even
enjoyable.

L. Weiss
"Philosophie et vie" (1951)

Humor and the physiological response to it, laughter, are universal. As Rabelais
is quoted in the article on French humor: "Laughter is what characterizes man."
While laughter, the main response to humor, can be defined, measured and
described, humor itself is an elusive concept. As with many psychological concepts, precise definitions are impossible. If you are asked to think about and
name someone who has humor and someone who doesn't, you can do it easily.
But when you try to define *humor*, it becomes much more difficult. For a scholarly
example about the difficulties inherent in definitions, one can read the article in
which Robert Miles tried to define the concept *definition*. He arrived at twelve
perfectly valid definitions of the term (1957).

If concepts in humanities are not easy to define, theories proposing to explain them are even more difficult. However, this did not stop some of the most brilliant philosophers from proposing theories of humor. Their work is fascinating but never completely satisfying. George Mikes, the British humorist, expressed it rather nicely. Talking about philosophers' efforts to create theories, he wrote: "The philosopher is like a good athlete on the double bar; his movements are beautiful; his skill is breath-taking; his achievement admirable. But when he jumps off, he is where he was before he started: he had achieved nothing, he had progressed nowhere. . . . There is not one single statement—however simple, innocuous and self-evident—on which philosophers agree" (Mikes, 1971, p. 19).

Theories on humor have a long history. Since Plato and Aristotle, philosophers such as Kant, Schopenhauer, and Hobbes, writers such as Baudelaire and George Eliot, and even humorists such as Leacock and Mikes have proposed theories to explain why people laugh. Diligent people have summarized and presented these theories in learned books (Greig, 1923; Piddington, 1933; Bergler, 1956; Keith-Spiegel, 1972). There are more than a hundred such theories, some of course following the classic academic dictum on innovative research: "Give old phenomena new names."

In full awareness of the danger, I shall nonetheless define humor, knowing perfectly well that not all will agree with the proposed definition. The definition is necessary in order to make the reader aware of what we, the writers of this book, mean by humor and the physiological phenomena most frequently accompanying it: laughter and smiling.

LAUGHTER, SMILING, AND HUMOR

Laughter is a daily phenomenon in humans, clearly visible and audible. It can be measured with great precision, and the best description of the physiological process of laughter was offered at the beginning of the century by Norbert Dearborn. He wrote:

There occur in laughter and more or less in smiling, clonic spasm of the diaphragm, in number ordinarily about eighteen perhaps, and contraction of most of the muscles of the face. The upper eyelid is elevated, as are also, to some extent, the brows, the skin over the glabella, and the upper lip, while the skin at the outer canthi of the eyes is characteristically puckered. The nostrils are moderately dilated and drawn upward, the tongue slightly extended, and the cheeks distended and drawn somewhat upward; in persons with the pinnal muscles largely developed, the pinnae tend to incline forwards. The lower jaw vibrates or is somewhat withdrawn (doubtless to afford all possible air to the distending lungs), and the head, in extreme laughter, is thrown backward; the trunk is straightened even to the beginning of bending backward, until (and this usually happens soon), fatigue-pain in the diaphragm and accessory abdominal muscles causes a marked proper flexion of the trunk for its relief. The whole arterial vascular system is dilated, with consequent blushing from the effect on the dermal capillaries of the face and neck, and at times the scalp and hands. From the same cause, in the main, the eyes often slightly bulge forwards and the lachrymal gland becomes active, ordinarily to a degree only to cause a ''brightening'' of the eyes, but often to such an extent that the tears overflow entirely their proper channels. (Dearborn, 1900, p. 853)

Fortunately, we are not aware that our body goes through such changes during laughter. We are conscious of the pleasure produced by it and by the special meaning transmitted in the humorous message which made us laugh. While physiologically laughter is well understood, psychologically it is certainly more complex, since it can communicate many things. For instance, there is social laughter, with which we intend to signal to others that we understood and appreciated a joke. There is laughter of derision, victory, embarrassment, and even hysteria. From this, it should be clear that stimuli other than humor can produce laughter.

Smiling can also be described from the physiological aspect. More than a century ago, Darwin wrote of the smile:

By drawing backwards and upwards of the corners of the mouth, through the contraction of the great zygomatic muscles, and by the raising of the upper lip, the cheeks are drawn upwards. Wrinkles are thus formed under the eyes, and, with old people, at the outer ends. . . . As in laughing and broadly smiling the cheeks and upper lip are much raised, the nose appears to be shortened, and the skin on the bridge becomes finely wrinkled in transverse lines, with other oblique longitudinal lines on the sides. The upper front teeth are commonly exposed. A well marked naso-labial ford is formed, which runs from the wing of each nostril to the corner of the mouth. (Darwin, 1872, p. 210)

As with laughter, the psychological meanings of the smile can be numerous and varied. A welcoming smile, a smile of recognition, and an expression of embarrassment are just a few examples.

Clearly, then, laughter and smiling are not exclusively responses to humor. However, they are the main reaction to it and thus can be used in a definition of humor.

Humor is therefore defined as a social message intended to produce laughter or smiling. As with any social message, it fulfills certain functions, uses certain techniques, has a content, and is used in certain situations. These aspects of humor can be understood as relating to the questions of *why* people use humor (its functions), *how* it is transmitted (techniques), *what* it communicates (content), and *where and when* it is communicated (situation). Some of these aspects of humor are universal, characterizing humor everywhere. Others are more influenced by culture.

At the present state of knowledge, theoretically one can see these aspects of humor on a continuum from universal to cultural. On this continuum techniques should be considered as most universal. There is no society in which humor has not been reported to exist. In all anthropological research in which cultures have been compared, the techniques of humor have been found to be the same.

Incongruity, surprise, and local logic (i.e., something that seems logical in a certain context) are the main elements in all humor. These are cognitive elements, and since cognitive processes are universal (as are the physiological ones involved in laughter and smiling), there are no reasons to expect national or cultural differences. Next on the continuum are the functions of humor. They are certainly universal because they reflect human needs. However, certain functions would be more dominant in some cultures than in others. Closer to the cultural end of the continuum we would find the contents of humor, which are more influenced by society. Probably societies differ most in the situations in which humor is used and considered appropriate. Since there are no differences in humor techniques between cultures and nations, we shall look into the functions of humor. The contents and situations will be detailed in each chapter concerning national humor.

THE UNIVERSAL FUNCTIONS OF HUMOR

Humor is a way of expressing human needs in a socially accepted manner. In *Jokes and Their Relationship to the Unconscious* (1905), Freud wrote about the ways humor can deal with social taboos. The two great social taboos are aggression and sexuality, and most humor expresses needs in these two areas. Expression of sexual and aggressive needs in a socially accepted way helps the individual to economize the psychic energy necessary to inhibit these pulsions and thus release psychological tensions. Theoretically, it can be expected that less aggressive and sexual humor exists in cultures where there are no taboos concerning these drives. Unfortunately, no research has been undertaken to determine cultural differences in the aggressive and sexual functions of humor.

Another theory concerning the function of humor was proposed by the French philosopher Henri Bergson. His book *Laughter* (1911) proposed what is known today as the social function of humor. In his view, we laugh at forms of behavior or thought that are contrary to what is socially expected and accepted. Therefore, laughter has a punitive effect aiming at correcting behavior. Satire may be the best example of humor fulfilling this social function.

As a defense mechanism, humor is used in order to laugh at things that frighten us. Death and illness are examples. When we joke about them, it seems for a short while that they are less terrible and we don't take them tragically. The proof: we can even laugh at them. "Gallows humor" or "black humor" expresses this aspect of the defensive function of humor. Another defensive aspect is self-disparaging humor, instances in which we ourselves are "victims" of the joke. We are thus able to laugh at ourselves, to see our sense of our own importance in a different way, and to laugh at the misfortunes we encounter. Some see in self-disparagement the essence of humor, the ability to see the ridiculous in our own behavior.

Finally, in all humor there is an intellectual aspect. By twisting the usual rules of logical thinking, humor allows a momentary feeling of freedom. Absurd humor, nonsense, and wordplay are examples of intellectual humor.

The theory concerning these functions of humor is presented in detail in one of my books (Ziv, 1984), and all the authors of the articles in this book used it in presenting and analyzing the humor of their individual countries. As a result, readers will be able to note the differences among national styles of humor in using one or another of these functions. Although these functions are universal, cultural histories and backgrounds influence them. Some cross-cultural research on humor has pointed out such differences. For example, hostile jokes were found to be more appreciated by American students than by Japanese or Senegalese since "aggression and violence are more prevalent and salient to Americans" (Goldstein, 1977, p. 167). Another research project found that when students were asked to report jokes they enjoyed, American students wrote more aggressive and sexual ones than Belgian and Hong Kong students (Cassell and Goldstein, 1977). In the chapters of this book, differences in national styles of humor are evident. For instance, while sexual humor seems an old and dominant trend in French humor, it is very rare in Belgian humor. Intellectual aspects are dominant in British humor but are less prominent in Yugoslav humor. The chapters of this book explain the reasons for these differences in the light of the historical trends in the development of these cultures.

THE ARTICLES ON NATIONAL STYLES OF HUMOR

As mentioned above, the greatest differences among cultures should be found in the contents and situations of humor. Researchers have found that while most American jokes are sexual and aggressive, Chinese jokes deal more with social interaction, and nonliterate cultures have more jokes about physical environment (Shultz, 1977). Although all chapters in this book are written about nations having in common what is called a Western culture, differences clearly exist. First of all, languages differ, but history and tradition also create differences. Because humor reflects a nation's life, differences among national forms of humor can be expected.

Some of the reasons for the differences in the humor of different nations can be found in social salience of diverse topics. For instance, one can find many jokes about drinking and fistfighting in Irish humor. Jokes on these topics are practically nonexistent in Israel. The social value attributed to humor is also different among nations: leaders in the United States use humor much more frequently than do those in France or Italy. Radio and television make great use of humorous programs in the United States and Great Britain. In Belgium, Yugoslavia, and Israel, such programs are rare. Pioneer nations, such as the United States, Australia, and Israel developed in the beginning certain styles of humor. Tall tales and exaggerations are typical of pioneer culture; they are rare in "older" nations.

These, and many other differences are presented and explained in the articles

STAFFORDSHIRE POLYTECHNIC LIBRARY

that follow. As this book is the first comparing national styles of humor, it is far from perfect and certainly readers will regret that a particular topic or a humorist did not receive the place it should. The selection of nations is not as representative as I would have liked. Because the serious study of humor is quite new in some countries, there was little prior research to draw upon and scholars were not available to undertake the task.

The way I found the collaborators of the book is not as fortuitous as it may seem. Among the 483 papers presented at the Five International Conferences on Humor (see appendix A), one finds the greatest number of contributors from the United States, followed by Great Britain, Israel, Ireland, Canada, and France. Other countries were represented by only a handful of scholars (less than five), a fact reflecting the paucity of humor research at this stage in these countries. As a first step in my research for collaborators, I contacted scholars from the six countries having the greatest number of presenters at the International Conference. Four of these are included in the book. Others worked hard and with great enthusiasm—hence the contributions from Australia, Belgium, Italy and Yugoslavia.

Again, the selection of nations is not as rich as I would have liked but the material presented is fresh and fascinating, and the authors diligently went about their research in a way designed to facilitate comparative study. Each chapter studies the historical development of humor with emphasis on the twentieth century and contemporary forms and trends. Included in the survey are traditional and popular forms of humor and humor in literary, performing and visual arts, and the mass media. As noted above, each author also assesses the national manifestations of the universal functions of humor. A bibliography of sources for further study completes each chapter.

It has been my pleasure to edit and present the combined efforts of these fine scholars, and it is my hope that the book will open up new avenues of research in cross-cultural humor. I also hope that it will reveal new horizons toward a better understanding of unfamiliar cultures. It is certainly a good way to understand others by looking into one of the forms of behavior most common to all people: humor and laughter.

REFERENCES

Bergler, E. (1956) *Laughter and the Sense of Humor*. New York: Intercontinental Medical Books.

Bergson, H. (1911) *Laughter: An Essay on the Meaning of the Comic*. New York: Macmillan.

Cassell, P. J. and Goldstein, J. H. (1977) "Social Occasions for Joking: A Cross-Cultural Study." In *It's a Funny Thing, Humor*. Ed. Chapman, A. J. and Foot, H. C. London: Pergamon Press, 193–197.

Darwin, C. (1872) *The Expression of the Emotions in Man and Animals*. London: Murray.

Dearborn, G.V.N. (1900) "The Nature of the Smile and the Laugh." *Science* 9: 851–56.

Freud, S. (1976) *Jokes and Their Relation to the Unconscious*. London: Pelican (originally published in 1905).

Goldstein, J. H. (1977) "Cross Cultural Researcher: Humor Here and There." In *It's A Funny Thing, Humor*. Ed. Chapman, A. J. and Foot, H.C. London: Pergamon Press, 1967–74.

Greig, J.Y.T. (1923) *The Psychology of Laughter and Comedy*. New York: Dodd & Mead.

Keith-Speigel, P. (1972) "Early Conceptions of Humor: Varieties and Issues." In *The Psychology of Humor*. Ed Goldstein, J. H. and McGhee, P. E. New York: Academic Press.

Mikes, G. (1971) *Laughing Matter: Towards a Personal Philosophy of Wit and Humor*. New York: Library Press.

Miles, K. L. (1957) "On Defining Intelligence." *British Journal of Educational Psychology* 27: 153–65.

Piddington, R. (1933) *The Psychology of Laughter: A Study in Social Adaptation*. London: Figurehead.

Shultz, T. R. (1977) "A Cross Cultural Study of the Structure of Humor." In *It's a Funny Thing, Humor*. Ed. Chapman, A. J. and Foot, H. C. London: Pergamon Press, 175–79.

Ziv, A. (1984) *Personality and Sense of Humor*. New York: Springer.

National Styles
of
Humor

Humor in Australia

Australian history is almost always picturesque; indeed, it is so curious and strange, that it is itself the chiefest novelty the country has to offer, and so it pushes the other novelties into second and third place. It does not read like history, but like the most beautiful lies. And all of a fresh new sort, no mouldy old stale ones. It is full of suprises, and adventures, and incongruities, and contradictions, and incredibilities; but they are all true, they all happened.

Mark Twain
Following the Equator (1897)

The authors gratefully acknowledge Vane Lindesay, Jeff Dugan, Andrew Williams, Vernon Teyrill, John Jeffries, Keith Dunstan, John Clarke, Ian McFayden, Jim Bridges, Johney Ladd, Ian Oshlack, Peter Weiniger, John-Michael Howson, Peter Tacthell, Phillip Adams, and the assistance given by the staff of the State Library of Victoria, Derek Whitehead, and Chief Librarian Moira McKennon. Special thanks to Jo Pittendrigh and Robert King Crawford for their advice and help.

BACKGROUND

"History," said Horace Walpole, "makes one shudder and laugh by turn." The history of Australia since the white man's discovery of the country in 1788 is small as histories go—and there is much to make one shudder—and yet, from its anguished and miserable beginnings, the background of Australian humorous expression evolved.

Australia was the last continent to be discovered by Europeans. The First Fleet, consisting of 750 Irish, Scottish, and English men and women convicts and children and 550 officers, marines and wives and children, clung to life made unbearable by isolation and hardship—and tenuously survived until the end of the century. In any assessment of Australian traditions, culture, and characteristics, the sheer size, remoteness, and emptiness of the country must be emphasized. The sixth largest country in the world, it is now, 200 years after the first white man landed, populated by *less* than 16,000,000 people.

It was from this tortured beginning that the whole tradition of humor was spawned in those first fledgling years. Apart from a small burp of ethnic influence, it is the same sardonic irreverence and lack of respect for authority which characterizes the mainstream of indigenous Australian humor to this day.

The humor of the colonial convicts typified their character and those who held them in captivity. The blend of isolation and the relentless demands of the elements is perpetuated in many stories and jokes of the early settlers. The underdog battling to survive in a hostile environment, and the realization that things are so lousy that you can only laugh, that you can't win, is a constant text in Australian humor.

The harsh and mysterious land, with its inhabitants of convicts and free settlers and law and judiciary, soon imprinted its character on the people. The Cockney twang and the soft lilt of Ireland and gentle vowels of English countries and Scottish inflections, all flattened together and became the laconic Australian accent. The land imposed its awesome mark on the settlers. Myths and traditions were formed and endured largely unquestioned until World War II.

The influences that shaped the Australian into a positive self-image were the brute fact of Australian geography and the tradition of "mateship," a consciously held substitute for religion. The he-man image weaves a thread throughout almost the whole psychological fabric of Australian society. The ribald aggressiveness of the humor finds expression in the mateship of segregation and does not include women in its aura. While most Australian men would probably deny it, there is vacillation in the creed of mateship that displays of soft core. In stories, folklore, and legends, the sacrifices recorded show a care that is devoted.

Anthropologist Robert Brain in his book *Rites, Black and White* (1979) says:

White Australian men, at certain periods of their life-cycle and also for long weary stretches of their history, have been deprived of women. A frank acceptance of Faute de

Mieux homosexuality has never existed in western societies with Christian traditions. In Australia its place has been taken by a very close form of institutionalized friendship known as mateship (p. 180).

The very nature of the settlement, combined with the scarcity of women (the ratio was five to one), suggests that the stories told among mates in the drinking places today reflect an ethos which has persisted from those early days of taverns, tents, wharves, isolated camps, and outback sheds of the early settlement. Men like to participate rather than listen.

Entertainments were few. Convict shows under the auspices of the authorities were occasionally performed in the first few years. "David Collins, the judge advocate wrote 'they professed no higher aim than humbly to excite a smile' " (West, 1978), but no evidence of any other entertainments exists until the end of the century. There was no training in the passive role of listening, and Australian men participated in songs and yarns between themselves. There is still some antipathy to comic peformers today—national acceptance has been reserved for few comics, and Australian women are divided in their acceptance of even these few. This is not surprising, given the background of male domination and the shortage of women.

At the time of the gold rush in 1851 the American tradition of the tall story was introduced into Australia, its essence of exaggeration, fantasy, and nonsense related to the spaciousness of the land, and the pioneering, anything-possible attitudes of the people in the bush.

As the nineteenth century drew to a close, the male/female ratio evened up, but the effects of male predominance were still very much evident in the humor. The mold had settled into an undeniably typical form: the ironic, understated deadpan humor.

With the Federation of the Australian States in 1901, the humor had matured, it had shape and style and a point of view, but the feeling persisted that everything worth producing was produced overseas. This included comedy and humor which saw overseas artists and imported plays dominate Australian entertainment. The comedy cringe persisted to a large degree until very recent years, when an awareness of Australian cultural worth brought a resurgence of national pride. These constant assaults from the earliest music hall entertainers, and the American and English television influences, have in no way dented the characteristic humor; Australians seem to be secure and content with what makes them laugh. The current wave of comics would find almost total acceptance from the early pioneers. This feeling earlier led to a particular attitude called "knocking" which denigrated almost everything—politicians, artists, writers, institutions.

The bush attitudes and humor stemming from the *Bulletin*, the magazine that had fostered local and humorous talent from the latter part of the last century, were expressed in the digger humor of the 1914–18 war against Germany. The self-mocking rebellious disrespect for authority was in the trench jokes and war wit of the Aussie soldier. The legendary glow of "Anzac" was to elevate the "digger" into a bold and bronzed demigod, the apotheosis of the bushman.

In the wake of World War I Australia was emerging as an industrial nation with great changes in the political, social, and economic fields. There was little change in the humor of the country except for a heightening of the national characteristics in the harsh days of the depression at the beginning of the 1930s.

The tremendous advancement in what Evan Esar called "Techno Comedy" (film, radio, video, etc.) were the major influences on American humor in the 1930s and 1940s (1978, p. 1), and the same can be said for Australia. In 1939, once again, the country was at war with Germany, and Australia's humor was reflected in the cartoon strip *Bluey and Curley*. The black and white artist, Alex Gurney, captured all the democratic humor of the digger, and indeed Australia, in the comic strip of the two soldier mates.

The national character of any country is nothing more than a description of the dominant group in it. The curious anomaly is that the dominant group in Australia today, the white-collar worker suburbanites who occupy 75 percent of the country's coastal cities, have not strayed from the fundamental elements of their historical background.

Since the landing of the First Fleet in 1788, there has been a slow and significant change in the direction of Australian humor. The basic style remained the same, but economic, political, and social changes influenced its direction. In the twentieth century, the booming economy of the fifties, the continual social changes of the sixties, the self-identification period of the seventies, all have been factors in the process. The democratic humor attitudes of the pioneers of Australia were prominent in this self-discovery humor scene. The comedy cringe, together with the cultural inferiority complex, finally all but disappeared in the eighties. The new nationalism that is being built is asserted by the traditional humor that now questions and confronts, and as Mark Twain said in 1897, still is full of surprises, incongruities, and contradictions.

TRADITIONAL FORMS AND EXPRESSIONS IN HUMOR BEFORE THE TWENTIETH CENTURY

Popular Forms

Humorous Language

By the very nature of the establishment of the colony, its convict origins, and what Geoffrey Blainey, Australian historian, calls the "tyranny of distance" (1968), the early settlers breathed in colloquialisms from the social environment air. It is the language which is originated and used by people seeking to deal with the contingencies of a world they have to endure, master, enjoy, or fall victim to. Through it, the national identity was expressed and recognized. Humorous expression has evolved and can boast one of the most original and individual colloquial languages in the English-speaking world. "Not much chop,'' meaning not very good, has survived since 1847. "She's Jake" and "She'll be right," which utilize the feminine gender to urge one not to have any concern, are now being replaced gradually to the less colorful "no worries." "Better than a poke in the eye with a burnt stick" is sometimes used to express stoic resignation.

Australians have an expression of singular nobility for the heroes of failure, whereas the British and Americans have only a language of admiration for success. "Battler" is the finest word in the Australian language.

Words are used with devastating effect against any form of pretension and hypocrisy. "Wowser," used since the early 1890s to depict a straight-laced fun-hating person, is still in vogue.

Aborigines

The first traditional forms of humor and expression belonged to the aboriginal. In their tribal life the aborigines of Australia possessed great riches in their philosophy and in the tremendous artistry of their culture. Beth Dean in "Folk-loric in Australia" (1974) says, "Their playtime folklore is inventive, creative and very funny. Among Aborigines, the art of mime is superb, their rhymes are intricate and their comedy delightful. Unfortunately little of the Aboriginal folk-lore has pervaded the white community" (p. 48).

Folklore

The traditional folklore of the early settlers would not have transplanted well to the vastly different environment of their origins, although some convict songs did survive about brutal overseers and harsh settlements.

There are four oustanding folk heroes of Australia: an outlaw, Ned Kelly; a sporting hero, cricketer Don Bradman; a flyer, Kingsford Smith; and an animal, racehorse Phar Lap.

Circus and Clowns

Worths, Ashtons, Bullen, Sole, Perry—these and other family circus names have entertained Australians since 1878. Before that date the great American circuses visited Australia. Geoff Graves (1980) describes the logistic problems of moving the great circuses in his chapter on train transport. Horse-drawn wagons became obsolete as the circuses became larger, and even though railways were opening up the country, they serviced only the main towns and cities. In 1876 St. Leon Circus was the first to travel by train. The inevitable problem that confronted every enterprise and influenced every endeavor was that of the immensity of the land and the sparseness of the population.

In terms of time, the young country of Australia has little in the form of its own traditional expressions of humor. There are some great events like the Royal Agricultural Shows and Australian rules football that capture all the excitement of the vigorous young country, but mostly the traditional forms are borrowed from Europe. Circus clowns, pantomimes, and carnivals are all part of Australia's heritage.

Humor in the Literary and Performing Arts

Theatre

The journey of writers, artists and poets, and those visionaries of future attitudes and customs has been anything but easy in the 200 years since the First Fleet landed. The comedy cringe covered the cultural creators like a blanket, and only in recent times have they derived warmth and recognition. Humor in the arts is not only being written and performed by Australian artists, but is drawing audiences in commercial and artistic successes.

In 1789 Australia's first play was performed in a hut by convicts. It was Farquhar's Georgian Comedy, *The Recruiting Officer*.

There is little evidence that the exciting social revolution that followed the discovery of gold in Victoria in the 1850s led to local satirical or comedic writings for the stage.

Influences in art in the Victorian era that were shaped by home movements in Britain gradually changed as a social pattern developed.

Plays written in Australia about Australia during the nineteenth century were in three categories—popular melodrama, comedy, and drama and light theatre.

Literature

Democratic satire and humor began in the very first verse printed in Australia. It appeared in the second issue of the *Sydney Gazette* in 1803, which was published by Australia's first author/editor, the literary-minded convict George Howe. The content of the verse, "A Rum Effect," was the scourge of domestic bliss of the time—rum.

With gifted writers like Robert Lowe, Marcus Clarke, and Australia's first woman novelist, Catherine Helen Spence, wit, sarcasm, and satire were the written word of the times.

Henry Lawson, who was known as the "bard of the bush" or the "people's poet," and Andrew Barton (Banjo) Paterson are the two most important Australian balladists. Lawson captured the native realism and comic spirit of the country. His sardonic humor and democratic emphasis on social injustices are evident in much of his bush balladry. The peak of Lawson's literary development is generally regarded as the Joe Wilson stories, and rich veins of laughter are trapped in the black burlesque humor of stories like "The Loaded Dog."

Andrew Barton Paterson captured the spirit of the adventurous times with a humorous, farcical ironic quality. His fatalistic good humor gave to verses a reality of the folklore of bush stories. Snatches of Paterson's verse are known in every Australian home, and poems like "The Man from Snowy River" and "Clancy of the Overflow" have become part of the folk history of Australia.

In 1984, Paterson wrote the words of "Waltzing Matilda." It became the national song and is identified with Australia more than any other poem.

One of Australia's most renowned impresarios of fun, humor, and playfulness was the eccentric and fascinatingly unique E. W. Cole, owner of Cole's Book Arcade. The first *Cole's Funny Picture Book No. 1* (1879) was advertised as the funniest picture book in the world and, after numerous editions, is still being sold today. Cole classed laughter as mankind's greatest gift, and in a later book, *The Fun Doctor*, he said: "In all ages of the world, it has been held by the almost universal consent of mankind, that one of the greatest blessings that man can enjoy is a good laugh. And the best of all medicines for the mind and the best of all medicines for the body, is a good, honest, healthy laugh" (p. 1).

In 1899 the novel *On Our Selection* by Steele Rudd (real name Arthur Howe Davis) was published. No other Australian comic character has had the impact of Dad Rudd: the father figure of the bushman versus the environment.

In 1899, Australia's first family of the arts, the Lindsays, gained national acclaim when Norman Lindsay, along with his brother Lionel Lindsay and fellow artists and writers, produced an extremely handsome, humorous, and superbly illustrated magazine, *The Rambler*. It was billed as the only penny comic, but because of poor distribution it did not see out the century. But Norman Lindsay went on to become a creative genius. As a graphic artist, he produced over 10,000 cartoons, comic strips, and illustrations for two publications alone; published thirteen fiction and four philosophical works; and was a superb painter in water colors and oils. He spent his life waging a war against wowsers who were responsible for censoring his creative talents.

Humor in the Visual Arts

Australian journalism has produced and developed many world-class draftsmen, and they have made a remarkable contribution to the satiric and humorous national achievement. Because these artists regarded the joke drawings as a serious contribution to art, the "Australian School" evolved; its difference from other countries, apart from humor and satire, was that the themes arose out of the attitudes, characteristics, and behavior patterns of the gold miners, rural laborers, and the early nineteenth-century urban dwellers.

The golden age of Australian Black and White art began with the *Bulletin* in 1880. It established the Australian black-and-white tradition in that nursery of hard-hitting humor which made Australia, in the second half of the nineteenth century, one of the most important centers of black-and-white art in the world.

DEVELOPMENT OF HUMOR IN THE TWENTIETH CENTURY

Popular Forms

Humorous Language

The hotel functions as a vernacular museum for verbal Australian humor. Beehives of indigenous oral comedy—Oz-lingo, rhyming slang, ockerisms, and larrikin slanguage—are integral parts of the speech patterns of Australians. The most popular is strong language, otherwise known as swearing, and its use is ambivalent. One use is as a term of endearment; "G'day you bloody old bastard" is a common form used by Australians when they greet one another. The other is a form of abuse, particularly against people in authority.

Censorship has been the main obstacle in the past preventing Australian humor surfacing because its essence is unprintable. Australians have a certain sense of shame about the crudeness of their humor. It is both a giving and sharing experience—but only for males. It is a thread of commitment that has developed into an entire subculture, which to this day remains largely untapped. Being highly colored, its one-dimensionality effectively maintains this humor as a male preserve.

Aborigines

Since coming to the continent 30,000 years ago, the aborigines lived as a hunting and food-gathering people until forced to adapt to European ways. Religion linked the people, their land, and nature through the ancestral beings, the preexistence and reincarnation of spirits, totemism, mythology, and ritual. They have considerable diversity and expressed themselves aesthetically through a rich heritage of art and a wealth of songs, music, literature, and the nature of their humor. This remarkable people, after almost two centuries of contact with the white man's civilization, is now seeking to establish its own racial image and identity and to preserve as much as it can of its language, beliefs, culture, and ceremony.

Folklore

The influence of the Irish has been mainly in the field of folklore, in the ballads, humorous anecdotes, and stories.

Folklore in Australia is influenced less by the European tradition of religious ceremonies or historical events than by the factors that principally shaped and molded the Australian character, the environment and the elements.

Royal Shows

The Royal Shows in the capital cities of the states of Australia are held to give both primary and secondary industry producers the opportunity to exhibit their products. It has been said "See the Royal Shows and you see Australia." That is because it is the nation's biggest single showpiece of the people. It has often been called the "shopwindow of Australia." Showmen or sideshow people have been a vital part of the Shows since the first plowing match in 1848. Their role, like that of society, has changed considerably over the years.

Humor in the Literary and Performing Arts

Theatre

Australia's first musical comedy star, Nellie Stewart, returned to the country to sing at the opening of the first Parliament in Melbourne on May 9, 1901. She had been away for some time and, on her arrival back, said "I'm really afraid that the Australian taste has degenerated. It has been ruined by modern burlesque" (Pearl, 1974). For decades from that time, the performances in our commercial theatres were largely imported musical comedies, and when an Australian playwright did break through, it was mostly "country cousin" comedy.

In 1955 Australia's national theatre arrived, with the founding of the Elizabethan Theatre Trust. The cynics would not have been at all surprised that the first play in our national theatre was by an English playwright, an English director and English principals, and supporting roles played by Australians. In the same year, they were embarrassed and shocked, along with the major percentage of our population, by the realistic vulgarity and uncouth truth of Australia's most successful postwar play, *The Summer of the Seventeenth Doll,* written by Ray Lawler. The egalitarian humor of situation, character, and vernacular stunned and stirred our emotions of recognition as Australians saw themselves mirrored on the stage, possibly for the first time. The story of the cane cutters' annual return to live it up with their women in Emma's boardinghouse is etched into the national consciousness.

George Wallace and Gladys Moncrieff starred in the first all-Australian musical comedy in 1934. Musical comedy was always one of Australia's most profitable, meaning also one of the most popular, theatre forms. Since the beginning of the century, about 310 musical comedies have been produced professionally. Of these, roughly 45 were written by Australians, but very few of them appeared in more than one state.

American accents are easily defined, and in England, humor and accents can differ within a few miles. In Australia, however, despite the vast distances across the land, there are no apparent or easily recognizable differences in accents, expressions, or humor attitudes.

Literature

In 1906 Ed Dyson published a fascinating and very funny book which turned a corner in Australian literature. *Fact'ry 'ands* was about the realities of living

STAFFORDSHIRE POLYTECHNIC LIBRARY

and working in a mainly impersonalized urban society. Dyson, the brother of cartoonist Will Dyson, was one of a number of writers building the foundation of an indigenous literature. Other authors were Tom Collins, E. J. Brady, Katharine Susannah Prichard, and Kodak (Ernest O'Ferrall).

C. J. Dennis began his literary career in 1915 with the writing of *The Sentimental Bloke*. The hero was a personification of the city-dwelling character of the larrikin. The book, a series of verse stories told in slang, sold 66,000 copies in 18 months. Dennis was called the "Robert Burns of Australia" by the then prime minister, A. J. Lyons.

In 1927, a critic from America, C. Hartley Grattan, made a visit to Australia and is on record for saying "Australian readers feel safe with a third-rate English or American book rather than with a first-rate Australian book" (Pearl, 1974, p. 168). Sadly, history shows that that was the case for the next 20 years. The exception was Lennie Lower's *Here's Luck*, published in 1930, which shocked Australian society with the hilarious naked truth of their suburban domestic scene.

In the mid-1940s, Australia's literature bloomed, with urban subjects and satire prominent, and brilliant writers like Alan Marshall, Vance Palmer, and Patrick White (the 1983 Nobel Prize winner for literature) achieving international notice. Alan Lawson, a lecturer in Australian literature, wrote of Patrick White, "Humour is essential to his vision of humanity—that vision is basically a comic one" (1982).

Though the period was a Camelot for Australian comic literature, very few writers were earning enough to call themselves professional humorists, and only one was having a great deal of financial success. He was Nino Culotta (real name, John O'Grady). In 1957 he wrote *They're a Weird Mob* to pull Australian legs. The book's key phrase, "owyergoinmate Orright," struck a humorous chord which was in harmony with the mood of nationalism in Australia at the time.

Humor in the Visual Arts

Will Dyson, indisputably the only genius in the Cartoon Hall of Fame, submitted his first cartoon to the *Bulletin* in 1897. Will Dyson was one of the robust minds of his age. In his irony and force he has been approached by no Australian cartoonist before or since.

In 1911, David Low (New Zealand) was engaged by the *Bulletin* to do caricatures of famous Australians, but his fame really rests with his drawings of the Australian prime minister, Billy Hughes. These were collected in his sellout book, *The Billy Book* (1918). He stayed with the *Bulletin* until 1919 and pioneered brushwork in Australia. His reputation and ambition led him to England, where he achieved an international reputation and became one of the most politically astute animals in all cartooning and earned himself top priority on Hitler's death list.

Stan Cross was the most famous of the Smith artists; his aboriginal and Dad and Dave cartoons are still remembered and laughed at today.

He later did *Wally and the Major* for the Melbourne *Herald* and became the highest paid newspaperman in the country. He also drew the famous "Stop Laughing This Is Serious" cartoon, which is considered the funniest Australian cartoon ever published. The drawing depicts two men who had been working on top of a building construction. But there has been a mishap, for now one is hanging by his fingers from a girder at a frightening height above the ground. The second man, to save himself, has firmly grabbed the trousers of the other, yanking them down over his ankles and, looking upwards, is convulsed with laughter, while the other implores 'For Gorsake, stop laughing: this is serious!"

Intense newspaper rivalry during the 1920s and 1930s resulted, with the object of circulation building, in a host of significant comic strips, many printed in color.

The most famous of all Australian comic strip characters was Ginger Meggs, created by Jim Bancks in 1921. The red-haired, orchard-raiding, football and cricket "champeen" fighting youngster with the "terrible right" was syndicated in 1929 in America, England, Canada, and South America. The adventures of Ginger Meggs, a small boy, and his ups and downs, knowing glorious victory today and bitter defeat tomorrow, was in line with Jim Bancks's view of humor, "You can't win." Ginger Meggs still appears in newspapers worldwide.

Public or Specialized Places for Humorous Expression

Pubs

The Australian pub was, and still is, the home of the country's true-blue dinky-di humorous expression. The first legal pub was opened in Parramatta, New South Wales, around the year 1796. At that time, they were called taverns and inns, eventually becoming pubs and hotels.

Without the tradition of many touring professional shows, no repertory or a provisional theatre, the pub became the stage for many amateur comedians, practical jokers, and raconteurs, locally known as wits, wags, and wackers. They would spin one another yarns, tell traditional stories and tall tales about tricksters, heroes, and hoaxers, all the time holding their small territory around a hotel bar in an ambience of mateship, eulogized in Australia as perhaps the single most important virtue that the Australian male can possess.

The Australian joke is very much like those told by Australians in pubs: always masculine, at times cruel, uncouth, disrespectful, and often racist. Australians rarely came into contact with the butt of their jokes, so there was little of the strident venom of the true racist; and more often than not, the jokes were dirty and quite often directed at themselves.

Vaudeville

Vaudeville and burlesque were the spawning ground of comedy throughout the world during the early part of the twentieth century, and Australia was no exception. Harry Rickards created the Tivoli Circuit in 1893, and in 1912 entrepreneur Hugh D. McIntosh became the country's capital laughter impresario when he brought to life the Tivoli Circuit, and vaudeville was reborn, killing in the process the free and easy form of entertainment that was fashionable up until that time. Three years earlier, in 1909, the hopeful fun and cheerful chuckles of variety entertainment were taken to the bush via trains, caravans, and traveling tent shows, beginning a long touring tradition.

Roy Rene teamed up with fellow comedian Nat Phillips in 1914, and for fifteen years they toured together as the Stiffy and Mo Revue. Roy was building up a reputation as a risqué double entendre, innuendo expert. According to Keith Willey, "Roy Rene, in his own private life, preserved the dichotomy between the prude and the prudent, or . . . the wowser and the ocker. As the public ocker, he appealed to the secret self of those many Australians who cherish the devil-may-care self-image of a rebel, while conforming, quite stably in their own lives to the observance of suburban society. Roy Rene was the legendary dinkum Aussie in reverse. While so many were outwardly respectable and inwardly (or bar-room) rebels, he paraded his rebelliousness on stage, while in private he revelled in domesticity and family life" (1984). Mo had no equal as a sketch comedian in variety theatre.

While Roy Rene was the city suburban ocker, George Wallace was the rural bush ocker with the same ability as Mo of making any everyday phrase sound ridiculously funny. Both Wallace's father and grandfather were successful comedians, along with his son George Wallace, Jr. Wallace was one of those rare performers where it was the comic and not the comedy that counted. His humor was both realistic and resilient, with the bush fiber of gallows and flavor of corn.

Though vaudeville just managed to survive through the thirties and forties, it never lacked great comedy talents.

Ethnic Humor

Radio 3EA in Victoria goes to air seven days a week and broadcasts in 54 languages. Despite the multicultural society and the contributions made in other areas of art and culture, there is no ethnic humor that has made a dent in the Australian mode. It suggests that, like a huge sponge, Australia absorbs all the humorous aspects of migrants and within a short time, perhaps only a generation, sqeezes out true-blue, dinky-di Aussie standards of humor.

The evidence of the absorption into Australian humor of ethnic influences is most noticeable in the career of Australia's most loved and funniest comic, Mo. H. Davis writes, "In his sketches he portrayed the downtrodden, the loser, but with 'chutzpah', the employee—never the employer" (1984, p. 4). The familiar character appealed to Australians because of his apparent lack of respect for authority. Mo would appear onstage with Jewish makeup to the tune of "oy oy oy oy Muzzletov" and make occasional references to his origins, yet it is doubtful whether Australians ever associated Mo with being anything but Australian to the very essence.

Social Satire Revue

In 1952, a man who was to become one of the main branches of the country's family tree of funny men, Rolf Harris, left the shores for the first of many trips to export his unique brand of Australian humor, which is a concoction of many comedy forms.

Two years later, in 1954, Roy "Mo" Rene died. It was also the year that heralded a new era of humor—the social satire revue. It started at the Phillip Street Theatre in Sydney, and the vital lampooning light behind it was producer Bill Orr. There had been university revues of similar sorts before it, thumbing their noses at all and sundry, but general theatre audiences had not seen themselves on a professional stage, sent up, mocked, and insulted like this.

Nightclubs and Cabarets

Nightclubs and cabarets, which multiplied during the forties as a result of the war, slowly began to disappear in the fifties. The comedy of the nightclub comedians was similiar to their vaudeville comic comrades, though their costume had gone from being brightly colored and extra large to a black bowtie and a tight fit. Add to this the fact that radio and television had changed the timing of their jokes. Though Australia never produced any innovative, intellectual, social and political comic geniuses like Lenny Bruce and Mort Sahl, it did produce an exciting assortment of talented nightclub stand-up comedians—Slim De Grey, Sid Heylen, and the most polished performer of them all, Joe Martin, who was one of the few comedians who got requests for jokes. The hub of Australia's nightclub and cabaret scene was an area known as Kings Cross in Sydney, which was also the most densely populated region in the southern hemisphere. At that time 60,000 people lived in a quarter of a square mile, most of them with the egalitarianism and antiauthoritarianism which were the so-called backbone of the legendary Australian character. So a walk along Darlinghurst Road in the Cross was street entertainment par excellence.

Humor in the Mass Media

Newspapers and Magazines

A national Australian humor was born with the birth of the *Bulletin* magazine in 1880. It broke the tradition up until then of what was accepted as funny— humor about England and middle-class English attitudes and values. The two men who steered it through its infancy and voiced pro-Republican sentiments were J. F. Archibald and A. G. Stephens. They also displayed a determination

and talent for unearthing democratic geniuses of outlook and literary abilities—
Henry Lawson, Joseph Furphy, Victor Daley, E. J. Brady, and D. O. Riley,
among others. It rapidly became known as the "Bushman's Bible" because of
its sensitive insights into the lives of ordinary Australians from all walks of life,
the shearers, drovers, jackaroos, wharfies and bush cooks, and both the rural
and city working classes. It highlighted the resilient dignity of the bushfolk and
the untamable independence of the Australian people overall. The *Bulletin*
brought to surface, for the first time, the roots of a humor that could be instinc-
tively identified with that which was different and distinct from the European
one. It raised the national consiousness to recognize a unique bush ethos.

March 1919 saw the second most powerful publication in Australia's history
in print, the illustrated broadsheet *Smith's Weekly*. It was a manifestation from
the minds of three men, J. F. Archibald, Claude MacKay, and Clyde Packer.
It quickly became to urban humor what the *Bulletin* was to bush humor and was
duly named the *Digger's Bible*. V. Lindesay says of it, "Editorially 'Smith's
Weekly' was blatantly jingoistic" (1979, p. 44). Naturally a lot of this was
reflected in the types of its humor: drinking and drunks; soldier humor; horse
racing humor; Dad and Dave rural humor; and a new departure in Australian
urban humor, the theme of divorce, interesting for its comic cynicism. This was
the dinky-di slang, and the chauvinism totaled up to a fairly correct picture of
Australian life, thought, and attitude between the wars. It attacked pomposity
with vigor and venom, moralizing but never apologizing.

On June 10, 1933, publisher Frank Packer placed on the newsstands the
Australian Women's Weekly. It soon became the magazine with the highest
circulation in the country. With its core of domestic suburban humor and its
array of artists and writers whose comic contributions were essentially Australian,
it mirrored social changes through the depression and the war years, never failing
to keep the masses laughing.

Nineteen fifty saw the death of *Smith's Weekly*, the paper that had encouraged
a tradition of sentiment, of laughing with the larrikin and the battler. Its main
theme—urban domestic humor, expressing marital discontent—reflected a re-
versal from the once all-male society to a wife-controlled one. It was the unholy
trinity, boss trained, newspaper educated, woman dominated.

Film

Carl Hertz brought motion pictures to Australia in 1896, and on September
28, Australia's first movie theatre called Lumière's Cinémotographe was opened
by Marvis Sestier and Walter Barnett, and November 3, Sestier made Australia's
first historic film when he took his cameras to the 1896 Melbourne Cup. But it
was another decade before feature films were being produced and the movies,
as a medium, were established.

There are three distinct categories of Australian humor in film: the bucolic
hayseed, forever in conflict with society, his family, and himself; the larrikin
with the gift of gab, usually running in tandem with situations awash with

sentiment; and with the new freedom of the cinema to pursue sexual mores, the aggressive ocker stud, forever in pursuit of new and exciting conquests. Wit, style, and elegance of verbal expression are practically unkown in Australian cinema.

America had taken control and was dominating the film industry. Australian entrepreneurs found it impossible to raise the necessary money to finance a film. They were ignored, even by the government of the day, until director Ken G. Hall proved a favorite adage of his, "When times are tough, make a comedy." In 1931 he did: a sound remake of the silent Australian classic *On Our Selection*.

But it was George Wallace who proved to be Australia's first comic genius of film when in 1932 he wrote, along with C. J. Dennis, and starred in the first musical comedy film, *His Royal Highness*. This was followed by a string of other hilarious and financially successful films. Ken Hall's last feature film was in 1946. The Australian Film Industry, though it had fought valiantly, was virtually dead, and it was a quarter of a century before it was to be resurrected. There were many reasons for its decline, but the overriding factor was that most of the distribution network was under foreign ownership.

Radio

In 1935 radio was expanding rapidly, helped by the fact that vaudeville was on the decline, resulting in the changing of creative direction by many prominent performers. One such entertainer was George Edwards, an eccentric comic dancer called by Nancy Bridges, in her book *Wonderful Wireless* (1983), the "Father of Australian radio." He produced, and starred as Dad in, the "Dad and Dave Show," among others. It ran for 15 years and 2,275 episodes. Radio variety was to survive for only 20 years, but in that period Australia was never lost for a laugh. The three giants of Australian radio in this era were Jack Davey, Roy "Mo" Rene, and Bob Dyer.

Television

With the arrival of television in Australia on September 16, 1956, the comedy cringe was never more evident. Television only highlighted Australia's comic economic philosophy: "If you can buy it for peanuts overseas, why risk diamonds making it at home?" Australians never saw the British or the American unfunny failures—only their best shows—and this prevented the emergence of local laugh makers. It did, however, sharpen and broaden the Australian's appreciation of the types and styles, forms and formulas involved in the chemistry of comedy. In the interfusion of foreign situation comedies, variety and talk shows, Graham Kennedy stumbled into the compere's seat of a program called "In Melbourne Tonight." Kennedy went on to become the king of Australian television. His comedy was innovative and confronting and like that of a naughty little boy who says things others would like to, but dare not.

CONTEMPORARY HUMOR AND TRENDS

Popular Forms

Humorous Language

Despite the inroads made by American film and television speech jargon, which has cracked the droll iconoclastic tradition, there still is a vast coloquial language that is part and parcel of everyday speech. It is comic, descriptive, and accurate.

Professor A. A. Morrison, writing under the pseudonym of Afferbeck Lauder, wrote a best-selling lexicon of modern Strine called *Let Stalk Strine* (Let's Talk Australian, 1965). The incident which made a disturbingly profound impression on him, he writes, was a report in the *Syndey Morning Herald*, November 30, 1964, that while the English writer Monica Dickens was autographing copies of her latest book as they were being bought by members of the public in a Sydney shop, a woman handed her a copy and said "Emma Chissit." Thinking this was the woman's name, Monica Dickens wrote "To Emma Chissit" above the signature on the flyleaf. The purchaser, however, in a rather more positive voice said, "No, Emma Chisset?" Eventually it became clear that she had been speaking Strine and used the Strine equivalent of the English phrase "How much is it?" The misunderstanding was due to the fact that while Strines are often able to understand and read English, they usually speak only Strine.

In the short history of Australia, national characteristics have been expressed more by humorous expressions than by any other means. The slanguage of the nation is used in the boardrooms of big business, in the power halls of politics, in factories and pubs, in the home, and in the schools.

Circus

The circus in Australia has seen its prosperous times and its bad times. Television dealt a body blow to the circus from which it never fully recovered until Michael Edgley and family introduced the Great Moscow Circus to Australia.

But the famous names like Worths and the others hold a special place in the hearts of all those who love the Big Top.

Circus Oz is like no other circus seen before. Except for the animals and ringmaster, all the traditional elements are there—aerial acts, clowns, jugglers and acrobats—but there is much more. It's hard to define, but critics have tried with phrases like multiskilled innovation, infectious light-heartedness, profound image making, and energetic versatility.

In 1979 The Murray River Performing Group worked with 120 children on an exciting circus project in a celebration of youth in the border towns of Albury and Wodonga which separate New South Wales from Victoria. This unique children's circus, the Flying Fruit Fly Circus, has developed with world-class professionalism.

Festivals and Fairs

Robert King Crawford, former superintendent of arts for the city of Melbourne, initiated and devised the concept of "Free Entertainment in Parks" (FEIP) in 1972. It has escalated from an involvement of 80 artists to 35,000 artists and is one of the biggest "free entertainment" programs in the world. There are spectaculars every Sunday over a seven-month period, which comprises 27 festivals.

In Melbourne, the Moomba festival of culture, comic, and sporting events takes place in March. The word *Moomba* is an aboriginal word meaning "Let's get together and have fun," but it was really a practical joke played on Melburnians 30 years ago by an aborigine who suggested the name. It was discovered that the word really translated into a rude comment about the white man's bottom.

One day each year the University of Melbourne holds a Humor Festival and becomes a Humorversity. For this one day this is the venue where comics, writers, and hu"Mo"rists present and perform humor and comedy. This event was initiated by the Humour Comedy and Laughter League, the Australian affiliate of Workshop Library on World Humour.

Humor in the Literary and Performing Arts

Theatre

In the fifties the cinemas closed, new auditoriums for live theatre were being built, but they did not prevent the evacuation of actors, producers and directors, and some of the cream of the country's theatre personnel. The fifties saw women take control of the previous male domain of the box office. Gifted stars like Toni Lamond, Gloria Dawn, and Jill Perryman became the main attractions of the musical comedy stage. From 1960, hundreds either in or connected with theatre left for foregin shores and seldom (if successful) returned, but many actors noted for their comic talents remained. This period of the early 1960s was one of struggling and striving in the Australian theatre fraternity in search of that Australian-ness, their unique and individual cultural tradition that had previously, theatrically, been ignored. It was also the period that saw the eruption of the Australian iconoclast Barry Humphries. Humphries left university to become an actor with the Melbourne Theatre Company and seven years later, in 1962, launched his first one-man show, *A Nice Night's Entertainment*. Through the sixties and right up to the present day, he has remained Australia's major satirist. Proclaimed a genius by London's West End critics, he has the almost surreal ability to slaughter the sacred cows almost before they become calves.

Humor and the Australian arts got a welcome and much-needed transfusion of funds from the Whitlam government, the first Labor government since the war. By increasing the number and value of writers' grants and fellowships, the government made it possible for writers to treat their profession as a job.

Jack Hibberd, Alex Buzo, Alan Hopgood and David Williamson, Barry Dickens, and Steve J. Spears are some of the humor playwrights finding great acceptance with Australian audiences.

The most successful humorous playwright of contemporary times is David Williamson. Three of his plays have been filmed, *The Removalist*, *The Club*, and *Don's Party*. Williamson, through his 20/20 observations and a subconscious understanding of Australian attitudes and idiom, a marvellously accurate ear for the rhythm and rhyme of the country's vocal expressions, has managed to capture mainsteam Australian humor. One of Australia's funniest comedy actors in live theatre is Max Gillies. Prime Minister Bob Hawke is only one of his comic political characters.

It is no longer necessary to have the imprimatur of overseas patronage of the arts; however, there is some concern that a reverse cycle may have begun and that some of the most gifted artists and directors are leaving to work overseas. Nevertheless, there is an incredible vitality in the arts, with many themes of humor in the productions.

Literature

Bill Wannan, the foremost historian of humor literature in the country, in his introduction to *A Treasury of Australian Humour* says, "In browsing through this anthology, the reader may note the almost complete absence of sophistication in the writers represented. Here are no Dorothy Parkers, no Woollcotts, no Sullivans. There is satire and much sardonic laughter but no out and out nonsense in the vein of S. J. Perelman. The trend is more often to the earthy than the elegant" (1960, p. 27). But the book did contain a comic concoction of some brilliantly funny short stories by Australia's literary laugh makers: the likes of E. J. Brady, W. T. Goodge, and A. G. Stephens, who represented the past; and Dal Stivens, Frank Hardy, Ken Collie, and Cyril Pearl, representing the present.

In 1970 the arts were using and appreciating the growing nationalistic boom, which is still evolving. Keith Dunstan, Thomas Keneally, Barry Oakley, Kylie Tennant, and other humor authors were enjoying popularity at this time. Geoffrey Lehmann, a humorous poet and editor of *Comic Australian Verse*, made this observation in his introduction: Australian humour is like the macadamia nut, a prized delicious centre contained by a hard case. It lacks soft tissue but is dangerous. It is what we would like to believe about ourselves. It is an extension of our republican stoicism, our Anzac spirit, our detestation of tall poppies, our hatred of cant" (1972, p. 4).

In 1977, Pete Crofts, ex-stand-up comedian, opened the Humour, Comedy and Laughter Book Shop in Melbourne, the first bookshop in Australia specializing in humor. Crofts and his bookshop have acted as a catalyst for the study of humor, comedy, and laughter in Australia. In an interview in *Gene Perrett's Round Table*, Crofts said, "I would like to see the study of humour as a university subject, if we can all learn a sense of humour the way we learn a sense of religion of a sense of politics—we are not born voting Democrat or Republican— we would all have a common sense'' (1984, p. 4).

Humor in the Visual Arts

In 1964 Robert Murdoch published the first national newspaper, *The Austra- lian*. Bruce Petty, the Academy Award–winning cartoonist for *Leisure*, worked on that paper and got wider coverage than a cartoonist had received since the days of the early *Bulletin*.

Michael Leunig is a graphic poet. Historically speaking, he shouldn't even exist in Australian journalism. His cartoons are dreamy, youthful, yet painful excursions into the Peter Pan world of the Me Generation.

Pat Oliphant, an ex-Adelaide cartoonist, went on to bigger things in the United States, where he changed the shape and thrust of American cartoon and was awarded a Pulitzer Prize for his efforts.

Other artists working with responsibility and pride in their craft are Wil- liam Ellis Green (WEG), Patrick Cook, Less Tanner, and Rolf Heimann (Lofo).

In 1985 the inaugural Bulletin Black and White Artists Awards were held in Sydney. The trophy was a sculptured version of the famous Stan Cross cartoon with the caption ''For Gorsake stop laughing—this is serious.''

Public or Specialized Places for Humorous Expression

Clubs

Australia was becoming a permissive society as the sixties began. The new morality shaped the entertainment in the few remaining nightclubs which existed in the capital cities. The growth of licensed machine poker clubs in New South Wales, around 1,600 at the last count (the only state with such a license), resulted in the profits from the poker machines allowing clubs to provide the finest entertainment at next to no charge to the patrons. This caused an exodus of comedians and variety performers in general from other states, as well as con- siderable numbers from England, Ireland, and a few from America, to Sydney and the club scene.

Australians have a reputation for not appreciating what should be national treasures, the wit warriors in the front line of the laugh battles—the stand-up comedians.

A new form of comedy entertainment emerged in Australia in the sixties, which was a combination of two elements—restaurant and recycled music hall— becoming the theatre restaurant.

New Wave Comedy

The seventies began with an upmarket modern trend in Australian humorous expression, spread by people who were monitoring mostly the American and, to a lesser degree, the English scene. They soon became aware that the country was in for a new comedy era.

Then, in the mid-seventies, contemporary underground comedy surfaced in Australia. Mostly from inner-city suburbs, underground comedy began in Melbourne and Sydney and then spread to the rest of the country.

In 1974, John Pinder, who has been called the father of Australian contemporary comedy, opened a small theatre restaurant in Fitzroy, Melbourne, called the Flying Trapeze. It went on to become a model for the new-wave comedy movement, resulting in a host of similar venues locally and interstate. The most famous are Sydney's Comedy Store and Melbourne's Comedy Cafe, along with the Last Laugh Theatre Restaurant and Zoo, and Le Joke.

Two individual, distinct brands of humor became apparent. In Melbourne, the influence was from trendy suburbs like Carlton and Collingwood (what some call Carl/Coll comedy today), fringe theatre, and university revue. The comedy became iconoclastic and nihilistic, and was built around character, situation, and production. The overall content was aristocratic.

Sydney, a much more cosmopolitan city than Melbourne, has a far broader background for live comedy, from vaudeville to burlesque to strip clubs to machine poker clubs. A large scale social club scene has always had a variety of comedy not available in other cities. So Sydney's contemporary comedy is truthful, aggressive, and risqué; is built around stand-up personality and technique; and the overall content is democratic.

The eighties opened with a comedy renaissance resembling the heyday of the vaudeville comedians of the twenties; actors, writers, buskers, and musicians were all calling themselves comedians. A turning point for popular humorous expression in Australia came in 1984, which marked the beginning of a self-discovery humor scene. In May 1984, 10,000 people turned up for the Rock Comedy Explosion Part II in the Sydney Entertainment Centre, which consisted of only Australian new-wave comedy acts. At last, Australians were laughing with Australians at Australians.

1985 provided another major attitude change regarding Australian humor. No longer the butt of the jokes, women were the joke makers at home and abroad, with the comediennes leading the comedians in international recognition two to one: Maureen Murphy and Pamela Stephenson for the ladies, and Paul Hogan, the sole male comic to gain world recognition in the last decade.

At present, the humor revival extends across the entire country, a volatile mix of classical comedy and new-wave comedy, performed in pubs, cabarets, nightclubs, theatre restaurants, laugh lounges, all-male revue shows, rock concerts, RSL (Returned Servicemen's League) and Leagues Clubs, smokos (Saturday morning football shows), fringe theatre, both male and female strip shows, university revues, and business seminars and conferences, where humor keynote speakers like Campbell McComas, body language expert Allan Pease, and former politician Fred Daly all provide a highly sought after commodity in Australia in the eighties: laughter.

Humor in the Mass Media

Newspapers and Magazines

The sixties began and rock and roll boomed. Australia was no place for the budding humorist. The moviemakers had ceased to exist. The newspapers had changed the cartoonist from a social funmaker to a political point-scorer; radio was virtually in the hands of the poop-poopy-doo disc jockeys; and television was in its infancy.

April Fools' Day 1963 was the day editors Richard Neville, Richard Welsh, and Peter Grose introduced their satire magazine, *Oz*. It reflected a change in Australian journalism and was in some ways a telescope focused on the increasing consciousness. Brilliantly illustrated by two young graphic satirists, Martin Sharp and Gary Sheed, it was published monthly and provided a much-needed lamp of laughter.

Dennis O'Brien, journalist for the *Bulletin* magazine, which was continuing to foster humor and its creators, in an article titled "What Makes Australia Laugh," wrote, "Certainly the supply of deliberate humour in the Australian Press is becoming short. Ross Cambell in Sydney, Kirwan Ward in Perth and (occasionally) Allen Fitzgerald in Canberra, are the best of a very few columnists employed to help make Australia laugh" (1968, p. 31).

The humorist newspaper columnists of the seventies and eighties are Ron Saw, Phillip Adams, Max Harris, Keith Dunstan, and Clive James.

Film

In 1969 Phillip Adams presented a report on behalf of the Australian Film Council to the prime minister of the time, John Gorton, who pushed the recommendation that an indigenous film industry be supported with government funding, and the dormant industry was suddenly revitalized. Phillip Adams's artistic experience, like that of so many other creative and performing artists of the preceding period, was gained from advertising. Adams is one of Australia's leading advocates of laughter and his books and articles support the view that in the final analysis the ultimate war on this planet will not be waged between east and west, black and white, communist or capitalist, atheist or agnostic but between those of us who laugh and those of us who don't.

As well as the arrival of the underground comic, the seventies saw the beginning of the third category of Australian humor in films: the aggressive ocker stud, forever in pursuit of new and exciting conquests. The first was *The Naked*

Bunyip, then in 1971 *Stork*, and in 1972 the ocker movies really arrived with *The Adventures of Barry MacKenzie*.

In the last few years, Australian cinema has achieved international acceptance.

Records and Novelty Songs

The recording industry in Australia has leaned heavily on British artists when it comes to making Australia laugh. And a glance through the catalogs of the 1930s, 1940s, and 1950s shows almost total domination by English music hall and movie performers. In the comedy section, the Australians were represented by Ward Leopold, who had great success with his "Here's Hooey" collection. Fred Dagg and Col Elliott also made some comedy records, and Robert King Crawford made a series of successful comedy-discs between 1950 and 1960 which included "How to Speak Australian."

Television

In November 1964, "The Mavis Bramston Show" exploded onto the television screens. And as well as using the techniques that journalism was using in this period, it managed to portray in performance the first glimpses of indigenous television comedy using sketches, review, interviews, burlesque, and impersonation.

The persistence of the ABC (Australian Broadcasting Commission) in its pursuit of comedy excellence on television was paying off when Maurice Murphy produced the "Auntie Jack Show" in 1972, starring Graham Bond and Rory O'Donohue, from which many spin-off shows resulted. The most popular was the "Norman Gunston Show," with Garry McDonald as Gunston, who was a parody of talk-show hosts. It was written by Bill Harding, and the keynote of the show's comedy was embarassment.

The most rewarding and certainly most successful achievement of Australian humor since the birth of the *Bulletin* was the discovery on television of the real ocker, Paul Hogan. He was Australia's Will Rogers, the first folk comedian, and with his devastatingly accurate insight into middle-class Aussie values, he lampooned, parodied, and impersonated his way into becoming a major part of the Australian comic culture. His reputation was made in Australia with a series of cigarette commercials, in England with a series of beer commercials, and in America with a series of travel commercials. Sandra Hill, in her book *Supertoy*, wrote, "The character Hogan developed in such nice detail, is formed young in Australia, in the schools, the football clubs and anywhere else where boys look to mateship and cunning as a substitute for the more conventional kind of academic competition which either bores or defeats them. It is a brotherhood which elevates the male rights of sport, drinking, womanising and gambling while being perfectly aware of what it is doing. The language of the jokes denigrates both the means of escape in a status bound world that makes escape necessary, and it would be an extraordinarily bitter sort of humour if it had not camouflaged its roots so well with the picturesque language and the carelessness of its delivery'' (1976, p. 133).

Death of the Comedy Cringe

Nineteen eighty-four was the year that the comedy and humor storm arrived, and down came the metaphors, the sight gags, the irony, the tall stories, the satire, the fun and laughter. The *National Times* newspaper ran a humor writing competition and reported that the entries covered the traditional and the topical. The favorite subjects were Americans, ASIO (Australian Security Intelligence Organizations), tax dodgers, outback towns, lust, the ponies, drunken mates, the counterculture, semiotics, and marriage.

The *Bulletin* gave over its cover to comedy on May 1 and an eight-page story titled ''What Makes Australia Laugh Now.''

The Australian Film Commission established a comedy fund in 1984 to foster comedy on film and television under the guidance of film director Bob Weis, film producer Karin Altmann, and humor writer and performer John Clarke (Fred Dagg). Clarke approached the Victorian State Library; the result was cooperation between the Comedy Fund and the Victorian State Library to create a humor collection which will be available throughout the Australian Bibliographic Network. It consists of books, records, scripts, illustrations, cartoons, and other documents. The first success of the Comedy Fund was a comedy television program called ''The Eleventh Hour,'' which they coproduced and financed, along with the Seven Network, in Melbourne in 1985. It was a series of eight one-hour current affairs send-ups utilizing all forms of comedy devices—shock, parody, change, surrealism, recognition, and self-debasement. And it certainly displayed that there are some Australians who have a sense of comedy and a sense of humor.

Paul Hogan's great international success in his first feature film, *Crocodile Dundee*, makes it seem certain that the Australian film industry has arrived. What is certain is that humor in the Australian media has never been healthier and that humor is assisting and may even be responsible for Australians' discovery of their nationalism.

UNIVERSAL FUNCTIONS OF HUMOR AND THE NATIONAL MANIFESTATIONS

Aggressive Humor

The aggressive function of humor in Australia is adamant and nonselective. It fires its aggressive arrows at every conceivable target—city slickers, country bumpkins; new immigrants, according to the current influx (Asians are the flavor of the year at present); aboriginals; pommy new chums; and Chinese. Nothing and no one is spared in the aggressive search for equality of Australian humor.

A very pompous pommy walked up to an Aussie in Sydney because he was lost and looking for the subway. He said, "Excuse me, old fellow, could you tell me how I could get underground?" and the Aussie said, "Sure thing, drop dead, you pommy bastard."

Vital targets also include authority figures, such as clerics, policemen, bosses, teachers, bureaucrats, politicians, and academics. One of the features of Australian humor is its leveling tendency. Tall poppies are aggressively knocked off what are perceived to be their pompous pedestals.

By far the most aggressive comedian on the scene is a comic calling himself "Austen Tayshus"; he is also known as the "comedy commando," which fits his machinegun-like attack. He wages a war of words, and his comedy weapons are shock, satire, insult, embarrassment, and mockery. His comedy content is controversial to anyone who confronts his point of view. His humor is angry and directed to anyone needing the piss taken out of them.

Sexual Humor

The essential feature of sexual humor is male dominance, and this was shaped to some degree by English attitudes toward the role of women. The colonial society was the ideal breeding ground for stronger and more virulent forms of these attitudes. Male dominance of the social, bureaucratic, and political structures was firmly established in the predominantly male convict society of the late eighteenth and early nineteenth centuries. In their strong, sexually deprived male environment, men formed their attitudes toward women to establish, in their own crude and rough manner, their dominance of the Australian language.

An Aussie approached a young lady and said, "What about sex?"
"No," she answered.
"Well, would you mind lying down while I have some?"

The convict era was well and truly over by the mid-1850s, even though some convicts were still being transported to Western Australia in 1868; but the pastoral and gold rush eras, which brought more females to the shores, merely modified male attitudes. Indeed, the institutions had been formed by males and remained firmly in male hands, and still do to a large extent today. Isolation also reinforced the subservient role of women: men worked planting crops, shearing sheep, droving cattle, and prospecting for gold, while women looked after children (often by themselves) on isolated properties. With the urbanization of Australia from the late 1860s until 1900, the isolation of men from women began to change and with it men's attitudes toward women. Australian sexual humor is sexist, unrefined, with an uncouth larrikin element that highlights the independent Australian male attitude.

Through all the titillating tales and shameless sagas, wanton fables, boastful reports, and questionable anecdotes, Australian sexual humor reveals profound anxiety about women and their relationship to men. The brashness, the bravado, and the jaunting arrogance of the larrikin are merely attempts to cover up his social awkwardness and sensitivity in the company of women.

The major content of most Australian comedians' material is sexually oriented, and Australia's top stand-up comedian at present, Rodney Rude, sets the example. Journalist Paul Mann said, "He is getting paid for doing what thousands of Australians do every day for nothing—being rude" (1982, p. 102).

Social Humor

If we are to accept that a large part of the character that makes up the Australian sense of humor is to be found in the tradition of mateship, then the social aspects of humor are of paramount importance. Whether it be in interpersonal relationships or in a group, this tradition is the main factor.

There is no wish to reform society; this they leave to the professionals. There is no great evangelical mission to change the order. By the very nature of the sardonic interplay, the "knocking" technique, the leveling process, the effect of reformation is achieved within the group automatically.

It is impossible to divorce social aspects of comedy from their origins in Australian geography. The social aspects must be related to the hatred of oppression, the fierce spirit of independence, and the very sardonic humor of the Irish convicts and political prisoners that mainly formed the genesis of Australian humor.

Australians generally have a total disregard for politics as a career and politicians as a class. The stoical attitude is not that they don't care about the state of the nation or the world, but that they are not going to win no matter what happens in politics. Politicians are perceived to be somewhat absurd, even stupid, and most of the nation's concerns are only complicated by their activities.

The Prime Minister's Lodge has never been the pinnacle of ambition for Australian youth. The present popularity of Prime Minister Bob Hawke has more to do with his ability to crack one-liners and his occasional references to once being "one of the boys" than with his political acumen, which is considerable. His intellectual larrikin image, together with an obvious sensitivity to and concern for the underdog and a sense of humor, has given him a popularity rating higher than that of any other leader in Australia's history.

Humor as a Defense Mechanism

The function of humor as a defense mechanism in Australian society is to provide a *defense against the environment*. The joke below is indicative of the way the outback farmer has used humor as a defense mechanism to cope with his environment.

A local farmer's wife had a baby and the farmer came into the hospital to see them for the first time.

"You've got a fine boy," said the sister, smiling, "but as you know, he is premature, so he is very small."

"Ah, well," said the farmer, "a season like this you are lucky to get your seed back."

This form of humor, which made outsiders laugh, derived not from mirth but from the reality of life in the bush.

The well-balanced Australian is a bloke with a chip on both shoulders. The pioneer, faced with the ravages of the environment, the dictates of bureaucracy and government, and the misfortunes of everyday existence, could either weep or laugh. He chose to laugh, so the Aussie uses humor as a defense mechanism.

Even in the way the Australian males greet one another, a defense mechanism is obvious. Instead of using terms of endearment, they use insults. They punch one another on the arm and say "Good-day, you old bastard" as a defense against their true feelings.

The theory that black humor is a defense mechanism that helps us cope with threats and fears, instead of surrendering to them, is evident in the stories, folklore, and jokes of the early pioneers. It is not surprising that the very nature of the colony forced early inhabitants to find an element in their humor which would allay their fears of the frightening harshness of the elements and the privations of their lives.

Intellectual Humor

It has been said that cartoons are popular in Australia because they are pictures and because they don't require much mental effort. Though intellectual humor is not highly regarded by the majority of Australians, it is enjoyed by some and appears in several forms, the most obvious being the tall story which is exaggerated to the point of nonsense. Even in the time-conscious society we live in today, this nonsense is evident in the miniature tall stories, or one-line exaggerations: "The harvest was so poor that the sparrows had to get down on their hands and knees to get at the wheat." Mentally stepping out of reality into fantasy has been necessary for many Australians to survive.

Another very popular form of intellectual humor is rhyming slang—mind playing with words. An example of straight-out rhyming slang is the man who tells his wife that he is just going around the Johny Horner to the rubbity dub to have a pig's ear (around the corner to the pub to have a beer). However, the aficionados only pronounce the first word, which in fact does not rhyme, so the intellectual exercise is to ascertain the second, follow-on word to obtain the rhyme, and from the rhyme, the meaning. For example,

1. I was having a quiet gunga and philla when a grass grabbed the aris, stuck it in his north and finished up Brahms.

2. I was having a quiet Gunga Din and philharmonic when a grasshopper grabbed the aristotle, stuck it in his north and south and finished up Brahms and Liszt.

3. I was having a quiet gin and tonic when a copper grabbed the bottle, stuck it in his mouth and finished up pissed.

INFORMATION SOURCES

Organizations Dealing with Humor

The Humor Comedy and Laughter League. A nonprofit organization formed in 1982 to research, study, and promote all aspects of humor, comedy, and laughter in society. President: Peter Crofts, *The Humor Comedy and Laughter League Yearly Newsletter Magazine*, 24 Station St. Sandringham, Melbourne, 3191, Victoria, Australia, International Ph. 61–3–598–3671. The primary aim of the league is to foster a comic spirit by developing a sense of humor in all people, thereby promoting happiness and peace.

The Echidnas. An association of comedians formed in 1974. They are based loosely on the English Water Rats and the American Friars. The Echidnas is a fellowship of comedians, comics, and artists whose prime purpose is to develop goodwill in the entertainment industry, support each other when necessary, and help in worthwhile causes. King Echidna: Dave Burke, P.O.B. 526, Castle Hill, 2154, NSW, Australia, International Ph. 61–2–634–3762.

The State Library of Victoria

The humor collection at the State Library of Victoria includes a variety of forms of internationally funny works, both from Australia and overseas. It includes literary humor, cartooning, comedy, and biographical material. Derek Whitehead, Acquisitions Librarian, The State Library of Victoria, 328 Swanston St., Melbourne, 3000, Victoria, Australia, International Ph. 61–3–669–9888.

TEN MOST POPULAR COMEDIANS LAST TEN YEARS

1. Barry Humphries—Live Theatre
2. Paul Hogan—TV, Films
3. Max Gillies—Live Theatre, TV
4. Rolf Harris—Live Theatre, TV
5. Rodney Rude—New Wave, Live, TV
6. Norman Gunston—TV
7. Reg Livermore—Live Theatre
8. Graham Bond—Live Theatre, TV
9. Col Elliot—Live Clubs, TV
10. Pamela Stephenson—Live Theatre, TV, Films

GLOSSARY

Afferbeck Lauder: Alphabetical Order (Strine)

Barbie: (Abbr.) Barbecue

Bunyip: A mythical monster of aboriginal legend, impostor

Cobber: Friend, mate

Digger: An Australian soldier

Dinkidi, Dinky-di, Dinkum: Used to describe that which is honest or genuine

Drongo: Someone who is stupid, worthless, clumsy

Drover: One who drives cattle or sheep

Jackaroos: A young man working on an outback rural property

Larrikin: A young street rowdy. Generally accepted explanation of its origin is that it was an Irish policeman's pronunciation of *larking*.

Ocker: Uncultivated Australian

Owyagoinmate orright: How are you going mate, all right?

Oz: Australia; Australian

Pom, Pommy: An English immigrant; an English national

REFERENCES

Afferbeck Lauder (1965) *Let Stalk Strine*. Sydney: Ure Smith.
Baker, J. S. (1945) *The Australian Language*. Sidney: Angus & Robertson.
Blaikie, G. (1966) *Remember Smith's Weekly*. Melbourne: Rigby.
Blainey, G. (1966) *The Tyranny of Distance*. Melbourne: Sun Books.
Brain, R. (1979) *Rites Black and White*. Melbourne: Penguine.
Bridges, N. (1982) *Curtain Call*. Sydney: Cassell.
———. (1983) *Wonderful Wireless*. Sydney: Cassell.
Brodsky, I. (1963) Sydney Takes the Stage. Sydney: Old Sydney Free Press.
Cole, E. W. (1879) *Cole's Funny Picture Book No. 1*. Melbourne: Cole's Book Arcade.
———. (1886) *Cole's Fun Doctor*. Melbourne: G. Routledge.
Collie, K. (1980). *Great Joke Book*. Melbourne: Argus and Australasian.
Crofts, P. (1984) "The Crofts of Comedy." *Gene Perret's Round Table* 4, no. 9: 4.
Davis, H. (1984) "On the Environmental Characteristics of Jewish Humour in Australia."
    Melbourne Chronicle Nov./Dec., no. 5 (447): 9–10.
Dean, B. (1974) Folkloric in Australia. Sydney: Pacific.
Dunstan, K. (1968) *Wowsers*. Melbourne: Cassell.
———. (1972) *Knockers*. Melbourne: Cassell.
Dutton, G. (1984) *Snow on the Saltbush*. Melbourne: Viking.
Dyson, E. (1906) *Fact'ry 'Ands*. Melbourne: Geo. Robertson.
Dyson, W. (1918) *Australia at War*. London: C. Parmer and Hyward.
Edwards, R. (1977) *The Australian Yarn*. Adelaide: Rigby.
Esar, E. (1978) *The Comic Encyclopedia*. New York: Doubleday.
Graves, G. (1980) *The Circus Comes to Town*. Sydney: Reed.

Hall, S. (1976) *Supertoy*. Melbourne: Sun Books.

Hornadge, B. (1980) *The Australian Slanguage*. Sydney: Methuen.

Irvin, E. (1971) *Theatre Comes to Australia*. Brisbane, University of Queensland Press.

Keesing, N. (1982) *Lily on the Dustbin*. Melbourne: Penguin.

King, J. (1976) *The Other Side of the Coin*. Sydney: Cassell.

———. (1978) *Stop Laughing, This Is Serious*. Sydney: Cassell.

Lawson, A. (1982) "Patrick White, Australian Explorer."
Age Saturday Extra May 29:11

Lehmann, G. J. (1972) *Comic Australian Verse*. Sydney: Angus & Robertson.

Lindesay, V. (1979) *The Inked-in Image*. Melbourne: Hutchinson.

———. (1983) *The Way We Were*. Melbourne: Oxford University Press.

Lindsay, N. (1918) *The Magic Pudding*. Sydney: Angus & Robertson.

Lockwood, R. (1985) *Humour Is Their Weapon*. Sydney: Ellsyd Press.

Lower, L. (1930) *Here's Luck*. Sydney: Angus & Robertson.

Luck, P. (1979) *This Fabulous Century*. Melbourne: Circus Books.

McGregor, C. (1968) *People, Politics, Pop*. Sydney: Ure Smith.

Mahood, M. (1973) *The Loaded Line*. Melbourne: Melbourne University Press.

Mann, P. (1982) "20 Questions Rodney Rude." *Playboy Magazine*. September: 80–83.

Moore, I. T. (1971) *Social Patterns in Australian Literature*. Sydney: Angus & Robertson.

Murray, S. (1980) *The New Australian Cinema*. Melbourne: Thomas Nelson.

O'Brien, D. (1968) "What Makes Australia Laugh," *Bulletin*, 4 May, pp. 31–35.

Parsons, F. (1973) *A Man Called Mo*. Melbourne: Heinemann.

Partridge, E. (1937) *A Dictionary of Slang and Unconventional English*. London: Routledge and Kegan.

Pearl, C. (1963) *The Best of Lennie Lower*. Melbourne: Landsdowne Press.

———. (1969) *Beer Glorious Beer*. Melbourne: Thomas Nelson.

———. (1974) *Australia's Yesterdays*. Sydney: Readers Digest Services.

Porter, H. (1965) *Stars of Australia's Stage & Screen*. London: Angus & Robertson.

Prout, D. (1963) *Henry Lawson*. Adelaide: Rigby.

Reade, E. (1970) *Australian Silent Films*. Melbourne: Lansdowne Press.

———. (1975) *The Australian Screen*. Melbourne: Lansdowne Press.

Ryan, J. (1979) *Panel by Panel*. Sydney: Cassell.

Scott, B. (1984) *The Penguin Book of Australian Humorous Verse*. Melbourne: Penguin.

Stone, W. (1984) *Folklore of Australia*. Sydney: Obelisk Press.

Tanner, L. and Coleman, P. (1967) *Cartoons of Australian History*. Melbourne: Thomas Nelson.

Turnley, C. (1974) *Cole of the Book Arcade*. Melbourne: Cole Publications.

Twain, M. (1973) *Mark Twain in Australia and New Zealand*. Melbourne: Penguin. (Facsimile of *Following the Equator*)

Wannan, B. (1954) *The Australian*. Adelaide: Currey O'Neil.

———. (1960) *A Treasury of Australian Humour*. Melbourne: Lansdowne Press.

———. (1977) *Great Book of Australian Folklore, Legends, Humour, Yarns*. Adelaide: Rigby.

West, J. (1978) *Theatre-in-Australia*. Sydney: Cassell.

Wilkes, A. G. (1978) *A Dictionary of Australian Colloquialisms*. Sydney: University Press.

Willey, K. (1984) *You Might As Well Laugh Mate*. Melbourne: Macmillan.

2

H.-W.D. AM ZEHNHOFF
AND J.-P. VAN NOPPEN

Humor in Belgium

BACKGROUND

Belgium is a small European country wedged between two large cultures (Latin and Germanic), and this uncomfortable position between two cultural and linguistic communities right across the boundary line has made it into the crossroads and battlefield of Europe. Since Caesar's times throughout the Middle Ages and the following centuries, up to Napleon's defeat at Waterloo (near Brussels) and the two World Wars in our century, Belgium has been the scene of many decisive battles, which changed the fate and the face of Europe, and has had a long history of foreign occupations: it belonged to the Roman Empire, it was split up between the French Empire and the Holy Roman Empire of the German Nation, it sustained Spanish, Austrian, French, and Dutch rules and in the twentieth century was invaded and occupied twice by Germany (in World War I and II). For 150 years Belgium has been an independent monarchy, and it seems to maintain this political structure, despite the permanent conflict between the French-speaking Walloons and the Dutch-speaking Flemings, and notwithstanding numerous internal problems due to the rift between linguistic communities, which repeatedly shakes the foundations of this small state.

A Belgian asks a Swiss, "Why does Switzerland have a Ministry of the Navy?," implying that Switzerland, which has no access to the sea, has no need for an administration of nautical affairs. To which the Swiss answers, "Why shouldn't we? Belgium, after all, has a Ministry of Culture." The story is symptomatic not only of the prevailing image of the Belgian, whose attitude toward existence is conditioned by his senses rather than his brain, but also of a fundamental inferiority complex resulting from Belgium's awareness of its smallness and its cultural dependence on neighboring nations and cultures. Doubt over a true identity leads to a form of humor in which small and earthy things are considered with fondness (the Brussels *Manneken Pis*, the small bronze statue of a little boy relieving his bladder; the popular *Smurfs*, the blue dwarfs in their toadstool village; and even Agathe Christie's Belgian detective, the short but cunning Hercule Poirot, with his Belgian turns of phrase, may be counted among the manifestations of this propensity for *nanification*). On the other hand, the conceit and bumptiousness of Belgians infatuated with the Dutch or French culture and standard language across the border, and who turn their backs on simple and honest dialect speakers, are the target of humor which seeks to relativize the clash of values.

TRADITIONAL FORMS AND EXPRESSIONS OF HUMOR

Popular Forms

We shall here tend to concentrate on the Northern part of the country, i.e., Flanders, because these counties are culturally more representative than the Southern territories for the Middle Ages. The Middle Ages undoubtedly qualify as the greatest period in the history of Flanders, especially after the region repelled an attack by France in 1302 and gained its independence. For centuries, the three cities Bruges, Ghent, and Ypres dominated the whole region between Picardia, Artois, and what is now called the provinces of Holland. Bruges, the court of the dukes of Burgundy, was at that time a powerful and radiant city, the center of the Flemish school of painters and the cultural and economic heart of Europe and the known world. (Even today Bruges is called the "Venice of the North" because of its many canals and its preserved splendor of medieval architecture.) It was only centuries later that the other Dutch-speaking cities like Antwerp and Brussels assumed a major role in the history of the Southern Netherlands, which received the name *Belgium* only 150 years ago. The splendor and the follies of the jesters, clowns, and jokers at the medieval courts and the carnival traditions and habits of the people have been described many times (Heers, 1983). These phenomena are largely similar to those in other European countries.

Nevertheless, there has always been a considerable difference between the Flemish and the Walloon carnivals. Up to the present day, cities in Flanders and

Wallonia have had carnivals celebrating their victories, their independence, or their privileges. They are, thus, more historical than humorous in character. On the other hand, Flemish carnivals have always stood closer to the carnival as it is known in the Rhineland area and Cologne. Probably due to a common history and a similar mentality, the medieval Rhenish conception of carnival has gradually advanced westwards to the southern parts of the Netherlands and the Dutch-speaking part of Belgium. This highly organized and complex form of carnival is unknown in Wallonia, where we still find the archaic festivities with stereotyped masks and customs which probably stem from the former Celtic and Gallic inhabitants of the region. The roots are clearly pre-Christian. The carnivals of Malmédy, Stavelot, and especially of Binche are famous, but are less marked by humor.

Humor in the Literary and Performing Arts

The whole history of Flanders has been marked by the struggle against the powerful political and cultural influences of France. Like other small cultures, there are today about 20 million speakers of Dutch, a minority situation not unlike that of the Irish/Gaelic culture in Great Britain. Once beyond the zenith of its Golden Age, Flanders had great difficulties resisting French attempts at cultural colonization and military occupation. In the Dutch version of the Latin satire *Isengrimus*, a courtly ''Animal's Farm'' of those times known under the name of *Van den Vos Reynaerde* (1250), we already find a significant deriding remark about the use of French at the court of Nobel, the lion-king of the animals. The vulnerable position of the Flemish/Dutch tongue with regard to the French language is a very important incentive in the production of humor, as will be discussed in further detail below.

The Dutch-speaking heritage has given Belgium and the world the character of the sly fox Reynaert. He is the leading figure in Willem's *Van den Vos Reynaerde*, which is an encoded satire about the moral state of medieval courts. The kingdom of the animals is an image of man's own society. The comic nature of this ebullient satire lies in the anthropomorphic behavior of the animals, the cunning actions of the fox, and the stupidity and naïveté of his opponents. Although he is a thief and a murderer, a dangerous intriguer and an immoral imposter, Reynaert always manages to get away with lies, tricks, and promises. And all this begs the question whether man does not actually behave like a beast. The text of *Van den Vos Reynaerde* has the function of a general ''key-novel'' to more than one medieval court and shows here that humor is a dangerous political weapon. The same function was fulfilled by Erasmus's satirical ''key-novel'' *Laus stultitiae* (Morum encomium, 1509), which harshly ridiculed the conditions of life of the contemporary clergy.

In 1556 the whole Belgian territory came under Spanish rule. The intolerant Catholic Spanish occupation forced out most of the leading Flemish writers, scientists, and artists, who fled to (Protestant) Amsterdam, where they prepared the Golden Century of Holland's culture. This emigration of the Flemish elite caused a serious decline in Flemish culture, especially in literature, where formerly the Flemings had been supreme.

Humor in the Visual Arts

A psychological by-product of the centuries of occupation is the Belgian's urge for freedom. *Tyl Uilenspiegel*, the hero of Charles de Coster's novel, is reputed to be the typical Flemish antipapist hero. With roguish wit and subversive humor he fights for the freedom of the people of Flanders against the Spanish Inquisition and Catholic tyranny. But not everybody can be a hero, and the more usual strategy of survival under repressive occupations has always been the keeping of a low profile. Thus the Flemings developed a very pragmatic attitude toward mundane reality. In Pieter Brueghel's painting *Landscape with the Fall of Icarus* this mundane reality takes up the whole foreground; the plowman tills the soil and the shepherd attends his flock while, unnoticed by both, the legs of Icarus inconspicuously disappear into the sea. Brueghel is not a comic artist, but his art bears witness to what all great comic art celebrates, i.e., the basic rhythm of life. All the rest is of minor importance. Armies will come and go, kings will rule and die, flying men will soar and fall, but "de boer ploegt voort" (the peasant keeps on plowing). As Michel de Ghelderode, the great Belgian dramatic writer, who excelled in eccentricity and satiric humor points out, Brueghel—in fact all the Belgian satirists—have painted the Belgian ugly and courageous. The Belgian dances because he has to live—and the peasants of Brueghel dance beneath the gallows. Belgians are more given to action than to tragic emotions: immobility is a concession to death, and in every circumstance, the primal human instincts endure. . . . "Stronger than the funerary oration which he is delivering, the Belgian feels the need to urinate." The typical Fleming—and on that point he differs not at all from the Walloon—is not an Icarus, Faust, Don Juan, or Don Quixote; he is a moderate in every way and tries not to get involved in other men's business.

DEVELOPMENT OF HUMOR IN THE TWENTIETH CENTURY

Popular Forms

As in any other country, cracking jokes is the most popular form of humor. But in Belgium the specific linguistic situation is particularly productive of dialectal jokes, which can be divided into Walloon and Flemish popular jokes.

There are hundreds of jokes in the dozen or so dialects in Flanders as well as in Wallonia. But their actual importance is hard to assess. It is striking to hear the well-known Flemish actor Romain De Koninck shifting from standard Dutch into his Ghentian dialect when he is cracking jokes in his radio shows on BRT, the Flemish broadcast corporation. The same thing happens with the only Flemish couple of clowns, Gaston and Leon from Antwerp. They produce slapstick humor *á la manière de* Laurel and Hardy on BRT television, on radio, and in several movies. The only language they know and use is Antwerp dialect. In most cases, dialect is an impediment for broad reception, but this is not always so. The anarchistic and infantile musical clown Urbanus van Anus from Brabant, known for his musical parodies in his local dialect, is extremely popular in Holland, where his inconceivable Flemish accent forms his trademark. He is loved there for his portrayal of the stereotyped underdeveloped, simple-minded, and coarse Fleming/Belgian. The widespread popularity of the musical parody group The Strangers in Flanders and Holland has never been hindered by their intentional use of the Antwerp dialect. Their specialty is parodies of current hits. In the last two cases, it is obvious that the form of humor used depends less on the use of local dialect than on the special form of representation and the choice of music.

On the French-speaking side, there are surprisingly similar but less frequent tendencies. Stéphane Steeman, a well-known Brussels actor in vaudeville shows, is famous for his jokes and parodic speech imitations of Belgian politicians. Although he uses French, his way of speaking, his accent, and his imagination are anything but French. He is of course influenced by the Brussels dialect, which is a rare blend of Flemish culture and French-speaking civilization. Such a blending is obviously possible only in a more or less bilingual capital like Brussels/Bruxelles. In the southern provinces, where only French (and perhaps a local dialect) is spoken, there is a tradition of Walloon storytelling and regional comedy theatre.

Humor in the Literary and Performing Arts

As we have seen above, the consequences of the Spanish Inquisition and occupation, followed by 300 years of foreign rule of the Belgium territories, were very negative, especially for the Flemish nation. This "beheading" of the culture changed Flanders into a "speechless" nation, i.e., a region without a standard language of its own, but with dozens of local dialects. Since that time there has been considerable linguistic defection to other cultures and languages, mainly French. Many famous French-writing Belgian artists, like Maurice Maeterlinck, Emile Verhaeren, Charles de Coster, and Michel de Ghelderode, were actually Flemings who wrote in French because of the lack of Flemish literary readership. This brain drain from Flanders entailed the loss of an eminent literary potential and the absence of a uniform language for political, scientific, and administrative purposes. When Belgium became independent, this linguistic gap was filled by the other national language, i.e., French. Only at the end of the nineteenth century did the Flemish language revive; and since that time it has been regaining its proper place in Flanders and the other Dutch-speaking provinces. But the supposedly "standard" language in which every Fleming is educated nowadays is regarded as an artificial tongue, coined mainly after Dutch as it is spoken in the Netherlands. Many Flemings do not feel at ease with this imposed variety, which sometimes differs considerably from their local mother-dialect and is therefore perceived as a foreign language. This situation has disastrous consequences notably for literary creativity as well as for linguistic competence in general. But the consequences of the loss of the Flemish elite during the Spanish occupation and the following centuries, combined with a great talent for pictorial communication (cf. the Flemish School, the Brueghels, Teniers, Rubens, etc.), devloped the famous Belgian school of "narrative" painters and drawers. Nowadays this pictorial propensity survives in the form of cartoons, caricatures, and comic strips like Tintin, Lucky Luke, The Smurfs, and scores of others.

It is obvious that the situation of French is quite different in Belgium. Although there is a variety of Walloon dialects, the attitude of the French-speaking Belgian toward his own language is much less complicated.

A major contribution to world literature is Tyl Ulenspiegel, the hero of Charles de Coster's *Légende d'Ulenspiegel* (1867). Tyl is a popular joker reflecting the rural population's rejection of, and opposition to, all forms of social or cultural domination. Although originally a character in Central European folklore (Till Eulenspiegel), Tyl is represented as an epic hero who travels throughout Flanders in the company of the obese and good-natured Lamme Goedzak. The ill-matched but closely knit assemblage is reminiscent of Don Quixote and Sancho Panza (cf. Don Camillo and Peppone, Laurel and Hardy); but the comical couple's enemies are no windmills: Tyl is soon involved in the political and religious struggle opposing the people of the Low Countries to the Spanish oppressor in the sixteenth century. The initial wag is transfigured into a champion of freedom and becomes the epitome of a people's conscience. But the character's status as a symbol in no way detracts from the folksy vitality of the original type. And it is perhaps this duality which constitutes the originality of de Coster's Tyl, as well as his national specificity. Neither misfortune nor violence can tear the joyful companion away from his homeland with its healthy lust and hence his craving for freedom.

One of the most popular novels of Felix Timmermans is *Pallieter* (1916). The name, which in modern Dutch means "wag," belongs to a typical Flemish farmer, who enjoys the good things of life and always has time to make fun of other people; he is philosophical and vital, religious and full of good-natured humor. It is certainly no coincidence that the popular Flemish nationalist satirical magazine *'t Pallieterke* (Little Wag) has adopted his name.

De Witte (the Albino) (1920), by Ernest Claes, is in a way the Flemish equivalent of Mark Twain's *The Adventures of Tom Sawyer* (1876) and *The Adventures of Huckleberry Finn* (1884). It is the well-known story of a boy in a small village who plays tricks on many people on many occasions.

On the French-speaking side, Michel de Ghelderode has been called the "theatre's Bosch" as well as the "Flemish Shakespeare." His dramatic oeuvre, though penned in French, offers a carnivalesque vision of the world inspired by Flemish popular history and the pictorial tradition of Brueghel, Teniers, and Jordaens. His satanic buffooneries depict hallucinatory visions with disproportionate, exalted characters, a burlesque theatre which qualifies as the epitome of Belgian black humor inasmuch as this "great comedy of appearances" is the grating instrument of a lonely man's exorcism of his fear of death and erotic obsessions.

Humor appears in the works of quite a few other French-speaking Belgians (Achille Chavee, Fernand Crommelynck, Henry Michaux, G. Norge, Jean Ray, etc.), but more often humor is a device to relieve wryness or disenchantment, or the effect of a distorted, fantastic, or surrealist vision of the universe, than a deliberate attempt to amuse or elicit laughter. In this respect, the critic's terms "serious farce" and "sad burlesque" are revealing. Jacques Sternberg creates a universe that has been described as "Kafka rewritten by the Marx Brothers"; Jean Muno in his latest novel, *Histoire exécrable d'un héros brabançon* (Abominable Story of a hero from Brabançon) (1982), brandishes laughter as a weapon against the narrow-mindedness and complacency of the Belgian bourgeoisie, as the largely autobiographic character is pictured at grips with his parents' mentality, the German occupation, and eventually with the language boundary running through his backyard.

It is striking to notice that the only songwriters worth mentioning in Belgium are French-speaking. World famous Jacques Brel became something of a national hero after his untimely death. While some of his songs such as *Le Plat Pays* (Flat country) narrate the beauty of the country, his satirical repertoire (*Les Bourgeois*, *Les Flamandes*, etc.) scoffs at the ugly sides of Belgian life: the obtuseness of the bourgeois, the senility of the clergy, the obesity and bigotry of the Flemish, the conceit of the upstarts, the injustices and hypocrisy of the rich, and, of course, the accent of the Brusselers. Julos Beaucarne puts his irony and humor to the service of a pacifist and ecological commitment (*The Fruit Tree Liberation Movement*) and occasionally draws on the resources of Walloon language and its popular tales. Annie Cordy and Le Grand Jojo definitely belong to the more commercial and less subtle "oompah" genre. They are, however, very popular in France.

On the other hand, the finest and most cultured musician, pianist, and composer is the Fleming François Glorieux. After a successful career as a serious pianist, he started about 15 years ago an "unserious" career as composer of musical parodies. He manages to compose and improvise piano pieces with melodies of the Beatles *à la manière de* Chopin, Schumann, Brahms, Milhaud, etc. His great talent, musical culture, and humor enable him even to play the famous "Für Elise" by Beethoven à la Mozart's "Allegro," or "A Maiden's Prayer" by Badarzewska à la "Invitation to the Dance" by Carl Maria von Weber. While one would expect him to be known only to an elite of insiders, Glorieux is rather popular and his concerts are well attended.

Brussels is the privileged place to observe the different currents of the nation's humorous production. The blend of the two (and even more) cultures in the theatre and verbal humor accounts for this specific identity. As we have seen, the nation's capital, with its French-speaking majority enclaved in the Flemish part of the province of Brabant, has grown into a separate area with its own humor and folklore, but it nevertheless embraces nearly all the nation's tendencies.

Humor in Brussels is popular at root, and has its origins in the proletarian Marolles quarter, where Pieter Brueghel the Elder lived, painted, and died. Only in recent times have its manifestations moved from the narrow streets around the flea market into more respectable sections of town. Like Brueghel's paintings, the Brussels stories and anecdotes show the small man at the bottom of the social ladder in the predicaments of everyday life (household rows over excessive drinking or late homecoming; cuckoldry and adultery; fussy landlords, bossy mothers-in-law, and zealous but incompetent constables) or at grips with authority, incarnated in the judge, the policeman, the tram conductor, or the post-office clerk. While the situations themselves may qualify as comical or farcical and are not infrequently marked by the Brussels *zwanze*, in which the superior-acting character is taken for a ride and thus ridiculed, the greatest amusement is elicited by the language in which the story is told: the Brussels dialect is a corrupt mixture of Flemish, French, and malapropisms larded with typical expressions and earthy imagery. The anecdotes come in book form (*Les Fables de Pitje Schramouille* or Quievreux's *Mes Mille et Un Bruxelles*), but weekly musings and dialogues also appear in popular newspapers (Jef Kazak in *Le Peuple* and *Vlan*, Virgile in the satirical magazine *Pourquoi Pas?*, the Belgian counterpart of the famous French *Canard Enchaine*).

In the dialectical genre, the traditional Toone puppet theatre (originally a cheap form of amusement in a cellar room furnished with wooden benches) brings classics (*Hamlet*, *Faust*, or *Carmen*) and historical plays (*The Four Sons of Aymon*, *The Three Musketeers*, *1830*) down to the popular level with naive emphasis on spectacular, spicy, and supernatural episodes, but the humor resides in the discrepancy between the seriousness of the themes and the straightforward earthiness of the language—in recent times with more emphasis on the accent than on the vocabulary, as the public is increasingly composed of non-Brusselers.

On the Brussels stage, where French comedies and vaudeville are popular, the local humor takes the form of dialectal comedies. Of the once proliferating genre, two plays have remained all-time favorites of the Brussels public: *Le Marriage de Mademoiselle Beulemans* (F. Fonson and F. Wicheler) in which a French-speaking employee is initially ostracized by a Brussels-speaking family but eventually weds the daughter, and *Bossemans et Compenolle*, the epic of a feud between opposing football teams.

The revues, or variety shows (Théatre de la Gaité, du Vaudeville, des Galeries, Molière), are an ephemeral but recurrent genre in which the satirical component is leveled at the public's favorite culprits (politicians, taxes, the police, and in recent times the national networks). Here as before, the dialectal element is important and adds spice to otherwise rather gentle mockery (Stéphane Steeman); malicious humor does not go down well with the public.

Humor in the Visual Arts

A first, albeit schematic, conclusion is that Flemish humor is not based on linguistic wit and mastery of the Dutch language; when Flemings resort to verbal humor—and they actually are full of good-natured laughter—they mostly relapse into their familiar local dialect. It is difficult to crack jokes in a language one does not truly master; and when Flemings seek to express their humor to those who do not speak the same dialect or language, they do not produce texts, but *pictures*. The language controversy, which pervades and poisons all of cultural and political life, may well have acted as a boost to graphic humor. The obvious reason is that it is not language-dependent, addresses both communities, and even reaches beyond the narrow confines of the kingdom. It is perhaps not by chance that cartoons and strips (see above) are today the most representative manifestations of Belgium's humor abroad.

Although there is a long tradition of painters and drawers of humorous and satirical scenes in Belgium, little is known about a genuine Belgian history of cartoons; e.g., there is no biographical information about the cartoonists of the nineteenth century. We have the legacy of their drawings, but nearly no names. Even the history of the cartoon in Belgium before World War II is in most cases an anonymous affair. We have here the names of the greatest cartoonists of the prewar era, but we shall concentrate on the period after 1945:   Hergé (Georges Remy, Brussels) is probably the most influential artist; he is the father of Tintin, the world-famous comic-strip figure, whose adventures have been translated into 30 languages and sold in more than 70 million copies. It is less known that in the beginning of his long career, Hergé was quite a popular cartoonist too. Unfortunately, his artistic skill is much more highly developed than his polemical talent. He has never felt the need to doubt traditional bourgeois values, and that is the reason why he lacks the necessary aggressiveness. His artistic style is more influential than his ideology, but he is nevertheless representative of the Belgian artists of his kind.

The Antwerp humorous painter and drawer Georges Van Raemdonck (Antwerp/Amsterdam) was one of the first Belgian cartoonists: he is the creator of *Bulletje en Bonestaak*, the first Dutch-speaking comic strip. His style is very accurate and realistic, his scenarios are inspired by everyday life, and the narrative elements are clearly influenced by his political vision. Joz De Swerts ("Joz") is regarded as the most talented drawer of his time. He worked mainly for the Catholic publishing house Goede Pers and the satirical magazine *Pallieter* (not to be confused with the satirical magazine *'t Pallieterke* of our day). His style is also characterized by accuracy and realism.

Frans Van Immerseel worked for the newspapers *Ons Volk* and *De Standaard*. His cartoons were less realistically elaborated, but his technique, which stresses the outlines only, is still very modern.

Jam (Paul Jamin), one of the few Walloon cartoonists, stands out above all others: he published in *Le Pays Réel*, the newspaper of Léon Degrelle, the leader of the fascist Rex-movement and one of the leading figures in the collaboration with the Nazi occupiers during World War II. Jam's technique is influenced by Hergé's, but unlike Hergé, Jam is gifted with a brilliant, razor-edged satirical talent. He was even active in the pro-German propaganda. In spite of his political past, but thanks to his skill, he is still very much in vogue and works for the small (French-speaking, conservative) satirical magazine *Pan* and for the big (Catholic, Flemish) newspaper *De Standaard* under the pseudonym Alidor. His style is invariably realistic and explicit; his satire is as profound as it is incisive.

After 1945, a whole new evolution took place in Belgian cartoon production. Owing to the Anglo-American competition and under influence of its models, quite a number of artists in the new generation turned to the production of genuine comic strips. From this period onwards, Hergé exclusively produced his world-famous *Tintin* comic strip, his *Quick et Flupke*, and *Jo, Zette et Jocko* series (Casterman, Tournai/Utrecht). Marc Sleen, a gifted cartoonist, concentrated fully on the production of his very popular *De avonturen van Nero en Co.* (The Adventures of Nero and Co., Scriptoria Antwerp/Standaard Uitgeverij Antwerpen/Amsterdam). Marc Sleen's productions reach the amazing number of 100 albums. Nero, the leading figure of the series, is a moderate Brussels bourgeois whose only ambition is to be left alone; yet he is always entangled in the most fantastic and unbelievable adventures all over the world, and thanks to his son Adhemar, a ten-year-old genius and multitalented scientist, he always makes a narrow escape from the most dangerous situations. Every strip ends with a homecoming to his family and a ritual coffee-and-wafer party in a warm and reconciled atmosphere. Sleen's characters are tenderly distorted caricatures, full of fantastic eccentricities and sheer madness. Sleen's technique (unlike Hergé's) is not realistic but caricatural; the outlines are exaggerated and not as clear as in the scanty scenarios of Hergé. Sleen has much more fantasy and is incomparably funnier, but he is not critical either. His colleague Willy Vandersteen is even more productive: in thirty years, he and his team have created about 130 books with the adventures of Suske and Wiske, an enterprising neice and nephew. They live in typical Flemish middle-class surroundings in an undefined family situation with their Aunt Sidonie and their Uncle Lambik, the most comical figure of the series. Suske and Wiske meet with the most fantastic situations, since they own a sort of time machine and are able to travel through history; in spite of the arrogant clumsiness of Lambik, they manage to survive all perils. Lambik is actually a negative caricature of the typical petty-bourgeois with all his failings: he is arrogant, incompetent, tyrannical, egocentric, lazy, etc., but all his defects put together make him extremely ridiculous and funny. All the characters of Vandersteen are heavily stereotyped, and the lack of artistic fantasy fits well the propagation of conservative Flemish middle-class values. His style too is influenced by Hergé, but he adds much more detail to the background. Sleen and Vandersteen are rather "Flemish-minded" and work mostly for the publishing group around the Flemish Standaard Uitgeverij. Nevertheless, there are translations for the French-speaking public, *Les aventures de Néron et Cie* and *Bob et Bobette*, which are very popular too.

Jef Nijs (sometimes Jeff Nice) also started his career as a drawer of humorous scenes, caricatures, and cartoons. He worked for the Flemish satirical magazine *'t Pallieterke*, a rare combination of high-quality satire, cartoons, and an extremely Flemish-nationalist, right-wing (close to prewar fascism) ideology. In this case "satirical" is not at all a synonym of "left-wing." *'t Pallieterke* is full of harsh criticism against the State of Belgium (which is an easy target) and openly propagates separatism, i.e, the independence of Flanders as an autonomous state. Nevertheless, the magazine is very popular in Flanders, and it has survived much competition from the political left. Left-wing satirical magazines tend to be very short-lived in Flanders. The last magazine to disappear was *De Zwijger* (The Taciturn). It was a very modern, well-made satirical review with excellent writers and cartoonists, but the Flemish public seemed to prefer the old-fashioned *'t Pallieterke*. On the French-speaking side we have a similar constellation: like *'t Pallieterke*, *Pan* is a small satirical paper which obviously belongs to the conservative wing. The famous Alidor—as we have seen above, a right-wing satirist with a fascist past—publishes his brilliant anti-Belgian cartoons here. Although *Pan* is small, it is influential, but in French-speaking Belgium it does not enjoy the status of a leading satirical magazine, as does *'t Pallieterke* in Flanders. The left-wing *Pourquoi Pas?* is of much more importance, and the French *Harakiri* and *Le canard enchainé* enjoy a large readership in Belgium as well. Jef De Nijs also eventually switched to a regular production of comic strips: *De belevenissen van Jommeke* (The adventures of Jommeke, a small boy). More than a hundred books have been published by Het Volk, Ghent. The charm of the series lies in the infantile humor of Jommeke and is aimed at a young readership. The style is influenced by Hergé but is less realistic.

While the most outstanding Belgian cartoonists are French-speaking, most Belgian authors of cartoons and comic strips are Flemings. This is probably the consequence of the systematic support of Flemish humoristic artists by the Vlaamse Toeristen en Automobilisten Bond (Flemish Association of Tourists and Motorists), which in spite of its name is a very significant cultural institution of the Flemish movement. In the winter of 1951–52 it organized for the first time a Salon van de Vlaamse humor (Flemish Humor Fair), which included an exhibition of Flemish cartoons. Since that time, the fair has been organized at regular intervals, and many Flemish artists were discovered there by the public and the press. Since 1964 the biannual World Cartoons Festival has taken place in Knokke-Heist; this festival is an international event. On the Flemish side there are quite a number of local exhibitions, and even in Wallonia (Namur) a cartoon festival was organized recently. Most laureates of these festivals embarked on international careers: Joke (Jo Lagrillière) published in *Playboy* (U.S.), in Holland, and Germany; Leon (Leon Van Roey) worked for *Stern* (Germany) and in Switzerland, France, Holland, Great Britain, and Scandinavia, and now lives in Denmark. Picha (Jean-Paul Walravens), first laureate in Knokke-Heist in 1964,

STAFFORDSHIRE
POLYTECHNIC
LIBRARY

where he beat Virgil Partch (VIP) as a finalist, is another prominent Flemish cartoonist who works for the international press and publishing houses. Another great name is Bob De Moor, a gifted cartoonist, former first assistant to Hergé, and after Hergé's death in 1983, his successor as chief editor of the Tintin productions. André Franquin is the creator of the popular character Gaston Lagaffe (Dupuis, Mons), a desperately lazy, absent-minded office boy with a natural talent for messing things up. Got (Gommaar Timmermans) is another famous cartoonist from Flanders; he worked for several magazines in Germany and had many exhibitions abroad. Ray Gilles is probably the most active cartoonist and designer, since he publishes his cartoons regularly in most European countries and has an international reputation as designer and painter.

The paintings and drawings of Belgian-born Jean-Michel Folon have met with increasing success, particularly in France, where the artist now lives (Baetens and Willemyns, 1981). The humor of his pictures resides in their unexpected associations and the metamorphosis of objects (in one album, drawings have been made on letters, in which the stamp and the address are integrated in the picture [Soavi, 1974], but also in their striking tenderness—a pair of lips viewed as a gondola, the earth listening to men walking on it). Often, the drawings seem to denounce man's cruelty to his environment or the absurdity of man's existential situation. The characters, often hatted and coated middle-aged men (cf. Magritte, the great Belgian surrealistic painter) made of bricks, seem to be floating in an indifferent universe, lost in bewildering mazes where they follow arrows into the void, or locked up in transparent bubbles which keep them from communicating. But there are occasional suggestions that the pain of loneliness is self-inflicted.

Young talents are Jean-Pol (Jean-Paul Vandenbroek), a conventional humorist; Kamagurka (Luc Zeebroek), a particularly aggressive satirist; Pierre Leterme; and Luk Tegenbos, laureate at the World Cartoons Festival in Knokke-Heist, 1970.

In addition to being the home of many a great cartoonist, Belgium qualifies, as we have seen, as the Eldorado of the comic strip. This is due not only to the unique concentration of artistic talent but to other reasons also. In France a 1949 law enforced censorship of the "bestial and immoral" American comics (*Tarzan*, *Batman*, *Flash Gordon*) departing too widely from the established morality, but Belgium never knew such limitations. Yet youth magazines like *Spirou* and *Vaillant* acquired a reputation of "seriousness" by adopting bourgeois patriotic values. *Pilote*, on the other hand, attracted the interest of the adult public by allowing talented caricaturists like Gotlib, Greg, and Fred to earn names for themselves, thus freeing the Belgian strip from its ideological conformity. Anyhow, whether bourgeois conformistic or not, strip albums rate among Belgium's favorite export products. In Hergé's famous *Tintin* series, the clean, well-shaven journalist-detective opposes his boy-scout idealism to crime and dishonesty throughout the world. The humor of the album resides in its general slight irony, secondary characters, and (heavily stereotyped) "cultural" allusions rather than in the plot of the stories: the hard-drinking Captain Haddock has a gift for powerful invective; inventor Tournesol's genius is counterbalanced by his deafness, which renders communication all but impossible; secret service agents Dupont and Dupond, as symbols of "Belgitude," are clumsy and echolalic twins. In the present days of international travel, *Tintin*'s national stereotypes often appear naive, if not offensive (Americans as cowboys or gangsters, Africans as childish primitives, Latin Americans as fickle banana-republic dictators, etc.)

Lucky Luke, by Morris and Goscinny (who are also the scenario writers of *Astérix and Obélix*), is a popular parody of American Westerns. Much of the fun of these albums stems from their parodic character, but the comic effect is owed also to the multitalented Jolly Jumper, Lucky Luke's horse.

Peyo's Smurfs, by their smallness, constant quarreling, and funny language use, are a microcosmic picture of Belgium itself. The point is most clearly underscored in *Schtroumpf Vert et Vert Schroumpf* (Schtroumpf = Smurfs), where the village is bitterly divided over linguistic usage and winds up with a language border running straight through gardens and houses.

Quick et Flupke, a production by the team of Hergé, pursues the tradition of Knerr's *The Katzenjammer Kids*, in that their rather innocuous gaffes constantly put them at odds with the neighborhood constable. A rare case of typical Walloon humor is Walthery and Cauvin's *Le Vieux Bleu*, which deserves a special mention as—like the Walloon dialectal theatre—it introduces a regional element: through the comic situations unfolding around a grandfather's passion for pigeon racing, the authors sketch the weal and woe of a village in the Liège area.

Belgian cartoonists and comic-strip authors work mainly for the big newspapers and magazines like their colleagues in other countries. It is worth mentioning that the local television and radio magazines *Moustique* (Télé-Moustique) and its Flemish counterpart *Humo* (Humo-radio), which have been around for 60 years, are a rare mixture of a radio and television magazine and a cartoon and comic-strip magazine, bringing together many styles and authors.

Public or Specialized Places for Humorous Expression

a. There is an annual Festival du Rire (Festival of Laughter) in Rochefort, which could have been one of the highlights of Belgian (French-speaking) humor. The festival, however, attracts much foreign participation, and its role as a boost to promising youngsters is mitigated by the jury's emphasis on inventiveness and renewal of the art rather than on comic quality. The festival takes place every year in early May.

Information: Festival du Rire, Mme. Deloncin, Hôtel de Ville, B–5430 Rochefort; Tel.: 084/212537.

b. The 25th World Cartoon Festival in Knokke-Heist took place in 1986; the theme was "Beer and Humor." The exhibition was open from June 20 to September 10, 1986. Prizes were given on June 20.

Information: World Cartoon Festival, v.z.w. Humorstad, Zeedijk Knokke, 660, B–8300 Knokke-Heist; Tel.: 050/606185.

c. The very interesting Musée International du Carnaval et du Masque de Binche is situated in the ancient abbey of the small Walloon city of Binche.

Information: Rue de l'Église, B–7130 Binche; Tel.: 064/335741.

The small private Museum van de Lach (Museum of Laughter) in the tiny city of Kuurne (West-Flanders), with its collection of cartoons, puppets, and humorously altered objects, has just ceased to exist.

d. The small city of Damme near Bruges is the legendary birthplace of Tyl Ulenspiegel. The Tyl Ulenspiegel Museum is situated here; there is a large collection of "Ulenspiegeliana," such as paintings, books and various historical material.

Information: Tyl Ulenspiegel Museum, Jakob van Maerlantstraat 3, B–8340 Damme; Tel.: 050/353319.

e. And there is the Ulenspiegel-Gezellen; this is the highly regarded association of Friends of Ulenspiegel, which deals with the historical study of the character of Ulenspiegel.

Information: Ulenspiegel-Gezellen, Chairman: Guy De Laander, Zwaanstraat 40, B–8340 Damme; Tel.: 050/351943 (Honorary Chairman: Danny Heyneman).

Humor in the Mass Media (Radio and TV)

There are two full-fledged radio and television networks in Belgium, one for the French-speaking community (the RTBF) and one for the Dutch-speaking community (the BRT). (Actually there is a third network for the German-speaking minority.) On the national RTBF television network, Bernard Faure's program "Zygomaticorama" features the ventriloquist Michel Dejeneffe with his wide-eyed animal doll Tatayet, whose gentle ridicule of the adults' serious world (the administration, the law, the school, and an occasional shot at taboos like the Church or death) provokes laughter and an occasional tear. Faure's candid camera ("La Caméra Invisible") places unsuspecting citizens in a universe where ordinary relationships of causality are disturbed, thus forcing people to react irrationally; but cruel or potentially degrading scenarios are avoided. The spectator, who finds himself in the role of a voyeur, laughs, while Zygo's victims show puzzlement, mild discontent, or surprising ingeniousness (thus confirming the widespread stereotype of the Belgian as resourceful and crafty). Anger is provoked only when limits of well-manneredness are trespassed upon (as when Zygo dips his croissant in a stranger's cup of coffee) or when people's (linguistic) freedom is jeopardized (e.g., when a bookstall attendant pretends a new law forces customers to buy a paper in each of the national languages).

A similar program on the Flemish network BRT "TV Touché," was a short-lived experiment that petered out after a couple of years. Flemish television seems to give preference to Anglo-American comedy-import products over its own productions. The main reason is that the "canned laughter" series from abroad are cheaper than the home productions. ''The Benny Hill Show'' (British) and many American series attract the average Flemish public in a sufficient way. There are sporadic attempts at humorous homemade TV productions, but only the series ''De college's'' (The colleagues) is worth mentioning. The series depicts the everyday life of office boys, clerks, and secretaries in one of the Kafkaesque ministries of the capital. The humor lies mainly in the funny dialectal way of speaking and in the well-observed psychology of the characters.

On the RTBF-radio, Stéphane Steeman amuses the public for hours with his phone call program in which people are made to participate in the strangest scenarios. On the BRT-radio, dialectal jokes are cracked in some very short shows of Romain De Koninck and Walter Capiau. Some years ago, Capiau caused serious political scandal when in his show he phoned some politicians imitating the voice of the Royal master of ceremonies announcing the visit of the king. Capiau was fired, but he is now back in show business, since he is extremely funny. A new talent is Kurt Van Eeghem, who has produced some series of shows on television. His humor is outright surrealistic and is sometimes reminiscent of the mad Monty Python humor. On the radio he is known for his careful parodies of the king's manner of speaking Dutch, as the monarch speaks the other national language in a way no one else does, since it is hypercorrect with an ever-so-slight French accent.

CONTEMPORARY HUMOR AND TRENDS

In general terms, the technical revolution of the latest decade provides new facilities, notably in the electronic reproduction of sound and image. There is a tendency among singers and showmen to resort to these techniques to entrance their multimedia parodies and imitations.

The general trend of cartoons is away from children's humor toward a more intellectual, but also more aggressive, adult genre in which an increasing place is given to the erotic and pornographic.

UNIVERSAL FUNCTIONS OF HUMOR AND THE NATIONAL MANIFESTATIONS

Aggressive Humor

It is quite normal that a bicultural, bilingual country like Belgium should be full of reciprocal resentment and rivalry between language communities. Walloons and Flemings both suffer from an inferiority complex. The former linguistic, cultural, and economic superiority of the Walloons and the French-speaking Belgians has now been reversed. Quite a lot of aggressive humor, mostly in the popular form of jokes, is exchanged between the language groups. Most likely it is a way to express each group's craving for superiority (Ziv, 1984, p. 7) or its desire to reachieve it. Belgium's history and present sociopolitical development seem to foster homemade bilateral aggression between the

French-speaking and the Flemings, although ethnic differences are not profoundly marked.

The differences between Flemings and Walloons are mainly marked by the different use of and attitude toward language (Baetens and Willemyns, 1981). Most Flemings are diglossic inasmuch as they speak both their local dialect and standard Dutch, and bilingual as they speak Dutch and French and often have serious notions of English and German as well. Flemings speaking four or five foreign languages are not exceptional, while the French-speaking Belgian hardly manages—or cares for that matter—to learn such a "bizarre" language as Dutch, albeit the other national language, and his proficiency in other foreign languages is rather limited. The consequence is that the French-speaking Belgian has progressively lost his predominant influence in Belgian politics and economy and that the former Flemish "underdog" nowadays takes charge of Belgian affairs.

A Flemish and a Walloon factory stand facing each other across the language boundary. One day, the Walloons fly a banderole from their factory with the slogan "Here we don't speak Flemish!" The next day, the Flemish factory exhibits a banderole with "Here we don't speak. We work!"

In spite of their agricultural, proletarian, and petty-bourgeois backgrounds, Flemings seem more ambitious, work harder, make more money and are in economic terms generally more successful than the Walloons; Flemings have a higher birthrate, they now constitute the majority in Belgium, their standard of living is one of the highest in the world, they are very culture-minded and have a splendid artistic tradition—and yet they *feel* envied, ridiculed, and belittled by the French as well as by the Dutch.

It is not immediately clear why Belgium's neighbors, the Dutch and the French, like to treat the Belgians as targets of their aggressive humor. Of course, the French have the tendency to ridicule the "petit Belge" because of his funny way of speaking French and his proverbial taste for beer, steak, and chips or french fries.

How do the Belgians torture their prisoners? By putting them in a round cell and telling them there is a french fried potato in a corner.

The Belgian dialectal realization of Dutch also comes across as funny and unsophisticated to Dutch standard-language speakers. But this cannot motivate all the aggressive humor against the Belgians. Besides, who are the Belgians? Most aggressive humor seems to be directed against the Flemings, and it is really hard to tell why they should be the favorite victims, since they differ little from the Walloons.

But Flemings are the culprits rather than the creators of aggressive and negative humor: they are depicted as coarse and underdeveloped, simple-minded morons. One or two generations ago, the Flemings were indeed in a very unfavorable situation: they were the underdogs in a state dominated by the French-speaking classes. Now they are rising in the social hierarchy, and the former image is falser than ever. (Compare Anglo-American jokes about Poles and Irish; and the German "Ostfriesenwitze," jokes about the East Frisians, a minority in the northern part of Germany.) Walloon jokes about the Flemish:

1. Why is the air so fresh in Flanders? Because the Flemish sleep with their windows shut.
2. Why do the Flemish enjoy scuba diving? Because deep down, they are not stupid.

Dutch joke about the Belgians (the Dutch have hundreds of similar jokes about the Flemish, but they always call them "Belgenmoppen," i.e., Belgian jokes):

1. How does a Belgian shepherd count his sheep? He counts the paws and divides the sum by four!
2. Why do Belgian farmers always strangle their plum-trees? Because they think that the plums will turn blue earlier.
3. Why do Belgians have scratched faces on Monday morning? Because on Sundays, they eat with forks and knives.
4. In the Belgian army: " . . . and be extremely careful with these explosives! Last year, some of them exploded during maneuvers in Canada and there were dozens of casualties." "Don't worry, corporal, it could never happen here: There are only five of us!"
5. How do you catch a Belgian? Slam down the toilet ring while he's drinking in the bowl.

Of course as Charlie Chaplin often said, all comedy is based on man's delight in man's inhumanity to man—but the negative image of the Belgian/Fleming made up by the Dutch is a grossly exaggerated distortion. However, the Belgians themselves use the same sort of jokes against each other, and for every joke there is anti-Walloon, anti-Flemish, and/or even an anti-Brussels version. The internal Belgian balance of humorous "victimology" has therefore struck an equilibrium. Main targets of Belgian jokes are the Belgians themselves: there are as many anti-Flemish jokes made up by the Walloons as there are jokes about the Walloons made up by the Flemings. It is very difficult to tell on which side these jokes are generated, but since the Flemings are not very creative in cracking jokes in standard Dutch, it is not unlikely that the anti-Walloon jokes are inverted copies of anti-Flemish originals. In that case, the jokes are exclusively self-defensive, and because of the lack of a direct verbal communication across the language border, they are meant for internal use only.

Sexual Humor

Apparently, Belgium is one of the rare countries where problems with sexuality, eroticism, and pornography are not manifest. Of course, all the problems exist, but in a bourgeois-Catholic society like Belgium they are sanctioned or hidden by a heavy taboo. It is really striking to see—compared with countries like Holland or Denmark—how old-fashionedly prudish and submissive the greater part of the population is with regard to these questions. The law is still very strict, and the sexual liberation of the sixties has left few marks here. People are not interested in such subjects, and their introduction in a conversation— albeit humorous—very often causes bewilderment.

The groups which are interested in sexual humor are consequently very restricted. Sexual humor flourishes of course among schoolboys, students, and soldiers, where it functions as an outlet for frustrations and/or nonconformism. On November 20, the anniversary of the foundation of the Free University, students have their own carnival-procession through town on decorated trucks, with anticlericalism and sex in its cruder forms as constant factors throughout the varying themes. The saucy songs sung at this occasion are collected in the songbook *Les Fleurs du Mâle*, its title a parody of Baudelaire's volume of poetry.

But the specific sociocultural structure of Belgium apparently has no need of such a thing as sexual humor. It fulfills no public function, not even funny subversion, and features no particular national character.

Social Humor

As we have seen above, the use of Walloon or Flemish dialects in the production of humor is very frequent. It is possible that the plethora of dialects mainly exists to protect speakers against external influence and intrusion. The local dialect can be regarded as a safe island where one can be isolated and left undisturbed. The fact that Belgians prefer to crack jokes in their local dialects can be interpreted as the wish to "include" some and "exclude" others by means of humor: if someone understands my dialectal joke, he belongs to the in-group; if not, he is a stranger (Ziv, 1984, pp. 26–43).

In the situation of Belgium, which is marked by mutual resentment between the two cultural groups, this including/excluding humor could have two effects. First, it separates clearly between Walloons (and French-speaking Belgians) and Flemings by means of ethnological themes and leitmotifs, i.e., the stupid Fleming or Walloon and vice versa. Secondly, it subdivides the two linguistic groups into in-groups and out-groups. Within the framework of such a twofold particularism, a whole range of social functions can take place: aggression, self-defense, inclusion and exclusion, and correction. In our opinion, a clear-cut division into all these aspects does not correspond to reality, because any humorous situation embraces more than one of these aspects.

On the other hand, it seems that the Belgian preoccupation with the other language community results in there being only a few racist jokes about North African, Turkish, or other immigrant workers. The number of these immigrants is very high, and in comparison with other countries one would expect more racist aggression. In comparison, Belgium is not at all a xenophobic country.

Humor as a Defense Mechanism

In our mainly ethnographic structure of humor, humor as a defense mechanism is relevant primarily within the national context. Probably because they feel concerned, there is hardly any humorous aggression by the Walloons and the French-speaking Belgians against other nations. There is of course quite a lot of aggressive humor directed against the Flemish, reflecting frustrations, complexes, and fears. But this is counterbalanced by the same sort of humor on the Flemish side.

Cracking jokes about the Dutch, however, is a popular pastime. This is mainly a Flemish domain, probably because the Dutch are at the same time so equal and so different. They belong to the same culture, use the same language, and very often have close family ties with the Flemish. And yet they have a considerably different mentality. The (preponderantly Protestant) Dutch have the reputation of being avaricious and close-fisted (cf. the jokes about Scots). The (Catholic) Belgian/Fleming, on the contrary, has a Burgundian way of life: he likes to drink lots of beer and exquisite wine, he is a gourmet, and if he is rich he will make no secret of it. His attitude toward life is very close to that of a Mediterranean epicurean, and he will therefore never understand his northern nieghbor's frugal way of life.

The fact of being so equal and so different causes an interesting psychological attitude. The Dutch and the Flemish subconsciously transfer the possible negative qualities they are afraid of onto their alter ego. The high-hearted and self-assertive Dutchman fears nothing more than giving a stupid and ridiculous impression. Therefore, his Flemish twin brother takes this role in the Dutchman's jokes. On the other hand, the cheery and vital Fleming hates miserliness and economic narrow-mindedness. His Dutch twin brother consequently plays this role in Belgian and Flemish humor. This helps them to cope with their own negative ego which belongs to the possibilities of their cultural background.

Belgian/Flemish jokes about the Dutch:

1. Four Dutchmen enter a Brussels café. What do they order? A glass of water and four straws.

2. Who invented copper wire? Two Dutchmen fighting for a cent in the street.

3. How did the Grand Canyon come into being? A busload of Dutchmen was told there was a cent buried somewhere.

4. An advertisement in a Dutch newspaper: For sale! Second-hand gravestone bearing the name of Jan Janssen (= John Smith).

5. Do you know the story about the Dutchman who committed suicide? He sneaked into the house of his neighbor and opened the gas tap.

6. What does a Dutchman do when he finds a living fly in his soup? He catches the fly and shouts: "Spit it out! Spit it out!"

7. In a Dutch newspaper: Dear Sir. If you do not stop publishing poor jokes about the

so-called Dutch thriftiness, I shall feel obliged to stop borrowing your newspaper from my neighbor.

Of course, Dutch avariciousness and Flemish stupidity are not objective fact but a total distortion. In fact, a Dutchman isn't avaricious at all; he is only extremely inventive in being economical. And the Flemish?

Intellectual Humor

One would expect that in a multilingual country like Belgium the contact and the mastery of the languages and the knowledge of various cultures would provide brilliant *jeux de mots*, multilingual jokes or other cross-cultural intellectual humor. The reality, however, is rather disappointing. To our knowledge, there are hardly an bilingual jokes, not even in Brussels. And the intellectual mastery of the languages and the cultural competence—which undoubtedly exist in Belgium—do not result in something like "intellectual humor" which is worth mentioning.

REFERENCES

Arendt, G. H. (1965) *Die Satirische Struktur des Mittelniederlaendischen Tierepos "Van den vos Reynaerde".* (The Satirical Structure of the Riddle Netherlandic Animal Epic "Reynaert Fox.") Koeln, dissertation.

Baetens, H. B. & Willemyns, R. (eds.) (1981) *Linguistic Accommodation in Belgium.* Brussels, U.L.B./V.U.B. Brussels Preprints in Linguistics, 5 March.

Bergen, A. (1985) "Le Rire, une chose tres serieuse" (Laughter: A Serious Affair!), in *Vlan* 24 No.1119, 6.

Bergson, H. (1981) *Le Rire* (Laughter). Paris: Quadrige Press Universitaires de France. Originally published in 1911.

Beyen, R. (ed.) (1980) *Michel de Ghelderode ou la Comedie des apparences* (Michel de Ghelderode or the Comedy of Appearances). Bruxelles and Paris: Editions du Centre Georges Pompidou.

Burniaux, R. and Frickx, R. (1980) *La Litterature Belge D'expression Française* (Belgium French Language Literature). Paris: Presses Universitaires de France, Coll. Que Sais-Je, No.1540.

Collective Volume: *Davidsfonds Kartoenboek* (The Davids Foundation Book of Cartoons). Knokke-Heist, (yearly publication of Cartoon Fair).

Collective Volume (1980) *Il etait une fois . . . les Belges* (Once Upon a Time . . . The Belgians). Bruxelles: Editions du Lombard & Paul Ide Gallery.

Collective Volume (1981) *35 Ans du Journal "Tintin", 35 Ans D'humour* (35 Years of *Tintin* Magazine, 35 Years of Humor). Bruxelles: Editions du Lombard.

De Decker, K. (1966) *Lachend Vlaanderen* (Laughing Flanders). Antwerpen: Vlaamse Toeristische Bibliotheek No. 57.

———. (1969) *Joz de Swerts, Grondlegger van de Spotprentkunst in Vlaanderen* (Joz de Swerts, Founder of Cartoon Art in Flanders). Antwerpen: Vlaamse Toeristische Bibliotheek No.104.

————. (1969a) *Jong Lachend Vlaanderen* (Young Laughing Flanders). Antwerpen: Vlaamse Toeristische Bibliotheek No.113.

————. (1971) *Twintig Jaar Salon van de Vlaamse Humor* (Twenty Years of Flemish Humor Fair). Antwerpen: Vlaamse Toeristische Bibliotheek No.141.

————. (1972) *Slalom van de Vlaamse Humor* (Flemish Humor Slalom). Hasselt: Heideland, Vlaamse Pockets No.259.

————. (1973) *Georges Van Raemdonck, Ambassadeur van de Vlaamse Spotprentkunst in Nederland* (Ambassador of the Flemish Cartoon Art in Holland). Antwerpen: Vlaamse Toeristische Bibliotheek No.161.

De Dobbeleer, W. (1984–85) *Het Komische Stripverhaal, Ean Poging tot Typologie* (Comic Strips: An Attempt at Typology). Brussels: Vrije Universiteit Brussels (V.U.B.) Undergraduate dissertation.

De Laet, D. and Martens, T. (1979) *De Zevende Kunst Voorbij. Het Cartoon in Belgie* (Beyond the Seventh Act: Cartoons in Belgium). Brussels: Ministerie van Buitenlandse Zaken, Teksten en Documenten No. 320.

De Ley, G. (1984) *Leen een ei: Moppen en Cartoons over Hollanders* (Borrow an Egg: Jokes and Cartoons on Dutchmen). Aartselaar: Deltas.

Durnez, G. (1964) *De Lachende Tekenpen. Grafiese Humor uit Vlaanderen* (The Laughing Pen: Graphic Humor in Flanders). Hasselt: Heideland, Vlaamse Pockets No. 147.

Durnez, G. (1970) *Mijn Leven Onder de Belgen* (My Life Among Belgians). Leuven: De Clauwaert.

Durnez, G. (1973) *Kijk, Paps, een Belg* (Look, Dad, A Belgian!). Leuven: De Clauwaert.

Durnez, G. (1985) *Klein Belgisch Woordenboek* (Belgian Pocket Dictionary). Brussels: Elsevier.

Filippini, H., Glenat, J., Martens, T., Sadoul, N. (1979, 1984) *Histoire de la Bande Dessinée en France et en Belgique, des Origines à nos Jours* (History of Cartoons in France and Belgium—From Origins till Today). Grenoble: Glenat.

Folon, J. M. (1975) *Lettres a Giorgio* (Letters to Giorgio). Genève/Paris: Alice Editions and Editions du Chene.

Geerolf, N. (1983). *Kuifie: een Semiotische Benadering* (Tintin: A Semiotic Approach). Vrije Universiteit Brussels, Undergraduate Dissertation.

Gerard, J. and Polet, D. (1976) *L'Union Fait la Farce* (Union Makes Farce). Bruxelles: Editions des Archers.

Glorieux, F. (1976). François Glorieux Plays the Beatles. Arcade 206 TI.

Glorieux, F. (1980) Piano Hits Revisited. CBS 84538.

Grossvogel, D. I. (1959) "The Depths of Laughter: The Subsoil of a Culture," in *Yale French Studies* 23: 63–70.

Heers, J. (1983) *Fêtes des Fous et Carnavals* (Fools' Day and Carnivals). Paris, Fayard.

Kervyn de Marcke ten Driessche, R. (1948) *Les Fables de Pitje Schramouille* (Pitje Schramouille's Fables). Bruxelles: Wellens and Godenne.

Lever, M. (1983) *Le Sceptre et la Marotte. Histoire des Fous de Cour* (Sceptre and Bauble: History of Court's Fools). Paris: Fayard.

Peleman, B. (ed.) (1968) *In Het Spoor van Uilenspiegel: Schalk en Vrijheidsheld* (Following Uylenspiegel's Footsteps: Way and Freedom Fighter). Hasselt: Heideland.

Plard, H. (1981) "Uylenspiegel Espiègle, Rebelle et Fils de la Lumière" (Wag, Rebel and Son of Light) in *Charles de Coster: La Legende et les Aventures Heroiques, Joyeuses et glorieuses d'Uylenspiegel et de Lamme Goedzak au Pays de Flandres et Ailleurs* (The Legend and Heroic Adventures of Uylenspiegel and Lamme Goedzak in Flanders and Elsewhere). Antwerpen: Vlamsee.

Quievreux, L. (1961) *Mes Mille et Un Bruxelles: Bruxelles et ses Brusseleirs. Métiers, Types, Ziwanze* (Brussels: Brussels, Its Inhabitants, Professions, Types, and Humor). Bruxelles: Chez l'auteur.

Reitsma, J. (ed.) (1982) *Hollanders- en Belgenmoppen* (Jokes on Dutchmen and Belgians). Aartselaar: Deltas.

———. (1984) *Holland, België* (Holland, Belgium). Aartselaar: Deltas.

Renoy, G. et al. (1978) *Bruxelles dans le 1000* (Brussels Millenium Hits the Bull's Eye). Bruxelles: Trois Arches.

Soavi, G. (1974) *Vue Imprenable. Essai sur le Monde de Folon* (Unobstructed View: Essays on Folon's World). Paris: Editions du Chene.

Steeman, S. (1962) *Encore des Memoires!* (More Mémoirs!). Bruxelles: Rossel.

Steeman, S. (1977) *Raconte une Fois . . . Les Vraies Histoires Belges* (Tell Me a Real Belgian Story, Will You). Bruxelles: Rossel.

Tremolin, J. (1963) "La Fête Belge" (Belgian Feast), in *Belgique*. Lausanne: Editions Recontre (Atlas des Voyages), pp. 84–89.

Van der Boute—Hen Train (1978) *Anthologie de L'humour Belge* (Anthology of Belgian Humor). Paris: Garnier.

Ziv, A. (1984). *Personality and Sense of Humor*. New York: Springer Publishing Co.

OTHER WORKS BY BELGIAN HUMOROLOGISTS

Nysenholc, A. (1979) *L'age d'or du Comique. Semiologie de Charlot* (The Golden Age of Comedy: Semiology of Charlie Chaplin). Bruxelles: Editions de l'Universite Libre de Bruxelles.

Plard, H. (1963) "Du Sublime au Ridicule: Hebbel et Nestroy" (From Sublime to Ridicule: Hebbel and Nestroy), in *Etudes Germaniques* 18, 4:397–418.

———. (1966) "Anatomie du Witz" (Anatomy of the Witz), in *Etudes Germaniques* 21, 1:87–90.

———. (1968) "De Coster et la Tradition" (De Coster and Tradition), in *Revue de l'Universite de Beuxelles* (Nouvelle Serie) 21: 5–7.

3 HENRI BAUDIN, NELLY FEUERHAHN, FRANÇOISE BARIAUD, AND JUDITH STORA-SENDOR

Humor in France

BACKGROUND

Like all the other countries of Europe, France has been a composite of various peoples since the time of the settlement of the Gauls on its territory. Gaul was conquered by the Romans in the first century A.D. The stability of Roman rule was disrupted by the invasion of Germanic tribes in the fifth century: the Burgundians, the Visigoths, and the Francs who finally conquered the country and gave it their name. All these influences shaped the French character: quarrelsome, egotistical, pleased with themselves but not with others, critical of those who govern, and also quick-witted, lively, and "bon vivant."

The spirit of the early Gauls lives on in what is termed "Gallic wit." This earthy, frank, and unrestrained laughter where jabs at the government are interspersed with jokes on sex and adultery is a constant feature of humor in France.

The longevity of this popular spirit is all the more surprising since, perhaps with the exception of China, no other country has placed so much emphasis on the elitist spirit. One may be the consequence of the other.

A centralized monarchy emerged early in France's history. It brought with it a series of measures which had a profound influence on the culture and the mentality of its inhabitants. It has left its mark on French humor. In 1539, French was decreed the official language of the country as a means of combating regional divisions. Academies overseeing language, the arts, and literature made their appearance as early as 1635. French as a language became codified, and as a consequence, the spoken language began to diverge from the written word. All the ingredients were thus present for the development of a culture reserved for a minority who perhaps spoke the same tongue as the common people but certainly not the same language. In the seventeenth century, the tone was set by Louis XIV's court in Versailles and the Paris salons where was born the "art of conversation," a French specialty like gallantry, fashion, and gastronomy. This new art was the impetus for what is called "the French wit," biting, sarcastic, light, where the fine-talker dodges within the subtle limits of refined language.

Oppressive authority provokes the revolt of the free-minded. The writers, living on the fringes of this artistocratic society and living off it as well, took up again the combative spirit of the Gauls directed against those in power. Molière's comedy in the seventeenth century, and Voltaire's irony in the eighteenth, vivified the somewhat stale atmosphere of salon discussion.

In 1789 the Revolution overthrew the Ancien Régime. But the Napoleonic interlude further strengthened the tendency toward centralization, still a characteristic of France today.

Thus, since the nineteenth century, the mocking French mind with its taste for the well-chosen word combines with the critical Gallic mind to give battle to politics and clericalism. The elite continues to express itself in a language which, despite obligatory education since the end of the nineteenth century, is not always understood by all. But the bitter polemics of the intelligentsia directed against current rule and hegemonies is different only in its form from the conversations in "Joe's Bar" ("Le Café du Commerce") where the habitués groan about the cost of living, taxes, and the officials who concocted them. Today, nobody makes mincemeat of the clergy, but people still derive a certain satisfaction from attacking the government.

As for the ribald spirit, the other facet of humor inherited from those distant ancestors, the Gauls, it has always had free reign, insinuating itself in all genres, from the discreet allusion to the more or less vulgar joke, and testifies to a remarkable constancy in the psyche of a people throughout the vicissitudes of its history. Despite diverse external influences, which will be presented later, the Gallic, now French, rooster has lost nothing of its individualism and individuality.

TRADITIONAL FORMS AND EXPRESSIONS IN HUMOR
BEFORE THE TWENTIETH CENTURY

Popular Forms

The Feast of Fools

During several centuries in the Middle Ages, France was not the only European country celebrating the Feast of Fools. However, in France the enthusiasm and the extravagances included in the playfulness and the parodies that invaded the streets and the churches during those days were particularly deep-seated, notably in the northern part of the country.

The priests themselves had introduced funny and unusual elements into church services which glorified the humbles; these services were held at the end of December and the beginning of January. Hierarchical roles were reversed, and the weakest members of the community were chosen as leaders: the "bishop" or the "Pope of the Fools". These plays slipped naturally into irreverence, parody, and satire. And during these centuries when religious taboos were overwhelming, at the Feast of Fools, priests disguised as women or fools could be seen dancing, grimacing, singing drinking songs and dirty ones, playing dice in the churches, and mocking church authorities. The celebrations continued before the church and in the streets (Bakhtin, 1970; Auguet, 1974). Laymen joined the merrymaking where indecent fantasies, grotesque masked parades, obscene songs, and garbage thrown on passers-by were combined with satirical farces against the powerful and mockeries of sermons and sacred services.

This sort of catharsis was admitted by the lower clergy. However, the higher authorities decided to put an end to this disrespectful gathering and the Feast of Fools finally disappeared during the sixteenth and seventeenth centuries. Being chased from the sacred places by the antireform movement, the celebrations became profane (Heers, 1983).

The Entertainment by the Mummers' Guilds

During the fifteenth and sixteenth centuries there existed in many cities of France groups called Mummers' Guilds ("Les Compagnies Joyeuses") composed of students, bourgeois or laborers (notary clerks, printers) who took upon themselves to organize popular entertainment. Many such groups were set up. They satirized and caricatured social hierarchies, putting at the head of the ceremonies such characters as "The Crazy Queen" (a role held by a male), "The Prince of the Fools," or "The Prince of Pleasure," rendering absurd justice. Processions traversed the cities, presenting on chariots disguised kings and other caricatures of powerful persons accompanied by "ridiculous music." The atmoshere was not really obscene, and the accent was on making fun of personal and public enemies by witticism. Standing on chariots in the city streets, the jolly companions presented sketches and satirical revues inspired by actual events, mostly of local nature. The targets of the fun making were individuals (cuckolds, hypocrites), groups (judges, lawyers, doctors, and clergy), or even the power play in the government (Mazouer, 1983). It is likely that this type of festival was later absorbed into carnival festivities (Heers, 1983).

The Street Entertainers (Les amuseurs de rues)

In the sixteenth century and later, the great urban fairs were in France, as in many European countries, the choice places for popular entertainment. People were coming to enjoy and laugh at jokes, puppetry, and dressed animals (Auguet, 1974). Singers presented with great success their political satire—a form of entertainment censured later by Louis XIV—and during the era of the Fronde, pamphlets against the people in power were sold in libraries, these being also prohibited later on. The hawkers were particularly appreciated by the public, and their jokes, often rather indecent, were told all over Paris. Some of these jokesters were real stars, and their fame reached the king's court. Among them, Turlupin, Gros-Guillaume, and the most famous, Tabarin. To his partner, Doctor Mondor, who was the caricature of the pompous and all-knowing medicine man, Tabarin opposed his role of the servant who used the common sense and earthiness of the common tongue, to the joy of spectators. Among these was a little boy who didn't miss a trick: Jean-Baptiste Poquelin, the future Molière. Tabarin's comic register did not lack breadth: non sequiturs, gibberish, puns, self-metamorphosis, sexual and scatological remarks (on the aristocratic bottom see Beauvais, in Fabbri and Sallee, 1982, p. 90: "this so between the cheeks verve that is a source of major trend in French popular humor"). Other popular entertainers are mentioned in the Paris Chronicles of the eighteenth century. In the fairs and markets (Les Halles, in Paris) colorful harangues and insults created a very popular style of verbal attack which made Madame Angot famous onstage (Faure, 1978). The washerwomen of the nineteenth century also used this way to get even with the powerful: men, the bourgeois.

Among the street entertainment forms, the puppet theater appeared in Lyon at the beginning of the nineteenth century. In 1805, L. Mourguet created Gnafron, a drunkard and noisy shoemaker (Fournel, 1975), and later the character of Guignol, who is still popular today. Guignol gently protested against injustices done to simple folks and served also as a kind of oral daily commenting events. Around the end of the century the Guignol was transformed into "public place entertainment" made for children.

The Carnival

Like many other countries, France has the tradition of the carnival. The carnival's history is complex (with many variations as function of time and place), incomplete (popular joys leaving few traces), and closely related to carnivals of other European countries such as Italy and Germany. The carnival is a collective form of merrymaking which expresses freedom from the social constraints, a temporary change in the daily rules, a way of expressing mass liberation—most of the time harmlessly, but sometimes revolt is introduced (Faure, 1978), or fights among different groups (Le Roy Ladurie, 1979). The laughter of the carnival is important to understand for what it shows, in the freedom from tensions, about morals and desires of the times.

For some of the scholars studying French carnival, its robots, like those of other European carnivals, are in the Roman Saturnalias, a pagan homage to nature's fecundity. It also inherited from the Feast of Fools and the parodies of the Mummers' Guilds (Heers, 1983). The church co-opted these excesses to oppose to them the rigors of Lent. The religious characteristics disappeared around the nineteenth century, and carnival kept the social meaning of a parenthesis of a joyful illusion in a life of misery and social injustice.

From its known beginning (see Heers, 1983, on the fifteenth and sixteenth centuries) carnival was *the* popular festival, including feasts, dancing, masked pageantry, parody and satire, theatrical representations, parade of chariots, and fancy dresses—all in an immense joy, hardly imaginable nowadays. The alimentary freedom had as symbol the personage of Carnival, the huge fat mannequin with a red nose who preceded the caravan and was usually burned at the end of the festival, after a mock trial. Frequently the theatrical representations of Carnival stressed the contradiction with fasting (Carême), which was represented as thin and joyless (Mazouer, 1983). The exaltation of food which characterized the festivities in the cities till the end of nineteenth century was a strong contrast to the daily poverty. With it, people associated the freedom of the body with a lot of scatological laughter: in language (dirty insults and jokes) and behavior (throwing of waste, dirtying clothes, and farting). Farting was considered great fun (Fauer, 1978). It was appreciated also later outside the carnival. At Moulin Rouge, during the "Belle Epoque," "the farting one" was a great success (in French, le Pétomane, the name used by Mel Brooks for the governor in the film *Blazing Saddles*) (Zeldin, 1981). Among the other amusements of the carnival were the practical jokes played on others. Here one can find the inspiration for the practical jokes of April 1 used till today. Parody was queen at the carnival in the comic effects of masked parades with sex inversions, grotesque figures of nobility, and known persons.

The Clowns

The clown's art, being based on pantomime, gestures, and situational comedy, does not require from the public the knowledge of a language or a particular sociopolitical context. Therefore, the history of this art in France is full of Italian, British, and other influences.

Formerly buffoons in fairs, the clowns appear in the circus at the beginning of the nineteenth century. In 1782 the British Astley, inventor of the modern circus, created the first one in Paris. In the beginning, the clowns were mute: horse riders and acrobats who introduced funny movements into their acts. When the privilege of dialogue reserved to the theatre was abandoned in 1864, talking clowns appeared in the circus. Around 1880, after a few years of groping, the personage of the Auguste was born (Rémy, 1945). Between 1890 and 1910, Footit and Chocolat created the first duo, caricaturing the domineering-dominated couple to denounce human misery and wickedness. Later on, the relation between the White Clown and the Auguste was modified in the sense of the revenge of anarchy over authority and self-assurance.

Humor in the Literary and Performing Arts

Middle Ages

Religion, war and courtly love are not good partners to laughter and smiling. Only when there was a bourgeois public (city dwellers, merchants, artisans, etc.) would folklore themes in which animals leading an anthropomorphic life be accepted (*Le Roman de Renart*, end of the twelfth century). This world of animal fables can be seen as a forerunner of our animated cartoons, using however a heavier humor. In other picturesque stories, the fable writers arrived to introduce into a human environment a few gags.

At the beginning of the thirteenth century, mixed lectures of the Gospel, using burlesque episodes, drinking feasts, and swindling, became popular. Later, banned from the holy lectures, these episodes gained autonomy, were slowly refined as "soties" and farces, the best known being *La Farce de Maistre Pathelin* (fifteenth century). Prose humor appeared during the fifteenth century in Bourgogne in such stories as *The Hundred New Novels*, lecherous stories about cuckolds, and *The 15 Joys of Marriage*, making fun of women (see Garapon, 1957, for a review of comical theatre from the Middle Ages to the classical period).

Renaissance Period

It was the century of prose tale-tellers. The greatest among them was Rabelais. The adventures of Gargantua and Pantragruel brought pleasure to the readers by presenting the amusing giant heroes, the flexible morals of the cunning Panurge, and the great love of life without any concession to whatever is against enjoying it fully.

Other known works of the period which should be mentioned include Amyot's fresh and acid translation of Longus's *Daphnis and Chloe*; Noël du Fail's *Tales and Discourses of Eutrapel*, which perhaps inspired La Fontaine; and finally Brantôme, with his mirthful and ribald *Gallant Women's Lives*. For a detailed review of Rabelais and his times, see Bakhtine (1970).

The Baroque Period

Wars of religion changed the previous certainty. The baroque plays on appearances and their metamorphoses (Rousset, 1953). New styles appeared: the rambling and presurrealistic style of Sigogne; the realistic and caricatural cynicism of Scarron in his *Comic novel* (Le Roman Comique), where gags and fights are plentiful; and Régneir's *Satires* (Blanchard, 1969).

Corneille's *The Comic Illusion* (1635) plays on the scenic illusion. In his comedy *The Liar* (1644), borrowed from the Spanish, gags are told and not played. Had they been played, they would have been the forerunners of burlesque in the movies.

The Classical Period (1660–1715)

The peak of classic comedy was attained by Molière. In his *The Lady's School* (*L'école des femmes*, 1662) the plot is refined by the flexibility in the use of rhymes which are poetic, brutal, or syncopated in the dialogue. In *Tartuffe* (1664) the attack on morality goes even farther, against bigotry and false religious persons who exploit religion for their own needs. *Dom Juan* (1665) juxtaposes the burlesque prose of Sganarelle with the brilliant prose of his seductive master. Mimicry and farcical disguises are combined with the fantastic and with moral degradation. Merrier, gay, and more alert is the scenic play in *Les fourberies de Scapin* (1671). *La Malade imaginaire*—Molière died during a performance of this play—has a scene in which Louison, the imaginary sick man's daughter is subjected to an obnoxious inquisitorial procedure. That the procedure becomes amusing testifies to Molière's greatness (Schere, 1952).

During this same period, the most exquisite form of comedy can be found in La Fontaine's tales and fables, in which he treated anew some of the saucy medieval stories, as well as some from the Renaissance. But it can be seen better still in the bantering pessimism of the writer's natural spirit as both an accomplished storyteller and a refined poet full of humor and vivacity.

Madame de Sévigné's *Letters* to her daughter and her friends are full of life alertness where comic descriptions are plentiful. Another witness of the great century, Saint-Simon, uses a dauntless pen on everybody (including himself). Less incisive but also moralistic, La Bruyère introduces us to a gallery of extravagant personages of his time (for a reveiw of the century, see Adam, 1949–1956).

The Enlightenment (Les Lumières 1715–89)

The Regency Period lifted suddenly the cloak of respectability and conformism maintained by Louis XIV till his death. Pleasure and wit became fashionable for the rich and the "philosophers." It appears with finesse and discretion in Marivaux's elegant comedies where spectators were more invited to smile than to laugh. In his plays, pleasant people were put in embarrassing situations caused by the internal contradictions between the prejudices of social class and sexuality (Deloffre, 1955). The king of irony, master of the pamphlet, and prince of insolence was Voltaire, poet of intelligent paradox, libertine storyteller, skeptic, and critic. His *Candide* gives the same pleasant and amusing reading today that it did when written. His *Philosophical Dictionary* has nothing didactic but a lively and dry style reflecting a lucid intelligence. The reign of Louis XVI was made cheerful more by Beaumarchais than by the cynical maxims and flippant anecdotes of Chamfort. Beaumarchais's dramatic spirit puts the personages of *The Barber of Seville* and *The Marriage of Figaro* in embarrassing situations. His satirical manner was adopted later by the presss. His polemical verve in the malicious exchanges of arguments (made in more or less good faith) was one of speech, tirade, formulations, and imagination.

The July Monarchy (La Monarchie de Julliet 1830–48)

Forty years without laughter? The revolution and the empire were not keen on humor, which had to wait for the émigré Rivarol and his brilliant paradoxes. The restoration, with its extremists and religious communities, was not funnier; the liberal P. L. Courier reinvented the Voltairean pamphlet. However, the July monarchy gave freedom of expression to a lively anticlericalism. Henri Monnier, in his short plays (or long sketches), concentrated on the behavior of the triumphant bourgeoisie, its best personification being his Joseph Prudhomme. Plays like *L'Enterrement* (the burial) and *Le Déménagement* (household removal) announced the derision and the talkative ways of Ionesco.

Romanticism is generally too serious, but it had its exception with Alfred de Musset, prince of imagination and libertinism. One finds libertinism in the brilliant beginning of *Namouna*, fantasy in *Comédies et proverbes* (Comedies and proverbs) where Fantasio, well-named farce player, is close to *Les Caprices de Marianne* (Marianne's whims). In *On ne badine pas avic l'amour* (One never banters with love), the characters of the drama are surrounded by puppet-characters such as the drunkard priests Bridaine and Blazius, as well as bony Madame Pluche. The baroness of *Il ne faut jurer de rien* (One should not swear on anything) and the marquis of *La Nuit Vénitienne* (The venetian night) make apparently absurd remarks, because of their incongruity within the dialogues. In Victor Hugo, the playwright of romanticism, one finds the union of the sublime and the grotesque, the latter in *Ruy Blas* personified by Don César de Bazan. But it was only after his exile that Hugo really showed his comic abilities.

Second Empire and the Third Republic (1852–88)

Hugo was the author of the engaging *Freedom theater* (*Le Théâtre en liberté*). He was also a poet "chansonnier" in *Toute la lyre* (All the lyre) (Guillemin, 1951).

Outside ideologies, there was a happy playwright who evoked laughter even from those he ridiculed in his "vaudevilles": Labiche. He recorded almost "live" the irrational and illogical behavior of the bourgeoisie. Plenty of absurd situations in which the panic-stricken characters of his plays find themselves, produce, as Anouilh said, "a curious laughter: happy and black" (Soupault, 1945).

Children's literature in which comic elements were included appeared only in the nineteenth century. The illustrations with the pioneers of caricature such as

Grandville, Gavarni, and Doré enriched comic literature for children and youth starting around 1830.

Music

During this period, music offers, in itself (and not with the help of texts or scenic action), comic resources. In "Animals' Carnival," Saint-Saëns gives us the turtles who slow down the rapid quadrille of Offenbach's *Orpheus in Hell*, elephants who crush on double-bass in Berlioz's "Sylfes' dance" and Mendelssohn's "Summer nights' dreams." Other "animals": the piano learners with their terrible repetitious scales, all create laughter from music.

With a similar lack of respect, some time before Saint-Saëns, Fauré and Messager rewrote in a reckless tempo of quadrille the themes of Wagner tetralogy.

Songs and "Chansonniers" (Satirical Song Singers)

Song as a term appeared for the first time in the eleventh century with "gesture songs" (les chansons de geste), epic poems more recited than sung. Until the nineteenth century the term designated a form consisting of a rhymed text in music. The term did not apply to a great part of the musical production, considered as more popular and having different names such as *mazarinades*, *Ponts-Neufs*, and *vaudevilles* (coming from voix de villes—i.e., city voices, meaning those who were singing in different streets of the city). These included songs of social and political criticism. From the eleventh to the fifteenth century, *Les goliards*, or wandering scribes, were composing in French and Latin epicurean songs, often rather indecent, which sometimes lampooned the Church. Profane, and sometimes improper, they were sung to religious music. The *mazarinades* (pamphlets directed originally against Mazarin in the seventeenth century) commented on recent events. Passers-by also enjoyed lecherous songs, ancestors of our lewd songs. The foundation of the Caveau (small cellar) by three jolly fellows—Piron, Collé, and Crébillon—in 1734 is the origin of the *Chansonniers*, satiric "singer-talkers" who composed their texts on popular tunes (Vernillat and Charpentreau, 1983). During the Revolution, primacy went to the political songs: the still popular "Ça ira" (it'll go well) was improvised by Ladré during the feasts of the Federation, to the music of a popular tune. The Pont-Neuf (one of the great Paris bridges) was the center of the satirical song till the Empire, when censure prohibited all criticism of those in power. Political songs took shelter in singing societies (les goguettes), which were very numerous till the arrival of Napoleon III, until censure intervened. After the First Empire, Béranger became the idol of the singing societies; his song made fun of royalty and censorship, and with him there was the passage from anonymous songs to signed ones (*chansons d'auteur*). The songs called "goguettes" combined imagination, love, good food, and politics; full of Rabelaisian tradition, the songs were better in their lively banter than in their lyricism (Brochon, 1979).

Under the Second Empire, most of the *chansonniers* changed their place to the Caf' Conc' (Concert coffee houses), which became the great popular show till World War I. It was a place for bawdy laughter and simple songs joined by all spectators. The singers derived comic effect not only from the scatological or burlesque texts but also from their physical, good-natured appearances and postures. Censorship encouraged sexual innuendoes, false rhyme, and droll pronunciation (Caradec and Weill, 1980).

The *chansonniers* did not disappear, and Montmartre became the center of satirical singing. In 1878, Goudeau created in the Latin Quarter Le club des Hydropathes, in which he gathered young, eccentric artists: painters, poets, actors, musicians, and students. A few years later he helped Salis open the first artistic cabaret, the celebrated Chat Noir (The black cat), where Bruant distinguished himself. Later Bruant opened his own cabaret where he inaugurated the insulting of clients (a style made popular today by Don Rickles). The bourgeois came to this place to be insulted in slang and to listen to his insolent, scatological jokes and to songs also appreciated by the ordinary people. At the end of the nineteenth century and the beginning of the twentieth, cabarets multiplied, were opened, then closed, reopened in Montmartre, in the Latin Quarter or on the Grands Boulevards (for their history, see De Bercy and Ziwes, 1951; Herbert, 1967). An entire folklore developed in these places. The most famous names of the period were Xanrof (author of student songs and responsible for the great success of some songs at the Caf'Conc') and Montoya (whose "hospital duty room" songs are part of a lewd tradition still existing today).

Beginnings of Visual Humor

In the nineteenth century, the best place for the artistic expression of graphic artists was the satirical press. Grandville not only illustrated La Fontaine's fables but continued the zoomorphic drawing, publishing many caricatures in the press, particularly in *La Caricature* and *Le Charivari*. His last works were later much admired by the surrealists: his drawings *Un Autre Monde* (Another world, 1844) and *Les Fleurs animées* (Animated flowers, 1847), which showed the successive metamorphoses from animal to vegetable to mineral, are considered masterpieces. Daumier is regarded as the greatest caricaturist of his times. The irreverent caricature of Louis Philippe as Gargantua, in 1832, earned him a few months in prison. The suppression of freedom given by the July monarchy sent Daumier to criticism of characters, his targets being the ridiculous bourgeois, the financiers, lawmakers, playwrights, and many others. Eight thousand engravings made by Gavarni were published in the satirical newspapers. Doré, a collaborator at *Le Journal pour rire* (Journal for laughter, founded in 1851), *La Caricature*, and *Le Charivari*, was mostly famous for his book illustrations. His style was fanciful and truculent: Rabelais with Pantagruel, Balzac with the droll stories (*Les Contes drolatiques*), and also Cervantes with Don Quixote. Other newspapers where caricature was triumphant starting in 1881 were *Le Chat noir*, directed by Alphonse Allais; *Le Mirliton*, created by Aristide Bruant; *Le Rire* and *L'Almanach Vermot*, which still published a humor based on puns.

DEVELOPMENT OF HUMOR IN THE TWENTIETH CENTURY

Popular Forms

Carnival

In his *Handbook of Contemporary French Folklore* (1947), Van Gennep pre-sents, as a result of a systematic survey, a detailed and almost complete de-scription of the carnivals in the different regions of France. In the twentieth century, the feast is more modest, disguises are less numerous, and the parade of chariots in town takes precedence over popular participation. However, many ancient customs are still in evidence, among them some dances with comic characteristics and the special place given to the character of the cuckold. In the dance of "soufflaculs," dancers in nightgowns and armed with big kitchen blowers try to blow in other people's behinds and under the skirts of girls, thus provoking great laughter. In the "tiou tiou" dance, practiced in the south of France, the participants, in Indian file, have to use a candle to light a little piece of paper attached to the preceding person's lower back.

Gaignebet (1974) stresses the fact that you cannot name a country where cuckolds are paid as much attention as in France. Even since the entertainment provided by the "Cornards" and the parades of "cornus" during the sixteenth century, the pratice of what is called "assouade" (parading the cuckolds mounted backwards on a donkey), still found in the nineteenth century, to crowning with horns in the twentieth, with this refrain: "if all cuckolds had little bells attached to their behind, we couldn't hear each other talk anymore."

The Clowns

The golden age of the clownish spectacle was "les années folles" (the crazy years). In 1925, the clown was king: his huge popular success held for about 20 years. It was the triumphal era of the Fratellinis (up to 1940), talented creators of gags, accessories, instrumental "cacophonies," and inventors of the comic trio. Each of the Fratellinis, according to Rémy (1945), impersonated "one of the three main aspects of the clownish comedy: François, the Clown, the last incarnation of Latin imagination; Paul, the Auguste, a type of German origin passed to French, Albert, the Fool, refuge of supreme exaggeration from the British pantomime." They were the poetry, the order and the 'moving catastro-phe' " (see Fabbri and Sallée, 1982). Also appreciated by the public from 1928 to 1948, the Dario-Bario opposed to the distinguished phlegm the big joviality of a drunken Auguste. Rhum played a little disabused man inspired by Buster Keaton; he excelled in parodies of theatre and movies as well as in great comical reviews of the Medrano circus ("Buffalo Bill," 1939; "Les Chesterfollies," 1943–44, etc.). Later, his talent as a mimic exploded on the cabaret scene. Many others, such as Boulicot at the Music-hall Circus, knew great success, and France received with joy and admiration the internationally acclaimed Grock.

The circus "consecrated the triumph of the show over the popular festival" (Auguet, 1974). However, after World War II, laughter little by little distanced itself from the ring, attracted by other, more intimate and verbal forms of humor. The time of the scenic comedians had arrived.

Humor in the Literary and Performing Arts

La Belle Epoque (1889–1914)

At the 1889 Universal Exhibition in Paris, a new world was signaling the twentieth century. A militant anarchism and insulting apparitions of young authors changed the existing literary climate. Claudel, future diplomat, translated his vigorous temperament into L'Endormie (The sleeping one), a kind of adolescent fantasy. Before the first war, he wrote a lyrical farce Protée; his greatest work, Le Soulier de satin" (the satin shoe), had a strong comic component combined with baroque art.

Jarry, poet and symbolist, wanted to throw out from the stage psychologism and realism, which were then predominant. He created what can be called for France "a new comedy" by using surrealistic situations and language. His trilogy about King Ubu was a milestone in the comedy onstage.

The humorist Alphonse Allais wrote in periodicals his highly original and comic inventions. Georges Courteline's humor, offering comic views of the conjugal, bureaucratic, judicial, and military life, were often presented (and still are) onstage. Georges Feydeau gave vaudeville the perfect mechanism of what is still called today in France "La comédie de boulevard." His best-known plays (Le Dindon, Le Fil à la Patte, L'Hôtel du Libre échange) were, and still are, extremely popular (for this and the following period of the theatre in France, see Baudin, 1981).

Les Années Folles (1918–30)

Refugees in Zurich, pacifist intellectuals and artists who declared war on war and its causes, used provocative mockery as their weapon. It was the Dada Movement, introduced in Paris in 1919 by Tristan Tzara, which prospered and developed into surrealism under the impetus of André Breton. At the same period, those who stayed home and those who came back from the war tried to forget the slaughter by indulging in the unbridled fantasy of poetry and shows. Even such a great intellectual as Jules Romains stressed the comic part of his work with pranksters typical of teachers' college (canulars). The comic was king in such plays as Knock, where the medical profession was the victim, Sacha Guitry, actor and son of a great actor, was brilliant in his boulevard plays which only give the appearance of being optimistic and superficial.

Marcel Pagnol, who started in theatre by writing social satire (Topaze), developed the Marseilles comedy to a masterful degree (*Marius*, *Fanny*, and *César*). He wrote his hilarious and delightful mémoires in the trilogy *The Glory of My Father*, *My Mother's Castle*, and *The Time of Secrets*.

In France, 1917 was a year of competition between original comic works. Apollinaire presented a burlesque farce, *The Breasts of Tiresias* (*Les Mamelles de Tirésias*). Cocteau created *Parade*, collaborating with the best: Satie wrote the music, Picasso painted the scenic background, and Cocteau himself wrote the text of this ballet. In the postwar period, imagination and anachronisms filled his theatre (*Orphée; The Infernal Machine*). In the same year, 1917, a collection of poems in prose was published by Max Jacob: *Dice Box* (*Le Cornet à dés*). Nothing was less conventional than this collection in which everything is fantasy, and most frequently funny, either by its verbal acrobatics or by conceptual absurdity and clever parody.

The newest style was dadaism, with its provocative anticonformism, attacking language and so producing joyful absurdities and incoherences. Many new forms of worldplay were created by Desnos, Péret, Aragon, Soupault, and Breton; the latter published his famous *Anthologie de l'humour noir* in 1939.

The Difficult Times (1930–50)

In *Intermezzo*, Giraudoux put children, long-forgotten characters, onstage in French theatre. Burlesque and fantasy are present in many of his plays: *The Bellac Apollon*, *The Trojan War Will Not Take Place*, *Electra*, and *Sodom and Gomorrha*. Rich and crackling paradox, the verbal elegance forgotten since Marivaux, Beaumarchais, and Musset, is back again. Giraudoux sometimes used unreal episodes, like the juggling of time in *Ondine*.

Vitrac wrote dadaistic sketches in 1922–23. A true surrealist, he wrote in 1930 a long incongruous play halfway between the burlesque and the tragic modes, *The Mysteries of Love*. His most famous play, *Victor, or Power to the Children*, introduced a huge nine-year-old child who poured ridicule on parents and adults, using obscenities to comment on events (on Dada and surrealism, see Bahar, 1967).

Anouilh at age 20 started with his "Pink plays," among them the exquisite *Thief's Ball*; and the contrasted fantasy of *Léocadia*, which is more accentuated in the "Brilliant plays," the most famous being *Invitation to the Castle*. The pessimism grew but always appeared in combination with comedy in his "Grating plays" (Pièces grinçantes), such as *Poor Bitos*. Aristocrats, resembling the ones in Musset's or Oscar Wilde's works, are delightful: old, arbitrary, and sympathetic ladies; puppetlike gentlemen, sometimes moving; young girls who are sometimes tigresses, sometimes doves; parents, petty and sour. In the novel, the eruption started in 1932 with the publication of Céline's *Voyage au bout de la nuit* (Trip to the end of the night), followed by his portrayal of the adolescence of Bardamu in *Mort à crédit* (Death on credit), where a somewhat lesser pessimism is completed by burlesque and saucy elements. The popular style of the ordinary (or extraordinary) horror in his German trilogy: *D'un Chateau l'autre* (From one castle to another), *Nord*, and *Rigodon*.

This eruption shadowed a similar attempt, from which, however, the visionary genius and the powerful language manipulation of Céline were missing. In 1933 Raymond Queneau published *Le Chiendent* (The trouble), but he became famous as a poet-philosopher with a popular song, "Si tu t'imagines" (if you imagine), as a storyteller with *Exercises de style*; and as a novelist (*Zazie dans le métro*, *Les Fleurs bleues*).

Less sophisticated, Marcel Aymé satirized rural life in *La Jument verte* (The green mare), provincial town life in *Le Boeuf clandestin* (The clandestine cow), the leftist bourgeoisie in *Travelingue*, the German occupation in *Le Chemin des écoliers*, and the liberation in *Uranus*. In addition, he wrote exquisite short stories with a science fiction taste *Le Passe-muraille* (passing through walls) and children's stories. A latecomer to theatre, Marcel Aymé was generally as funny and as critical of realities as in his other works. His famous plays were *The moon's birds* (Les oiseaux de lune), *Clerambard*, and *The others' heads*. (For a critical view of his works, see Dufresnoy, 1982.)

In poetry, the current language takes a satirical spirit and an incomparable verbal virtuosity in Prévert's poems: *Paroles* (Words), and *Histoires* (Stories). The rich creativity of Henri Michaux introduces us to imaginary misfortunes in *Un Certain Monsieur Plume* (A certain Mr. Plume) and the hilarious and parodic touristical ethnology of *Voyage en grande Garabagne*. One has also to mention the writer who synthesized in his brief creation, in the best way, the main tendencies of the "new French humor": Boris Vian (Baudin, 1973).

Cartoons and Children's Literature

Humor for children developed in children's magazines where stories accompanied by drawings appeared. In this form was published in 1889 in the *Le petit Française illustré*, the "Fenouillard Family," an illustrated story by G. Colomb, known as Christophe. It was followed by "Le Sapeur Camember" and "Le Savant Cosinus." However, Louis Forton's "Les Pieds Nickelés," which appeared between 1908 and 1934 in *L'Épatant* (The amazing), and "Bibi Fricotin" (1924) were the most famous. These "stories in images" showed a great comic invention as well as a popular verve in which slang was king. In *Suzette's week* (La semaine de Suzette) the little daughters of the bourgeoisie could read "Bécassine," by J. P. Pinchon. Bécassine was a young, silly, and simple provincial servant who took every expression literally and who, despite all her goodwill, came into all kinds of comic troubles. St. Ogan created *Zig and Puce* (1925), which mixed naïveté with many extravagant situations. In 1923 *Gédéon*, the first illustrated album of B. Rabier was published. Rabier created many gags in his drawings which appeared in *L'Album drolatique* (The funny album), and he is known for his drawings of laughing animals. Animals were also the heroes of *Les Contes du chat perché* (The stories of the perched cat) by Marcel Aymé

(The rose stories, 1937, and the blue stories, 1963). The main quality of his animals was that they were always for children and against adults.

The Francophonic culture gave the French the opportunity to enjoy the Belgian illustrated stories in their original language. The Belgians produced the best-known "bandes dessinées" (comics), among them Hergé's *Tintin*, which started in 1923 but became appreciated by the French public mainly after 1947 when they were published in book form.

Songs and Singers (Chansons et chansonniers)

Entertainment Songs

Around 1900, Paris offered the world the image of the city of pleasures during the Universal Exhibition. This was also the golden age of the concert coffeehouses (Le Caf'Conc') which inspired many caricaturists: Toulouse-Lautrec immortalized in his drawings the great singer Yvette Guilbert. Other famous painters who drew her were Cappiello, Sem, Léandre, and Steinlein. This was also the golden age of posters and satirical newspapers.

A new genre of comedy appeared with the "soldier comedian" (*le comique troupier*). He was a naive simpleton who told funny stories and was much appreciated (a variation of this type was the "peasant comedian"). Many such comedians followed each other, from Polin to Fernandel in 1922. Dranem, a great star in 1900, had an undersized jacket, oversized trousers, ruddy cheeks, and enormous shoes that reminded the public of the clown. In his burlesque show composed of inept and indelicate songs, he imposed himself with his unique style. Mayol, who created more than 500 songs, was one of the last stars of the Caf'Conc'.

Just before World War I, Georgius abandoned the excessive makeup style and appeared in a white suit. His parodies and imitations brought him an increasing success which continued until World War II (Brunscwig, Calvet, and Klein, 1981). A new wave started with the light, syncopated music of Mireille, followed by the great Charles Trenet. He introduced new rhythms and surrealistic poetry borrowed from Max Jacob and Charles Cros. Nonsense and onomatopoeia replaced the old style of the Caf'Conc'; absurd humor on a swinging background was "in."

Chansonniers

Chansonniers are not real singers; they use popular melodies and make up satirical or comical lyrics for them, which are more "told" than sung. The great epoch of the cabarets from Montmartre, where satirical humor took all forms of expression, was renewed by the newcomers who, back from the front, are less ironic than their predecessors. Dorin was the speaker for the middle-class Frenchman with his "chansons poilues" (soldier's songs). Pierre Dac wrote in 1917 his first song, "Victory with Close-Cropped Hair" (*la victoire aux cheveux ras*), made exciting by the novelty of its absurd humor. During World War II, Noël-Noël and Jean Rigaux used comedy for veiled satire of the German occupants, and Raymond Souplex made fun of the restrictions of daily life.

Humor in the Visual Arts and the Press

Between 1881 and 1914, graphic expression was at its apogee in caricature and in posters. Aesthetic research, in which Toulouse-Lautrec excelled and Capiello was a brilliant representative, was closely related to caricature and publicity posters. The Caf'Conc' stars appeared on posters as well as in satirical reviews. *L'Assiette au beurre* (Butter on platter), the most celebrated satirical publication, between 1901 and 1912 gathered all great names of drawings: Jossot, Willette, Steinlein, Faivre, Forain, Caran d'Ache, Léandre, Hermann Paul, and Grandjouan. The main targets of the caricatures were the poverty of the proletariat as contrasted with the arrogance of the rich of the Belle Epoque, clericalism, and the two parts of the population divided during the Dreyfus Affair, when a strong anti-semitic trend appeared, reinforced by a xenophobic attitude before World War I. It was the end of a great period.

Founded in 1915 by Maurice and Jeanne Maréchal, *Le Canard enchaîné* (The chained duck—still the greatest satirical newspaper today in France) marked a radical change in the satirical press. Caricatures were less important, and ironic texts took central place. The cartoonists of that period were characterized by a gentle and poetic humor, such as Peynet with his couples of lovers and Effel with his series on the creation of the world. Bellus invented a type of small, fat bourgeois, nice and well-intentioned. The most creative cartoonist at the beginning of the century was Dubout, with his celebrated couple, the big authoritarian woman with the fragile little husband. His illustrations of famous literary works of Villon, Rabelais, Molière, Courteline, Pagnol, Cervantes, and Daudet combined a taste for accumulation and hugeness with texts which celebrated pleasures and excessiveness.

Related to the surrealistic movement, Maurice Henry, who contributed as journalist and caricaturist to more than 200 newspapers, introduced black humor and irrationality into satirical drawing. Verbal absurd humor before the war was best represented in *L'Os à moelle* (The Marrow bone), a newspaper founded by Pierre Dac, which proposed nonsense humor with the motto "against all that is for and for all that is against." Immediately after the war, a new group of cartoonists appeared—Chaval, Bosc, and Tetsu—who used mostly black absurd humor. Barberousse reintroduced anthropomorphic animals in drawings, and Tim, of Polish origin, started a long career of political cartooning; their best themes were expressed during the time of de Gaulle.

Movies

"Until 1914, French comedy dominated world cinema" (Sadoul, 1949, p. 79). Emile Reynaud with his praxinoscope, or optical theatre, was the inventor of animated cartoons. His first movie, *The Clown and His Dogs*, was made in 1881. *L'Arroseur arrosé* (the wet gardner), by Louis Lumière (1895), the inventor of the Cinématographe, as simple as it was, was the first comic story in the history of the cinema.

Compared with the "realistic" school of Lumière, Méliès can be considered as an "illusionist" moviemaker (Kral, 1984). In a magician's style, Méliès created a fantasy world in his films, the best-known being *Voyage to the Moon*, (*Voyage dans la lune*, 1902), where the spectacular and the story were combined for the first time in cinema. He was a master of trick shots; his acrobatic actors changed their image as they wished and the suprising effect of their movements and gestures was reinforced by unexpected apparitions and disappearances. Negation of the real world, the unforeseeable, and a certain naïveté made Méliès's movies cinematographic fairy tales.

Most comic creations in the earliest movies followed the same pattern. To the trick shots, fairy-tale quality, and the nonsense inherited from Méliès, the good humor of French farce and the clownish and acrobatic traditions were added. Most of these films were shot in the streets of Paris, with characters who seemed to ignore the laws of gravity; all this made a lasting impression on young Mack Sennett.

Max Linder added a new conception to the comic tradition of movies of the times. He was the first to create a real comic character: a dandy and womanizer, enjoying life, always dressed to kill, and using sure and elegant gestures. Max portrayed with dignified melancholy the resourcefulness so typical of the French spirit (which was later to be used and reused by contemporary comedy). His gags were mostly original, and the plots were based on misunderstandings (*quiproquos*) taken from the themes of the boulevard comedies. His first success, *The Beginnings of a Skater* (1907), was followed by the series of Max, the most perfect being *Max Victime du Quinquina* (Max victim of quinquina) (1911). Max Linder was the greatest movie comedian in the world before World War I.

The international importance of French cinema started to dwindle after the war. The new impressionist school had no one of the stature of Méliès or Max Linder. It is on the fringe of this school that René Clair, the most original director of the French cinema, appeared. He made the connection between the silent and the talking movies, producing in both real chef d'oeuvres. Already his first silent movies (*Paris That Sleeps*, 1923; *An Italian Straw Hat*, 1923), René Clair showed an exceptional talent in using possibilities of the new media. He fought the tendency of certain filmmakers to make realistic "filmed theatre" and declared that cinema was not "theatre in conserve tins." In *Under the Roofs of Paris* (1930), his first talking movie, followed by *The Million* (1931) and *A nous la liberté* (Let's Be Free, 1932), as well as many others, he showed that the silent movie technique was still valuable and that it was the image and not the words which created life on the screen. His "Fantastic in French style" was highly appreciated in movies he made overseas: *Ghosts for Sale* in England (1935), *I*

Married a Witch (with Veronica Lake in 1942) and *It Happened Tomorrow* (1943) in the United States.

The light ironic comedy, filmed with all the technical advances offered by the camera, seemed to be the sign of the one and only René Clair. With his departure in 1934 this cinematographic style emigrated for a while to America, where it found new masters. There remained Sacha Guitry, who excelled in this style, but movies he directed based on his plays were scorned by critics who considered them too much as "filmed theatre."

Like Guitry, Marcel Pagnol was rediscovered by the "new wave" in the mid-fifties. During his own time, critics were savagely against him, calling his movies "canned theatre." This did not stop the huge international success of his movies. When he directed his own plays or wrote the movie scripts based on his plays, the perfect dialogue, often with a deep Southern accent, of his picturesque characters, combined with an excellent cast (Raimu, Delmont, Charpin, and Fernandel) made Pagnol famous in the gallery of French comedies for two decades. His most important film comedies were *Marius* (produced by Korda in 1931), *Fanny* (produced by Marc Allegret in 1932), *César* (1936), *Topaze* (1936), and *The Baker's Wife* (1938). Jean Vigo's *Zéro de conduite* (Bad behavior, 1933), which was a burlesque and poetic chronicle of a boys' boarding school, had a great influence on the future development of comic movies.

Between 1930 and 1945 the French school of cinema, known as "poetical realism," did not produce many comedies. Marcel Carné, using Jacques Prévert as a scriptwriter, made in 1937 *Drôle de drame*, ("Bizarre, bizarre"), a burlesque and ironic thriller starring the best actors of the period.

The Rules of the Game (*La Règle du jeu*) by Jean Renoir (1939), misunderstood when first presented, is considered today as one of the greatest films worldwide. "To produce a gay drama was the ambition of my entire life," said Renoir (Sadoul, 1949, p. 285). In this comedy of human passions, all moral rules are violated. The ironic tone in which the fundamental social and human problems are dealt with made this subversive and profound movie a comedy in the most authentic meaning of the term, comparable to Beaumarchais's *Figaro's Marriage*.

Music

With Erik Satie we have a musician who for 25 years showed the comic in music, but more in the words than in the notes (e.g., the titles of his works). However, for Cocteau's ballet *Parade* he included comic elements in the music using such "instruments" as sirens, revolvers, and typewriters (in a way similar to the introduction of concrete objects in cubist paintings). His musical writings mix popular forms, brass-band music, syncopated ragtime, and rapid valses; he invented "repetitive music." Naturally, this Sage of Arcueil attracted young composers (known as "Les Six," the group of six) who wanted to create "good humor music." Cocteau's *Rooster and Arlequin* was the manifesto of this group, which contributed to the music of his *Marriage on the Eiffel Tower*.

The most prestigious musician touching the comic vein was Poulenc. He introduced into his "serious" works (except the religious ones) many humorous elements.

As for Ravel, his deadpan humor found, after *Natural Histories* by Jules Renard, a choice terrain with Colette. In *The Child and Sortileges*, language becomes rhythmic sound-play where cakewalk, foxtrot, and Chinese- and shepherd-sounding music are all mixed, creating astounding effects (on music see Jankelevitch, 1961).

CONTEMPORARY HUMOR AND TRENDS

Popular Forms

Carnival

Many say carnival is dead. Not altogether, but it is true that it is nowadays a pale reflection of its glorious past. There are many causes for this: massive urbanization and industrialization; improved economic standards; greater freedom, which diminished the need for cathartic expression of frustration; and of course the arrival of new forms of entertainment.

However, in many parts of France, tradition continues in some towns for historical, social, and touristic reasons. Nice is certainly the best known; also, Dunkirk with the parade of "fishermen bands" and other cities with old local "glories" try to keep up traditions. But parody and satire are not so lively anymore. Paris no longer has a carnival. In recent years, youngsters in small groups attempt to renew the tradition of disguising and throwing flour on unappreciative passers-by.

Carnival is not the only festival which our century has snuffed out. Flourishing during the nineteenth century and the beginning of the twentieth century, the ball of the four arts, the cavalcades, and students' rag processions, the feasts for the anniversaries of the Free Commune of Montmartre, have no modern equivalents.

The clowns

The clown's virtuosity, so difficult because it asks for many kinds of expertise (dance, acrobatic, juggling, mime, music), suffers nowadays from the crisis of the circus in France. Some artists prefer to try their chances on scene as what Fabri and Sallée call "excentrics." Others defend the tradition with great passion. Known by all, Zavatta has performed the "popular Auguste" for more than half a century, in his own circus. Wonderful "Yoyo" of his film, Pierre Etaix has directed since 1972 the National School of Circus with a charming and illustrious partner from a great dynasty: Annie Fratellini.

In theatre and cabaret, others, finding inspiration in the clown's art, invented new styles: Farré, by disparaging the musical universe; Carl, on the classic theme of the fight against hostile objects (the microphone), with the extreme precision needed in order to gather so many blunders. Among other facets in their art, there is something of the clown in Rufus, Haller, and Devos. Nor should one ever forget that one of the greatest French comedians, Fernand Raynaud, was first a mime in the circus; and even at that time, with his beret pushed down over his ears, he imitated the simpleton he would later portray in his sketches to combat human stupidity.

Humor in the Literary and Performing Arts

The "new theatre," strongly marked by derision, translates the world's and society's absurdities with a mixture of clownish comedy and biblical pessimism in Beckett and a dose of tragedy, parody of chattering, and a dreamlike quality in Ionesco's works. In *Waiting for Godot* by Becket, the household fights between the two vagabonds, the delirious talking resembling an out-of-order computer, the missed suicide, the metaphysical farce of the unending waiting for the absent God—all this is more ridiculous than pathetic. *End of Party* offers the same desperate vision that comedy renders less desperate.

With Ionesco, the absurdities of the dialogue, the actions, and their interrelations characterize *The Bald Soprano*. More dreamlike, the parody of professorial discourses in *The Lesson* allows expression of the worst compulsions. *Amedee, or How to Get Rid of* shows a couple in conflict with a huge corpse which continues to grow. *Rhinoceros* is a burlesque and satirical painting of totalitarian arriving in a small, originally sympathetic, and absurd small town.

René de Obaldia in his plays keeps a verbal and imaginative fantasy, which his lyricism does not attenuate. Roland Dubillard, after the sympathetic and erratic characters of *Naive Swallows*, finds a tone where farce and despair alternate, the first more important in *The Beetroot Garden*, the second in *The Bone House*. Finally, Jean Tardieu, a poet who writes little philosophical tales, offers a "Chamber theatre," highly amusing because it built on a very formal performance for each play. (On the new theatre, see Esslin, 1963.)

Alone in the "new novel" trend to present comic elements, Robert Pinget brings familiar talking, colorful anecdotes with doubt in their inherent contradictions. The renewal of the narrative art passed also through some experimentation in Georges Perec's work. Active member of Oulipo, founded by Raymond Queneau, he wrote *Things* and *Life: Direction for Using*; in this novel constructed like a puzzle, anecdotes about the inhabitants of a Parisian building are the pieces (see Oulipo, 1973).

In science fiction, Jacques Sternberg accumulates preposterous, anachronistic, witty, and satiric ideas (for science fiction, see Cahiers Comique et Communication, 1984). Thrillers and detective stories have a funny Rabelaisian language and a wonderful humor in the books of Frédéric Dard about the adventures of St. Antonio. More recently, Jean Vautrin has brought comedy to this genre using Queneau's language, more specially in *Billy Ze Kick*.

Cartoons, Comics, and Children's Literature

Morris, a Belgian cartoonist, was the father of the celebrated *Lucky Luke* comics (in French, *bande dessinée*). Since 1955, Goscinny has written the words; he also created the texts of *Little Nicolas* (1954) with drawings by Sempé. Goscinny and Uderzo are also the authors of the famous *Astérix* (1959), in which a Gallic mythical community evokes our contemporary problems as well as our political reality in a brilliant parody. Since Goscinny's death, Uderzo has continued alone the creation of Astérix, putting the signature of his friend and collaborator, along with his own, on all his work.

The reading of these comics brings together children and adults, leaving to each the enjoyment of humor on his/her own level. Originally, these works were not created for children, and their success as humorous works appreciated by young people astonished the authors, who found a new tonality and a new public.

Zazie in the Subway (*Zazie dans le Métro*, 1959), the most famous comic novel of Queneau, presented to the readers a young heroine as insolent as able to play with words and inventive with language. The book appeared later (1977) in a children's edition, after its success as a movie.

In the sixties, some texts were presented to younger children, among them Ionesco's tales, a series of four albums where the talent of the artists illustrating them created a great interest in a production inspired by François Ruy-Vidal and edited by the American Harlin Quist. This experiment in liberating graphic art and bringing it into imaginative works for children was a financial failure.

The success of Pierre Gripari with *The Tales of Broca Street* in 1967 continues even today, thanks to the incongruous charm of a material world animated by the most absurd intentions. Philippe Dumas introduced a new irreverent style, extremely well accepted by children, with his *Reverse Tales* (*Contes à l'envers*). Pef, in the beginning a drawing artist, like Dumas, started short stories in which wordplays are the stars.

Tomi Ungerer, with his talent first acknowledged in the United States, produced children's albums (comic books), among them *The Three Brigands*, where nonconformism and unbridled imagination make fun of the works usually meant for children.

However, the main trend of the humorous production is found in the comics of Roba, with *Boule and Bill*, and Franquin, with *Gaston Lagaffe*. They use visual gags where naïveté mixed with a disparaging taste wins in the banal adult world. A latecomer, Frank Margerin, knew how to impose his character, Lucien, a popular antihero whose adventures mix the sordid with a megalomaniac attitude which doesn't take even itself seriously.

The Plastic Arts

Dada found in France a forerunner in Marcel Duchamp, who wanted to ruin the value "Art" by poking fun at it. He and Picabia put a mustache on a copy of Mona Lisa; he signed "ready made art" (putting his signature on public lavatories, bottles, doors, etc.).

Surrealism grouped a bunch of major artists, frequently strangers living in Paris. The most prolific but very marginal artist in the group was Picasso. Let's remember his bull's head made of a bicycle seat, on which he put the handlebars as horns. The most inventive by his themes was Max Ernst, with his absurd and burlesque collages. The most amusing was Miro, whose work makes us think of children's graffiti and forms. The most imaginative was Dali in his baroque compositions: "soft watches" spilling on tables, a female bust with a baguette bread on her head, or the living room, which viewed from the side represents Mae West's face. (For these arts, see Passeron, 1968).

The "girls" (Les nanas) of Niki de Saint-Phalle, the graffitic compositions of Jean Dubuffet, more recently the "free figuration," closely related to comics style, all these represent what Baudelaire called "The childhood freely found anew," Tinguely makes absurdly self-destroying (not dangerously) machines. The social criticism inspired the Malassis (Cueco, Tisserand, etc.) paintings against the consumer society: the Medusa raft on an ocean of beefsteaks, french fries, and plastic bottles.

Songs and Singers (Chansonniers)

Songs

In the fifties a wave of humor penetrated the songs in France, with Boris Vian (500 songs) and Francis Blanche (400 songs). It was the epoch of delirious, clownish, and parodic songs. A few singing groups specialized in absurd and satirical humor, the most famous being The Jacques Brothers and The Four Bearded Men. The funny costumes and presentation of the songs added to the comic effect, and they sang Prévert as well as Francis Blanche. Among the singers one should mention Henri Salvador, who for a time was teaming with Boris Vian, both coauthoring many songs. Pierre Perret sings about topics taken from daily life, caricaturing and exaggerating them, making them extremely funny by using a popular and racy slang.

Annie Cordy, a true female clown, has been entertaining since the fifties. Bobby Lapointe renewed in the seventies a style of comic song with wordplay, inventive breaking and changing of words, playing with the absurd, but unfortunately without great popular success. After 1968, Brigitte Fontaine with Areski and Jacques Higelin inaugurated a new style where gags and nonsensical dialogues turn the usual language around, with a background of African music mixed with jazz.

Follower of Prévert and Bobby Lapointe, Yvan Dautin sings with a dry humor where puns play with a popular language. Marie-Paule Belle with many varied songs presents the character of a not-so-dumb provincial girl who comes to Paris, keeps her common sense, and faces with humor the snobbish style of the great city.

Singers (Chansonniers)

The success of the chansonniers continued during the fifties, and during the sixties with the help of radio and records. Their choice themes were politics (Edmond Meunier, Robert Rocca, Jacques Grello, etc.) and sex (Roméo Charlès, Jean Rigaux). Among the singers were some funny storytellers too (Robert Lamoureux, Roger Nicolas).

Slowly, however, the places where chansonniers performed closed up; only very few remain in Paris, and they do their best to enrich and vary the show. Some of the stars continued their careers elsewhere: music hall, television (Roger Pierre, Jean Marc Thibaut, Anne-Marie Carrière).

Political attack has become attenuated. Why has this happened? We can only advance some hypotheses: the confusion that the colonial conflicts created in the political and moral values in France; self-questioning (something that Frenchmen don't usually do in a humorous way); the passage with a new generation to other forms of fun making, more militant or more oriented toward the absurd; and finally, too, in recent times the emergence of new social representations of politics and politicians and the large diffusion (by newspapers and radio among others) of a daily critical attitude toward political behavior in a serious and sometimes ironic form.

In a renewed style, Jean Amadou, Maurice Horgues, and Jacques Maillot continue the chansonnier tradition in the eighties.

Graphic Expression and Press

Hara Kiri or as its subtitle announced, "mean and nasty newspaper," appeared in 1960, reviving the graphic expressions and the anarchism of the Belle Epoque: a provocative humor. Under the direction of Cavanne, whose objective was to "demystify stupidity, even if it has good intentions," it had the collaboration of great cartoonists such as Reiser, Gébé, Cabu, Topor, and Wolinsky. A monthly which added many weeklies to its main edition, from 1969 on, it brought publications which were considered scandalous and pushed derision to the extreme, touching on the horrible. It was imitated in Germany by Pardon and in Italy by Archibrachio, until its great popularity diminished around 1976.

The Indochina War, followed by the war in Algeria which sent an entire generation of young people to fight outside France, provoked violent antimilitaristic reactions, best expressed in a newspaper entitled Siné-Massacre in 1963. (Siné, director and main cartoonist of the newspaper, was accused and judged for each of the nine numbers the journal published). Siné expressed himself again in 1968 in The Enraged by writing libertarian and iconoclastic satire. Drawings featuring despair and nonconformist humor were produced by Reiser,

Soulas, and Topor. Roland Topor, however, seemed to prefer bizarre and fantastic imagery.

Interrupted between 1940 and 1944, *The Chained Duck* (*Le Canard Enchaîné*) represents a certain kind of anti-power'' vis-à-vis the great influence of so-called serious media. Many great cartoonists collaborated or still collaborate on this great satirical newspaper: Gus, Guilac, Grove, Pol Ferjac, Moisan, Escaro, Kerleroux, and Cabu. Their illustrations accompanied texts, which went from irony to false naïveté, bypassing parody and pastiche.

The venerable newspaper *Le Monde* slowly gave in and also accepted cartoonists in its ranks, Chenez, Konk, and Plantu being the most famous. Their candid style in approaching political events forces lucidity from the viewer.

Faizant draws an editorial cartoon for the daily *Le Figaro*. For many years previously he had drawn cartoons of funny old ladies living in a universe of outdated ideas.

The art of the poster nowadays more often includes photography than drawings. However, Raymond Savignac introduced visual gags to help the publicity messages, as did Hervé Morvan and André François.

The edition of books of comics and cartoons (called *albums* in French) gave the opportunity to many cartoonists to exploit their production for themselves. This helped many such as Sempé to gain recognition not only from the press but also from the large public who got to know him from his funny drawings about little people fighting against a hostile environment and losing. Claire Brétécher, the only female humorous cartoonist, writes and draws for the weekly *The New Observer* (*Le Nouvel Observateur*); her series became famous and now appears in the States. Desclozeaux, another collaborator on the same journal, founded in 1967 with Bonnot a society for the protection of humor which continued till 1976.

Cinema

Robert Dhéry started a troupe called Les Branquignols which revived the tradition of French burlesque. Their humor was delirious, nostalgic, and neo-realist. Among their most famous films were *Les Branquignols* (1949), *La Belle Américaine* (1961), and *The Little Bather* (*Le petit baigneur*, 1967) with Louis de Funés.

With Jacques Tati, France had, for the first time since Max Linder, a comic genius. Monsieur Hulot, the unforgettable character created by Tati, appeared in *The Holidays of Monsieur Hulot* (1953) and *My Uncle* (1958). Monsieur Hulot was an absent-minded, clumsy character, constantly at odds with the accepted behavior of his environment, be it the bourgeois on the beach or the air-conditioned and mechanized world of an executive's family. The supreme comic character of the type resided in his boundless willingness to adapt, which pushed him to do too much. His next movies, *Playtime* (1967), *Traffic* (1971), and *Parade* (1974), did not have the success of his previous ones. Pierre Etaix had also a small public success with his films in which he was author and main actor. With *The Pretender* (1962), *Yoyo* (1964), and *Land of Plenty* (1971), he continued the tradition of burlesque based on clownish attitudes drawn from the circus, to which he finally returned.

How can the financial failure of the only two authentic French comics, Tati and Etaix, in the seventies be explained? The answer may be found perhaps in an article on comedy in France entitled ''The dictatorship of fun,'' by Jean Luc Douin (1974). This dictatorship is the one established by the box office: for two decades French comic movies have been disparaged by critics and adored by the public. What the critics do not like in these movies is undoubtedly what makes the public run to them: lack of subtlety and innovation, a soothing niceness, and a lack of subversive humor. The French comic films allow Frenchmen to identify with a positive self-image. It was not by chance that the greatest box-office success after the war was *La Grande Vadrouille* (Going on the loose), made in 1966. The script shows how, during the German occupation, the French were able to make fun of the Germans and thus prove their own great ability to manage (*se débrouiller*), one of the characteristics French people admire most in themselves. The producer, Gérard Oury, and his two main stars, Bourvil and Louis de Funès (both great actors), formed the most triumphant trio of the French comic cinema. The financial success of comic films is due mainly to the stars, for the public rushes unconditionally to see them: Les Charlots, Jean-Paul Belmondo, Pierre Richard, and Coluche, all very talented as comedians. The problem seems to reside in a certain facility adopted by the world of comic moviemakers in order to avoid financial failure. The ''new wave'' of comics coming from the coffee theatre (Gérard Jugnot, Michel Blanc) has not yet contradicted this orientation. This general tendency, however, has led to the production of a few good movies, but compared to the Italian comedy or to the creations of American comic authors such as Woody Allen or even Mel Brooks, French comedy in the movies is rather weak.

Television and Radio

Television was technically ready in the thirties, but its public history is more recent due to the high costs involved and the war between 1939 and 1945. The fifties, the wonderful period of radio where the spirit of Pierre Dac and Francis Blanche sparkled, presented many funny and marvelous programs, with terrific gags, wonderful short sketches, and serials which were extremely popular and continue to live in the memory of many. Inventor of telephonic gags (forerunner to ''Candid Camera'' on TV), Francis Blanche animated humorous programs in a way that gave certain radio stations their unique character. Among the many broadcasters working in humorous radio production, Maurice Biraud should be noted for his disconcerting inventiveness.

Starting in the fifties, television produced programs that combined the cabaret and chansonnier style with nonsense. The best-known stars were comic actors such as Raymond Souplex, Jean Poiret and Michel Serrault, Pierre Dac, Francis Blanche, Jeanne Sourza; they worked at the same time in radio presenting similar broadcasts. One program taken from the radio, "Five Pencils before the Judge" (Cinq crayons en correctionnelle, 1952), brings five cartoonists before a mock judge (Saint Granier). This parody of people before judges was presented in many variations, notably on the radio by Claude Villers in the eighties, where interviews of celebrities were mixed with many gags, and nonsensical interventions in the style of Pierre Dac.

Between 1958 and 1968, because of political conflicts, laughter was no longer "in." Some new programs, the most famous being "The Green Grapes" by Jean-Christophe Averty, started a great polemic mostly about scenes where dolls were destroyed in a meat grinder. Most of the humor in this program was visual and nonsensical, and it was not appreciated by the great public. In 1968 "The Shadoks" by Jacques Rouxel started another controversy; it showed strange, imaginary, and stupid animals doing insignificant and funny things on a bizarre planet, all commented on by the ironic voice of Claude Piéplu.

In the seventies, Jacques Martin presented a show entitled "Opera Glass" (La lorgnette) in which the insolence of cabarets was revived, but in a short time the tone became rather coarse. In 1979, Stéphane Collaro invented the "Collaroshow," followed later by "Cocoricoboy," where humor is mostly a staging of puns. With his "Little Theatre," Philippe Bouvard introduced the popular language in miniparodies, which satirized daily life and sometimes politics. Another famous humorous program by Roland Topor and Jean Claude Ribes entitled "Thank You, Bernard" presented a series of funny and daring sketches.

An excellent program for children was created by Topor, "Télé-chat," a parody of the television news presented by anthropomorphic animals in a children's time spot, where incongruity and imagination turn around the logic of the universe of objects so that humans do not know what to do anymore.

Since 1972 "The Ear in the Corner" (L'oreille en coin), animated by Jean Garretto and Pierre Codou, has adopted a new radio style. They prepare very elaborate and malicious sequences combining the unusual with humor. One of these sequences on Sunday morning continues the tradition of the Montmartre chansonniers.

Coffee theatre (Le Café Théâtre)

While the chansonnier and coffee-concert shows were less and less attracting the public, a new style of theatrical activity appeared in the euphoria of the sixties: the coffee theatre. It emerged on the fringes of the classical and boulevard circuits and in some ways an extension of the cabaret to theatrical creation.

In 1966, Bernard Da Costa created in a Montparnasse coffeehouse, the first coffee theatre in Europe. This style developed at a tremendous pace during the seventies. With little financial support, in unusual and small places (coffeehouses, lofts, cellars), young actors, authors, directors—frequently being all these things at the same time—created humorous plays or a series of comic sketches in groups like the "chums" at the Café de la Gare and later the clan at the Splendid or alone: the one-man show had existed before in the guise of a monologuist, but it was here that it gained the popularity it enjoys today.

Humor is omnipresent: in the unconventional and marginal spirit; in the demystification of brilliance and bluff; in the disparaging attitude toward everything, including oneself; in the climate of play and intimate complicity with the public. Themes vary, going from the daily life (such as men-women relationships, in the shows of "the Jeanne") to the delirious and black imagination of Romain Bouteille, passing by the absurd or the sad destiny of antiheroes (Dominique Lavanant, Josiane Balasko, Sylvie Joly). To note, the absence of politics. Here women took a place they had never before in humor creation, using comedy to attack the accepted stereotyped sex roles or to affirm an identity which is not part of the privileged status (like being fat, ugly, or frustrated).

From its origins, the coffee theatre has been a hot bed of talents (see Joyon, 1977; Da Costa, 1978; Merle, 1985). Many of today's comic and music-hall stars had their beginnings there. Others became movie stars and famous singers. During the "good years" around 1977, Paris had about 50 such coffee theatres, and success passed to the provinces; this art first performed during theatre festivals but now has festivals of its own. Even if nowadays the public is less enthusiastic, partly due to the fact that the stars left for the movies and major theatres, that evenings before the TV sets are taking up more time, or to the effects of economic crisis, the coffee-theatre is still well installed, and there are 12 places for it in Paris today. Faithful to the spirit of the beginnings, hostile to the bosses of "show-biz," Romain Bouteille dominates coffee theatre with his great talent; paradoxes, wordplay, digressions, brilliant soliloquies attacking the absurdities of the social system are the trademark of his shows.

One-man Shows

This chapter, necessarily incomplete, would be even more so if we did not evoke, even in only a few words, the comic format which during the last decade passed to the rank of superstar in the music halls, theatres, or television: the one-man show. The greatest comic star of the eighties is undoubtedly Raymond Devos, genius of verbal absurdity. Others among the best are Guy Bedos, bitter and sympathetic political critic (with texts written by Jean-Louis Dabadie); Bernard Haller, whose humor moves between the grotesque and the pathetic; Zouc, who touches the depths of anguish and drama with an extraordinary talent for imitation; Jacques Villeret, a pudgy dreamer; Jean Yanne and Colouche, who broke down social conventions in the media by their insolence and humorous rudeness; Pierre Desproges, with his acid, absurd verbosity; and the newest, Michel Boujenah, very talented in Jewish humor.

UNIVERSAL FUNCTIONS OF HUMOR AND THE NATIONAL MANIFESTIONS

Aggressive humor is very French: making fun *of others* and not of oneself (as in Jewish self-directed irony) or at the same time of others and oneself (as in British humor). The main victims are, since the first documents (literature of the Middle Ages),

—women in general
—the powerful (oppressive and repressive): clergy (twelfth to sixteenth centuries; eighteenth century; 1830–1950); magistrates and police; politicians and heads of state since the Revolution
—the marginal: physical deficits in more ancient times; or social class characteristics depending on epoch and perspective (peasants, bureaucrats, etc.) from the point of view of the dominant ideology; average Frenchman from the point of view of the temporary victors of May 1968; and deviant minorities such as snobs, "artists," hippies, etc.; "strange" accents, sometimes rural, sometimes from different provinces
—the foreigners: less than new immigrants of today (except when they were part of French colonies) than the ancient ones (Italians before the war) and mostly people from neighboring countries and "hereditary enemies" (British, Spanish, Germans after 1870, then Italian fascists, and German Nazis). Finally, peaceful neighbors (mostly Belgians, but also the Swiss) and also, now and then, some exotic ones. This helps the French keep a superior image of themselves.

Sexual humor is a constant in France; sometimes open and clear (during the Renaissance, the beginning of the Baroque Period, and the last fifteen years), sometimes more hidden, using more or less delicate allusions. Jokes on adultery were always macho style, making fun of the cuckold or the deceiving lover. There are popular scatological jokes about all kinds of bodily needs (excretions, dirt, fart), but also jokes about overeating and of course drinking (always with some kind of complicity).

Humor as a defense mechanism was nonexistent for a long time; no gallows humor (one practices the stoical style), and black humor stayed for a long time in the professions demanding a certain dose of cynicism (medical professions) before it found in modern times an intellectual form.

Social humor, as we have seen in its aggressive variant, is directed against corporate, or ethnic groups that differ from the dominant norm. However, when congenial, it has great importance as a means of facilitating social contacts by implying familiarity and conviviality. It takes the form of impersonal jabs and funny stories. At banquets it appears as crude jokes, ribald songs, and gags (more veiled than in the Germanic countries). In literary circles it expresses itself in brilliant and sophisticated verbal retorts. Political satire and humorous social criticism have been a French tradition since the Middle Ages, and the chansonniers made it a popular art. But humor, rarely used by politicians themselves, in politics is seen as something exotic.

Intellectual humor in France is chiefly verbal humor. As the popular song goes, "in France everything begins with words and ends with songs." Sometimes, on the way, new ideas are encountered, ideas to which frequently people arrived by using wordplay, sometimes of the worst kind. "Pun is the dropping of the flying spirit," said Victor Hugo, a great punster himself (*Les Misèrables*, book 3, chapter 7). A century after his death, this still holds true, and the titles of our newspapers aim frequently more for the amusing turn of phrase than for clear and precise information. The aim is not humor in the Anglo-Saxon sense of the word, but rather facetiousness, where the open laughter of popular banter mixes with the subtle or perfidious smile of the "clever word."

CONCLUSION

The millenary history of French laughter covers a great variety of manifestations of this universal human phenomenon. However, this diversity, which is also synonymous with richness, is not just a disorderly abundance. The spirit of a people having a common history in the same territory is naturally expressed in its artistic creation. In literature, oral or written, one can find its world vision, its manner of living, loving, and of course, laughing.

Since its beginnings, from medieval farces to the latest television shows, French humor has displayed an extraordinary freedom in the choice of its themes. Gallic wit is the opposite of the puritan mind; it is an open and free laughter, frequently loud, coming from a person who accepts his body and its needs. In this laughter, pleasure and rejoicing are together, and even the poor cuckold, the permanent laughingstock of French humor, accepts his fate with a resigned good humor.

Rabelais, the great master of this lecherous and smutty tradition, was also the ancestor of another rich tendency in the history of French laughter. Lover of life, he was also a lover of language. While he loved to inundate his writings with a torrent of words, his descendants devoted themselves with the same joy to finding the right word, the only one which falls exactly on target. Whether the victim is destroyed or only scratched a bit is not so important. What is crucial in French *wit* (rather than *humor*) is that the word has to sparkle with all the glitter of its author's intelligence. The most refined intellectual shares with the less bright punster, not always consciously, a profound satisfaction in using a so beautiful, rich, and expressive language. The best French spirit expresses a triumphant sentiment which is based not simply on successful play of words but on a true delight in language and its use.

Pleasures of words, pleasures of senses. These two tendencies do not sum up French laughter. But their lasting character brings precious information about what could be called the soul of a people.

REFERENCES

Adam, A. (1949 to 1956) *Histoire de la littérature française au 17ème siècle* (History of French Literature in the 17th Century). Paris: Domat.

Adhemar, J. (1971) *Le Dessin d'humour du 15ème siècle à nos jours* (Humorous drawings from the 15th century till now). Paris: Catalogue d'exposition de la Bibliothèque Nationale.

Auclert, J. P. (1981) *La Grande Guerre des crayons: les noirs dessins de la propagande de 1914–18*. (The great pencil war: the black objectives of propaganda in 1914–18). Paris: Robert Laffont.

Auguet, R. (1974). *Fêtes et spectacles populaires* (Popular festivals and shows). Paris: Flammarion.

Bachollet, R. (1979) *Satire à volonté* (Free satire) in *Le collectionneur Français*.

Bakhtin, M. (1970). *L'Oeuvre de François Rabelais et la culture populaire au Moyen Age et sous la Renaissance* (François Rabelais's work and popular culture during the Middle Ages and Renaissance). Paris: Gallimard.

Baudin, H. (1973) *Boris Vian humoriste* (Boris Vian the humorist). Grenoble: Presses Universitaires.

———. (1981) *La Métamorphose du comique et le renouvellement littéraire du théâtre français de Jarry a Giraudoux* (Metamorphosis of the comic and renewal of theatrical literature from Jarry to Giraudoux). Lille: Presses Universitaires.

Béchu, J. P. (1980) *La Belle Epoque et son envers. Quand la caricature écrit l'histoire* (The other side of the Belle Epoque. When cartooning writes history). Monte Carlo: A. Sauret.

Behar, H. (1967) *Étude sur le théâtre dada et surréaliste* (Study of the dada and surrealist theatre). Paris: Gallimard.

De Bercy A., Ziwes, A. (1951) *A Montmartre le soir: cabarets et chansonniers d'hier* (Evening in Montmartre: yesterday's cabarets and singers). Paris: Grasset.

Blanchard, G. (1969) *Anthologie de la poésie baroque et précieuse* (Anthology of baroque and affected poetry). Paris: Seghers.

———. (1969) *La bande dessinée. Histoire des histoires en images de la préhistoire à nos jours* (The comic strip. History of the picture stories from prehistory to our days). Verviers: Marabout Université.

Brochon, P. (1979) *La chanson français. Béranger et son temps* (The French songs: Béranger and his times). Paris: Editions Sociales.

Brunschwig, C., Calvet L., and Klein, J. C. (1981). *Cent ans de chanson français* (A hundred years of French song). Paris: Seuil.

Caradec, F., and Weill, A. (1980) *Le café concert*. Paris: Hachette.

Carrière, J. C. (1963) *Humour 1900*. Paris: J'ai lu.

Da Costa, B. (1978) *Histoire du café-théâtre* (History of the coffee theatre). Paris: Buchet-Chastel.

Deloffre, F. (1955) *Une Préciosité Nouvelle: Marivaux et le marivaudage* (A new preciosity: Marivaux and Marivaudean dialogue. Paris: Belles Lettres.

Dixmier, E. (1974) *L'assiette au beurre. Revue satirique illustrée* (Butter on a plate. Illustrated satirical journal). Paris: Maspero.

Douin, J. L. (1974) "La dictature de la rigolade" (The dictatorship of laughter). *La Revue du Cinéma* Mai: 21–34.

Dufresnoy, C. (1982) *Langage et dérision; le comique dans l'oeuvre littéraire de Marcel Aymé* (Language and disparagement: The comic in Marcel Aymé's literary work. Lille: Presses Universitaires.

Dumur, G. (Ed.) (1981) *Histoire des spectacles* (History of shows). Paris: Gallimard.

Esslin, M. (1963) *Le théâtre de l'absurde* (Absurdity theatre). Paris: Buchet-Chastel.

Fabbri, J., and Sallée, A. (1982) *Clowns et farceurs* (Clowns and funny men). Paris: Bordas.

Faure, A. (1978) *Paris Carême-Prenant: du Carnaval à Paris au 19ème siècle* (Paris during carnival in the 19th century). Paris: Hachette.

Fournel, P. (1975) *L'histoire véritable de Guignol* (The true story of the Guignol). Lyon: Fédérop.

Gaignebet, C. (1974) *Le carnaval: essai de mythologie populaire* (Carnival: an essay on popular mythology). Paris: Payot.

Garapon, H. (1957) *La fantaisie verbale et le comique dans le théâtre français du Moyen Âge à la fin du 17ème siècle* (Verbal fantasy and the comic in the French theatre from the Middle Ages to the 17th century). Paris: A. Colin.

Guillemin, H. (1951) *L'humour de Victor Hugo* (Victor Hugo's humor). Neuchâtel: La Bacconière.

Heers, J. (1983) *Fêtes de fous et carnavals* (Fool's days and carnivals). Paris: Fayard.

Herbert, M. (1967) *La chanson à Montmartre* (The Montmartre songs). Paris: Editions de la Table Ronde.

Jankélévitch, V. (1961) *La musique et l'ineffable* (Music and the unutterable). Paris: A. Colin.

Joyon, C. (1977) *Pleins feux sur le café théâtre* (Full light on the coffee theatre). Paris: Editions du Parc.

Král, P. (1984) *Le burlesque ou morale de la tarte à le crème* (Burlesque and the morality of the cream pie). Paris: Stock.

Le Roy Ladurie, E. (1979) *Le carnaval de Romans* (Romans' carnival). Paris: Gallimard.

Mast, G. (1973) *The Comic Mind: Comedy and the Movies*. Chicago: Chicago University Press.

Mazouer, C. (1983) ''Théâtre et carnaval en France jusqu'à la fin du 16ème siècle'' (Theatre and carnival in France till the end of the 16th century) *Revue de l'Histoire du théâtre* 35: 147–61.

Melot, M. (1975) *L'oeil qui rit: le pouvoir comique des images*. (The laughing eye: the comic power of images). Fribourg: Office du Livre.

Merle, P. (1985) *Le café-théâtre* (coffee-theatre). Paris: PUF.

Mitry, J. (1980) *Histoire du cinéma* (History of the cinema). Paris: Jean-Pierre Delarge.

Oulipo, R. (1973) *La Littérature potentielle* (Potential literature). Paris: Gallimard.

Passeron, R. (1968). *Histoire de la peinture surréaliste* (History of surrealistic painting). Paris: Livre de Poche.

Ragon, M. (1960) *Le dessin d'humour. Histoire de la caricature et du dessin humoristique en France* (Humorous drawings. History of cartoons and humorous drawings in France). Paris: Fayard.

———. (1972) *Les Maîtres du dessin satirique en France de 1830 à nos jours* (Masters of satiric drawing in France from 1830 till today). Paris: P. Horay.

Rémy, T. (1945) *Les Clowns* (The clowns). Paris: Grasset.

———. (1962) *Entrées clownesques* (Clownish entrances). Paris: l'Arche.

Rolandaël, G. (1985) *Petite encyclopédie du dessin drôle* (Little encyclopedia of the funny drawing). Paris: Cherche Midi.

Rousset, J. (1953) *La littèrature de l'àpe baroque en France*. Paris: Corti.

Sadoul, G. (1949) *Histoire du cinéma mondial* (History of world cinema). Paris: Flammarion.

STAFFORDSHIRE
POLYTECHNIC
LIBRARY

Scherer, J. (1952) *La dramaturgie classique en France* (Classical drama in France). Paris: Nizet.

Simoën, J. C. (1978) *Le livre d'or de l'assiette au beurre* (The golden book of the butter on the plate). Paris: Simoën.

Simon, J. P. (1979) *Le filmique et le comique. Essai sur le film comique* (The film and the comic. Essay on the comic film). Paris: Albatros.

Soupault, P. (1945) *Labiche, sa vie, son ouevre* (Labiche, his life and work). Paris: Sagittaire.

Stoll, A. (1978) *Astérix. L'épopée burlesque de la France* (Asterix. The burlesque epic of France). Paris: Complexe.

Tulard, J. (1982) *Dictionnaire du cinéma. Les réalisateurs* (Dictionary of the cinema. The producers). Paris: Robert Laffont.

Van Gennep, A. (1947) *Manuel du folklore français contemporain* (Handbook of contemporary French folklore). Paris: Picard.

Vernaillat, F., and Charpentreau, J. (1983) *La chanson français* (The French song). Paris: PUF.

Weill, A. (1984) *L'affiche dans le monde* (The poster in the world). Paris: Somogy.

Zeldin, T. (1981) *Histoire des passions françaises 1848–1945. Goût et corruption* (History of French passions 1848–1945. Taste and corruption). Paris: Seuil.

Studies on Laughter and Humor

Aimard, P. (1975) *Les jeux de mots de l'enfant* (Children's wordplay). Villeurbanne: Simep.

Bariaud, F. (1983) *La genèse de l'humour chez l'enfant* (The development of children's humor). Paris: PUF.

Baudin, H. (Ed.) (1983–1987) *Cahiers Comique et Communication*. Grenoble: CERCC.

Bergson, H. (1900) *Le rire* (Laughter). Paris: Alcan.

Escarpit, R. (1963) *L'humour* (Humor). Paris: PUF.

Guiraud, P. (1976) *Les jeux de mots* (Wordplay). Paris: PUF.

Jankélévitch, V. (1964) *L'ironie* (Irony). Paris: Flammarion.

Jeanson, F. (1950) *Signification humaine du rire* (Human meaning of laughter). Paris: Seuil.

Laffay, A. (1979) *Anatomie du rire et du nonsense* (Antaomy of laughter and nonsense). Paris: Masson.

Pagnol, M. (1947) *Notes sur le rire* (Notes about laughter). Paris: Nagel.

Stora-Sendor, J. (1984) *L'humour juif dans la littérature de Job a Woody Allen* (Jewish humor in literature from Job to Woody Allen). Paris: PUF.

Victoroff, D. (1953) *Le rire et le risible: Introduction à la psychosociologie du rire* (Laughter and the laughable: an introduction to the social psychology of laughter). Paris: PUF.

Ziv, A. (1979) *L'humour en éducation: approche psychologique* (Humor in Education: A Psychological Approach). Paris: Éditions Sociales Françaises.

Ziv, A., and Diem, J. M. (1987) *Le Sens de l'humour* (Sense of humor). Paris: Dunod.

4

JERRY PALMER

Humor in
Great Britain

BACKGROUND

The fundamental ethnic mixture of the British was settled in the distant past. The Roman invasion (55 B.C.-fifth century A.D.) unified the southern and eastern parts of these islands and left the western and northern Celtic fringes intact. Subsequent invasions from Scandinavia, and crucially the Norman Conquest of 1066, settled the ethnic stock from which the British would develop. From this point of view, the subsequent history of these islands consists fundamentally of the English subjection of the Celtic fringe and the imposition of its cultural and political forms upon those populations. Political unification was complete by the seventeenth century, partially so from the fourteenth, despite brief rebellions in Scotland in the eighteenth century; the military subjugation of Ireland was complete by the seventeenth century, but Southern Ireland fought for and won independence in 1921; the relationship between Great Britain and Northern Ireland has hung in the balance again since 1969. Subsequent immigrations into Great Britain have had relatively little impact upon our basic institutions or culture.

The relatively early settlement of our national boundaries and their relative stability (Ireland is the exception) are no doubt partially responsible for our homogeneity and political stability. The political form of representative democracy, albeit with a very limited franchise, was adopted in the seventeenth century, after our last violent revolution; the franchise was extended in stages during the nineteenth and early twentieth centuries. Women were the last group to get the vote.

From the point of view of cultural forms, this history has resulted in two main phenomena: first, the dominance within our boundaries of the English language; second, the dominance of cultural forms deriving from the bourgeois revolution of the seventeenth century.

Of the various non-English languages originally spoken in these islands, only Welsh is still a living language: it has its own TV channel, and much education is now conducted in Welsh; it is widely spoken as the normal everyday language. Cornish is so completely dead that it cannot even be deciphered, Gaelic (Scottish) is very little spoken, and although Erse (Irish) is used in the Republic of Ireland, it is little spoken in the North. Regional dialects of English are also virtually extinct, although some regional accents are relatively impenetrable for inhabitants of other areas.

The bourgeois revolution of the seventeenth century inaugurated the cultural forms that still dominate today: the theatre in its modern form, representational perspective painting, the novel, the school, the newspaper, etc. Although many of these had been in existence before, particularly during the sixteenth century, it was the politicl settlement of the last seventeenth century which confirmed their existence and the application they would have: the creation of a national culture dedicated to binding together the landed gentry and the mercantile class through a common language, set of values, and political and legal system.

The Industrial Revolution of the nineteenth century confirmed the British path toward a society in which the aristocratic, landed interest would not predominate, toward a middle-class, secular society devoted primarily to the creation of wealth and political stability at home; militarism was primarily for overseas consumption. The Industrial Revolution also created the working class and urban society in their modern forms. It was in this process that both universal compulsory education and the mass media of communication were born, as was commercial entertainment for the majority of the population.

It is difficult to trace direct links between this history and the nature of British humor. Certain institutional links will be traced later in this chapter. However, certain generalizations can be made.

First, distinctly regional styles of humor are a thing of the past. No doubt jokes get slightly modified for different audiences, and certain social types are only recognizable locally; but these differences are superficial compared with the profound regional differences that fissure other nations. The noteworthy exception to this rule is Ireland, dealt with in another chapter.

Second, the quasi-universality of the English language within our boundaries means that linguistically complex humor is accessible to the great majority of the population. Insofar as there is any divide between styles of humor based on different degrees of linguistic complexity, it is probably between those who have studied beyond the minimum school-leaving age and those who have not.

Third, the fact that we are largely a secular nation means that religious humor is not controversial in the way it would be in a fundamentally nonsecular society. There is little distinction between religious themes in humor and other general intellectual themes in this country; nor is religion a particularly popular topic for humor. Perhaps this statement is not true for subsections of the British population such as British Jews and British Muslims, were religion is more important in everyday life.

Fourth, our relative political stability and homogeneity is perhaps the reason why humor is relatively little used as a political weapon. Certainly politicians tell jokes and make humorous remarks, often at each other's expense. But in comparison with the vitrioloc, scurrilous ridicule which was commonplace in our politics two hundred years ago, such humor is muted.

HUMOR IN GREAT BRITAIN FROM THE MIDDLE AGES UNTIL WORLD WAR I

Popular Humor

The first known ''professional'' humorist in Great Britain was called Hitard. We know his name because it is recorded that in 1016 King Edmund Ironside gave him the town of Walworth (now part of London) as a reward for his humor. Hitard was Edmund's domestic fool, or jester, and in the Middle Ages all royal families, as well as many other rich families, kept a domestic fool. Sometimes these were men (no female fools are recorded) who were genuinely mentally peculiar, perhaps schizophrenic, sometimes men who pretended to a degree of folly. They would do such things as dance on the tables at dinner, fall off horses, and speak nonsense; they also had the license to criticize and insult their patrons in a way that nobody else could. What was appreciated in the fool was the occasional pearl of wisdom that appeared in absurd guise. By tradition—probably established in the late Middle Ages—the fool wore ''the motley,'' a costume of variegated color, with a long pointed cap covered in small bells, and carried a stick with an inflated bladder on it, which he used to hit people. This costume passed into modern theatrical and entertainment tradition with the character of Harlequin in the Commedia dell'Arte (see below), and subsequently the clown.

Mental defectives and the insane were in general regarded as objects of laughter in the Middle Ages, and the court fool was a privatization of what was public property in the country at large: the ''village idiot'' as a figure of fun has gone down in folklore. The activities of fools were widely imitated in the roles that formed the play-acting element of medieval festivals, the Christmas midwinter festival and the festival of spring, for example. The activities of fools, in all spheres of life, seem to have consisted of simple antics, exaggerated gestures and clothing, and babbling nonsense; it was recorded in the fifteenth century that the fool Scoggan (who also taught at Oriel college, Oxford) once stood under a waterspout for some hours for a bet of £20.

The names of many royal fools are recorded, from the eleventh century to the seventeenth. The Puritan Revolution of 1642 and the changes in the English monarchy that it inaugurated spelled the end of the court fool or jester. The new frame of mind associated with the Renaissance in any event evaluated *folly* in a manner incompatible with the medieval conception that underpinned the habit of easy laughter at the fool. However, the seventeenth century diarist Pepys recorded on February 13, 1668, after the restoration of the monarchy following the demise of the Puritan republic, that one Tom Killigrew had

a fee from the King's wardrobe for cap and bells, under the title of the King's fool or jester, and may revile or jeer anybody, the greatest person without offense, by the privilege of his place. (*Diaries* (1919) 4: 353)

The last record of any domestic fool refers to one retained at Hilton Castle, County Durham, until 1746 (Doran, 1858; Swain, 1932).

Troupes of jesters toured the country during the Middle Ages, performing at fairs for the benefit of all and sundry. Fairs were extremely common in those days, as they were the main place for the sale of goods; it is recorded that in Yorkshire (admittedly a trading county) there were around 300 fairs each year. Certainly there was a distinction between "pleasure fairs" and "market fairs," but is unclear when this distinction arose, and whether forms of entertainment were exclusively associated with the former (Richardson, 1961). In any event, antics which amused kings were also available to the lower orders of society. Eventually, the role of the fool passed into literature and the theatre (see below).

Traditional English folklore and customs were largely stamped out by the policing of leisure that accompanied the Industrial Revolution, and such folkloric forms as have survived are distant relics of this lost culture (Malcolmson, 1973). The best-known forms that still survive are April Fools' Day, Punch and Judy shows, and clowning.

April Fools' Day (April 1) is traditionally the day on which it is permissible to play practical jokes on people with impunity; it is probably the remnants of the "saturnalia" system of the preindustrial English countryside when it was permissible to be extremely rude to, or funny at the expense of, one's elders and betters on certain public holidays. The habit of these practical jokes seems to have declined considerably during the last thirty years, but traces are still to be found: on April 1, 1957, BBC television broadcast a short film about the spaghetti harvest in Northern Italy, in which peasants were shown collecting festoons of spaghetti from trees; on April 1, 1984, the *Sunday Times* included a report about a new generation of radio-guided self-driving buses being developed by London Transport. In neither case was there any formal indication that these items were not to be taken seriously.

Punch and Judy is a puppet show of highly ritualized violent encounters between Mr. Punch (who traditionally has an enormous red nose) and his wife, encounters that also involve a dog (or a crocodile), a string of sausages, and a policeman (it used to be a hangman). Dickens refers to one in the streets of the City of London in *The Old Curiosity Shop* (ch. 37) attracting spectators of all ages and conditions; nowadays that would be impossible, as street entertainments are by and large forbidden, and anyway only children would be interested. Punch and Judy is now exclusively a children's entertainment.

The traditional role of the clown in the theatre and traveling shows has succumbed to the forms of the modern mass entertainment industry. Much of the clown's skills passed into silent cinema, via the music hall, which thereby captured the bulk of the clown's audience. The massive Victorian theatrical shows, with animals and clowns, have become the modern circus, which is now the only venue for traditional pure clowning in the older manner, complete with Pierrot costume. In recent years the circuses have found economic survival extremely hard: they have become increasingly large and spectacular, probably as a result of public expectations being raised by exposure to film and TV versions of the "biggest and best" circuses, and correspondingly expensive. A visit to the circus is now a rarity for most children.

Last, pantomime. Originally this term referred to any mime show, as performed in classical antiquity and known throughout the Middle Ages; however, in the post-Renaissance period, this term came to refer to a specific type of theatrical performance. The comedy of the Roman Empire—for example, the plays of Plautus—conventionally featured a series of intrigues involving frustrated young lovers, severe fathers, ingenious slaves, mistaken identities, etc. In the Renaissance these stories were widely imitated and in Italy gave rise to a particular form of theatre called Commedia dell'Arte, in which the roles became entirely conventionalized and were even given standardized names: Harlequin, Columbine, Pantaloon, etc. (in their English versions). These plays consisted of more or less fixed scenarios on the basis of which the actors improvised the actual stage movements and dialogue, a performance based on a massive memorized knowledge of an entire tradition, analogous to the knowledge of the forms of peroration and the stock of commonplaces to fill them that was taught in rhetoric at the same period (sixteenth-eighteenth centuries); or—to take a modern parallel—analogous to jazz improvisation. The Italian troupes that performed such plays toured the whole of Europe. In England they performed before the court in 1578, and there are fragmentary records of earlier visits which refer to "dancing, antics and various other feats" (Nichol, 1963, p. 168). The English theatre was completely closed down by the Puritans (1642–60), but with the reopening in the Restoration the Italian troupes reappeared. They were less successful here than elsewhere in Europe, especially France (where they had their own permanent theatre until the Revolution), but were imitated in brief entr'actes, and by the mid-eighteenth century were known as pantomime. Also known as masquerades, they were enormously popular among the aristocracy and the lower classes but were condemned as frivolous and immoral by the more sober and moralizing rising middle class. The comedy was broad and often scatological (Nichol, 1963).

In the early nineteenth century pantomime still formed part of the stock-in-trade of the troupes of traveling players that toured the countryside, performing at fairs, race meetings, inns, and anywhere else that would pay them (Vicinus, 1974, p. 242). But as the century progressed, it became increasingly associated with Christmas, and since World War II exclusively so. In the evolution that followed the demise of the Commedia dell'Arte at the end of the eighteenth century, pantomime adopted many other scenarios as well as the traditional Commedia ones, in particular versions of the fairy tales collected by the Brothers Grimm or written by Hans Christian Andersen. Nowadays these stories (*Cinderella, Mother Goose*, etc.) are the basis of star-studded spectaculars with musical and humorous interludes, the young hero always played by a girl *en travesti* and the elderly women—especially the ugly sisters in *Cinderella*—played by men, preferably large well-known comedians adorned with voluminous skirts and enormous false breasts.

Humor in the Literary and Performing Arts

Humor in English literature starts with the beginnings of modern, i.e., non-medieval, English literature. This is not to say that there is no humor in medieval literature, but that none of these texts would nowadays be considered classics of humorous literature. The first modern English author is also our first humorous classic: Geoffrey Chaucer, whose *Canterbury Tales* (late fourteenth century) includes much comic writing in a traditional earthy vein. Shakespeare's works include fourteen plays which are labeled comedies, but in Renaissance terminology a comedy was any play with either (or both) a happy ending or a cast of characters drawn from the lower orders. Much of these texts is signally unfunny, at least to modern audiences, and this raises the problem, much debated in modern criticism, of the relationship between comedy and laughter (Palmer, 1987, ch. 1). It should be said that sympathetic production can restore the mirth in appropriate places in Shakespeare, and that on occasion—for example, *The Comedy of Errors*—there is pure farce of the broadest kind. Literary historians agree on the debt Shakespeare owed to the Commedia dell'Arte and other revivals of Roman comedy. More conventionally comic is Jonson's *Volpone* (1606), which is felt by many critics to be the finest comedy in English. Volpone pretends to be at death's door, and his neighbors, in anticipation of future receipts from his will, bring him more and more expensive gifts; he manipulates their greed to greater and greater extremes, making them victims of their own vices, but is eventually caught out.

The restoration of Charles II in 1660 ushered in a period of English culture marked by sexual license and a taste for humor. The best drama of the period is comic, and several of these plays still feature in modern repertories, notably

Congreve's *Way of the World* (1700), about a successful, sharp-tongued, and beautiful woman who is in love but does not want to "dwindle into a wife." This style of comedy—a little ribald, aristocratic in tone, sharply critical of provincialism, middle-classness, the comfortable complacency of middle age— lasted, in a slightly more sedate version, into the late eighteenth century: Goldsmith's *She Stoops to Conquer* (1773) and Sheridan's *School for Scandal* (1777) are remembered and still figure occasionally in the repertory.

The Restoration Period and the eighteenth century area also noted for their satirical poetry, nowadays more admired for its literary technique than its destructive wit: the author who has survived best is Alexander Pope, whose *Rape of the Lock* is a mock-heroic epic about a feud between two families over a stolen lock of hair. The satirical spirit of the century is best shown in Jonathan Swift, whose *Gulliver's Travels* (1726) was originally intended as a series of political satires on the follies of his age. They are chiefly remembered for the elements of fantasy in them. His *Modest Proposal* is the most ferocious satire on England's conduct in Ireland ever written. Also well-remembered is Fielding's *Tom Jones* (1749), a picaresque romp through all the levels of English society by a young orphan in search of welath and happiness, both of which he eventually finds. It was made into a successful film in 1963. Recently rescued from critical obscurity is Sterne's *Tristram Shandy* (1760–67), a novel which adumbrates modernist techniques.

Despite the overwhelming seriousness of nineteenth-century culture, the Victorians bred some of the greatest of English comic writers. Charles Dickens is both one of the greatest of English novelists and also one of its great humorists: his novels contain an entire gallery of affable fools and hilarious rogues, such as Mr. Micawber in *David Copperfield* (1849–50) and Mrs. Gamp in *Martin Chuzzlewit* (1843–44); equally remembered is the ferocious irony he directed at hypocrisy and self-serving public institutions such as the Circumlocution Office in *Little Dorrit* (1855–57), which stands for the law at its most obtuse.

The Victorian era also bred what are arguably our two greatest nonsense writers: Lewis Carroll and Edward Lear. Lewis Carroll's *Alice's Adventures in Wonderland* and *Through the Looking-Glass* (1865 and 1871) have remained standard children's books but are also recognized as nonsensical explorations of basic philosophical puzzles. Edward Lear's *Book of Nonsense* (1846) has continued to serve as a model for nonsensical poetry ever since.

Also a product of the Victorian era is the wittiest of English playwrights, Oscar Wilde. Although of Irish origin, Wilde wrote all his best work in London, and his subject matter is society life and the English upper classes: "The English country gentleman galloping after a fox—the unspeakable in full pursuit of the uneatable." On his deathbed in a cheap Paris hotel, he is reputed to have looked at the wallpaper and said "One of us has got to go." *The Importance of Being Ernest* (1895) is still performed and has been made into a film.

Finally, the late Victorian era produced the beginnings of George Bernard Shaw's long career as dramatist, essayist, and ideologue. In his prolific output of plays he used every device, especially comedy, to put across the ideas of a group of socialist intellectuals, the Fabians:

Mendoza: I am a bandit, I live by robbing the rich.

Tanner: I am a gentleman. I live by robbing the poor. *Shake hands*.

Shaw's plays have not worn terribly well, as the dialogue is often stilted, and many of the issues no longer seem very relevant, at least not in the terms in which he discusses them: it is typical that *Pygmalion* (1913), intended as a denunciation of the class system in England, should have become that ultimate in triviality, *My Fair Lady*.

Mention should also be made of the novels of Jerome K. Jerome: *Three Men in a Boat* (1889) and *Three Men on the Bummel* (189-?) are light-hearted accounts of the misadventures and most un-earnest philosophizing of three middle-class young Victorians; occasionally rising to farcical hilarity, they have survived better than most Victorian humor.

The comic operas of Gilbert and Sullivan were also the most successful productions of the late nineteenth century. Their popularity endured until after World War II, but has declined considerably since.

Humor in the Visual Arts

The modern cartoon has its origins in the satirical engraved print and woodcut whose chronological origins somewhat postdate the invention upon which they depend, the printing press. Dorothy George, historian of English graphic social satire, sees roughly a century of "sporadic activity" in this field preceding the appearance of the first great English cartoonist, Hogarth, in the early eighteenth century. The popularity of such prints is beyond doubt; despite their relatively high price they were to be found in even the poorest of homes. Hogarth's favorite theme was one commonly found among contemporary moralists: the pernicious effects of an idle and immoral life. In series of prints such as *The Rake's Progress*, *The Harlot's Progress*, and *The Idle Apprentice* he shows previously innocent young men and women dragged down by dissipation to an early death on the gallows or through disease. These prints and others from the same period are difficult to decipher now, for it is difficult to understand what is ordinary realism—for example, the neutral portrayal of what appear to us grotesque excesses at table—and what is a satirical observation of something like vulgar dress or gesture:

It is difficult now to realize the eighteenth century co-existence of stylized formality and elegance with (tolerated) grossness and eccentricity. (George, 1967, p. 13)

Artists who followed Hogarth are Gillray, Rowlandson, and Cruikshank. In this tradition, which preceded the newspaper cartoon of the nineteenth century, the predominant features, at least to a modern reader, center around the grotesquely ugly caricatures of individuals and social types. George tells us that many of the individuals would have been recognizable to contemporaries, and many of the types are illustrated by recognizable individuals: this extreme of personal ridicule was considered normal, apparently. As the eighteenth century turned into the nineteenth, social divisions in the country became more visible, social life became increasingly politicized, and the cartoons became increasingly concerned with directly political issues. With the foundation of *Punch* in 1841 Britain acquired its first publication specializing in humor, and especially in cartoons.

HUMOR IN THE MASS MEDIA

A hundred and fifty years ago the institutions of popular culture lacked the respectability they have since acquired. In part this was due to their sheer difference from the cultural institutions of polite society, in part due to the upper classes' fear of popular disorder and revolution, and the role that the institutions of popular culture might play in this process. This significantly affects the history of comedy and humor in this country, for its nature is closely bound up with the institutions in which comic performances were given, and the history of humor and comedy during the last century is the history of the acquisition of respectability.

The central institution of humor in Victorian England was the music hall, which became the prototype of the modern mass entertainment industry (Waites, 1981). Music hall synthesized earlier forms of popular humorous (and musical) performance into a commercially viable form, which was just sufficiently acceptable to the authorities to receive legal recognition in the form of licenses to allow public performances. The earlier forms were the "song-and-supper" clubs of the big cities, inhabited by upper-class young males and demimonde, the "free-and-easy" entertainments organized in pubs by groups of amateurs, and the groups of traveling players. The earliest music halls, in the late 1840s, were rooms attached to pubs, and although from an early date some small admission price was charged, the main commercial attraction was the massively increased consumption of drink. At this stage, the staple entertainment was musical, but many of the songs were comic ones, and this remained a feature of music hall. Examples of the words of such songs are to be found in Martha Vicinus, *The Industrial Muse* (1974). A typical program, in the early days, consisted of some 30 songs, lasting from 7:00 till 11:00 P.M. By 1868 there were 39 music halls in London and some 300 in the British Isles as a whole (Mander and Mitchenson, 1965, pt. 2).

Music hall's relationship to the cultural politics of Victorian Britain is complex. On the other hand, it attempted a higher standard of decorum than its competition and predecessors like the song-and-supper clubs, and in the south at least it eschewed the radical politics of the northern broadside ballads and entertainments based on them. On the other hand, it never lost "the atmosphere of relaxed, slightly risque social behavior . . . " (Vicinus, 1974, p. 246); it was associated with prostitution, and never gained the approval of those concerned with moral improvement. In general, music hall was associated with drink and Toryism (the alcohol business was predominantly Tory in the nineteenth century), whereas Liberalism was associated with the sacred choir, the dissenting churches, and the concert hall. More broadly, Liberalism was associated with the desire for improvement, freedom, and democracy; Toryism, with pleasure, deference, and a fatalistic acceptance of the existing social hierarchy (Vicinus, 1974, ch. 6; Waites, 1981, p. 47). In this divide lies the origin of many fundamental features of modern commercial entertainment. Thus, despite the music hall's association with disreputability (notably drink and bawdiness), it was nonetheless within the limits of what the British authorities were prepared to tolerate, especially as the fear of political revolution receded after 1848 and working-class loyalty to the throne became clear in the last quarter of the century.

By the high point of music hall (1870–1900 approximately), the comic sketch had become an integral part of the program alongside the comic song. These songs commonly involved mild satire of the upper classes, sexual innuendo, and irony about the hardships of working-class life; the most famous of all of these comic songs, Marie Lloyd's "My Old Man Said, Follow the Van," is about moving at night to avoid paying the rent:

We had to move away
'Cos the rent we couldn't pay,
The moving van came round just after dark;
There was me and my old man
Shoving things inside the van
Which we'd often done before, let me remark . . .

My old man said "Follow the van,
And don't dilly-dally on the way!"
Off went the cart with the home packed in it,
I walked behind my old cock linnet,
But I dillied and dallied, dillied and dallied,
Lost the van and didn't know where to roam.
I stopped on the way to have the old half-quartern,
And I can't find my way home.
[Half-quartern = a large slug of spirits]

Although the subject is poverty, there is no indication of anger: music hall songs in general appear to accept the status quo (Vicinus, 1974, ch. 6; Waites, 1981, p. 47). Music hall managements had lists of forbidden topics for humor, such as foul language and the Royal Family.

The comic sketches appear, from printed descriptions of them, to be a mixture of clowning and miniature comic plays. Here is a brief description, taken from

a newspaper report of the Royal Command Variety Performance at the Palace
Theatre in 1912:

. . . Pipifax walked off with his foot through a drum which he had thus shattered by a
fall into the orchestra. . . . Mr. George Robey—as the Mayor of Mudcumdyke . . . told us
of his municipal glories, of his speeches, and more than all, of his costumes. When he
appeared before his wife, the Mayoress, on November 9 he was scarcely prepared for
her remark, "Sebastian, why are you four days too *late*?" (Mander and Mitchenson,
1965, pp. 32–33).

The clowning sketches went straight into silent cinema: both Stan Laurel and
Charlie Chaplin, to take two examples, started in the London halls. The miniature
comic plays passed eventually into radio and television. George Robey was later
to receive a knighthood, and a London pub is still named after him.

HUMOR IN THE TWENTIETH CENTURY, FROM WORLD WAR I TO THE 1960s

Humor in the Mass Media

Music hall survived, under the title "Variety," until after World War II, when
it eventually succumbed to television. However, it was already in decline by the
end of World War I, ousted by ragtime, which killed the older musical style of
the halls, and by revue, with its greater emphasis on glamour and dancing. One
variety theatre survives in London—the Palladium, often televised—and in the
summer, variety shows are put on in small theatres in English seaside resorts.
The style, however, has been substantially modified by television.

Between the two World Wars, cinema was the mass media par excellence: in
Britain broadcasting did not reach the mass of the population until wartime.
Despite Hollywood's dominance of world cinema, Britain was still able to produce films, especially comedies, with sufficient local appeal to make production
financially viable. These films usually starred comedians and comediennes who
were already established in the variety theatres; the most famous were Gracie
Fields and George Formby. Just as music hall management had excluded any
material likely to be regarded as subversive, so the British Board of Film Censors
ensured that film comedy was respectable; the films made by music hall comedian
Ernie Lotringa from the more radical northeast, for example, were constantly
censored for inpugning British institutions (Aldgate, 1981, p. 14).

Variety was also affected by the birth of broadcasting, though this effect was
cushioned by the disinclination of the BBC to broadcast "pure entertainment"
until World War II. Moreover, theatre managers and agents fought hard against
broadcasting, which they were convinced would kill the theatres by giving the
public free exposure to comedians' material. Comedians themselves were fright-
ened of broadcasting because in the theatre they could repeat the same act over
and over again, whereas the nature of broadcasting demanded constant innovation. Broadcasting, too, maintained strict control over the propriety of humor.

World War II had a profound impact on the nature of British broadcasting in general, and the role that comedy played within it changed beyond recognition. Wartime radio devoted an entire channel to light entertainment, which remained after the war; its style was markedly more popular than anything the BBC had done before, audience participation was increased, an attempt was made to build audiences by regular scheduling—something the BBC had on the whole largely refused before—and it even included American imports, especially Bob Hope and Jack Benny. The percentge of radio time devoted to light entertainment rose from 5.76 in 1938 to 14.73 in 1942, an increase of around 250 percent (Scannel and Cardiff, 1981, p. 34).

Wartime radio comedy was dominated by one show: "ITMA" ("It's That Man Again," a popular prewar newspaper phrase for Hitler's activities). "ITMA" started on July 12, 1939, and ran until well after the war. It was a show based on nonsense, fast puns, catchphrases and recurrent situations. Tommy Handley, who was already an established radio star, played the mayor of a small seaside town, constantly threatened by a Nazi spy called Funf and attended by Mrs. Mopp, the charwoman. The show pioneered the use of elaborate sound effects as an integral part of radio comedy.

The experience of wartime radio led to a dramatic increase in the amount of radio comedy: "on a typical Thursday evening in 1953 you could hear four shows" (Took, 1976, p. 103). In the postwar period, radio comedy assumed the form that broadcast comedy still has. Previous radio comedy had largely been broadcast theatre, but now comedy was written specially for radio. The scripwriter, who had previously been no more than a supplier of individual gags to a stand-up comedian, became central, for he controlled the nature of the program. This role was established in what is probably the most influential comedy radio show of the postwar period: Muir and Norden's "Take It From Here." This show was innovative in other respects too: wartime comedy had been morale boosting, and nothing resembling social criticism was allowed, but "Take It From Here" was directly satirical; previous radio comedy had relied heavily on established variety stars, but the new comedy used unknowns who were launched by being radio comics.

The best remembered show of the postwar period is undoubtedly "The Goon Show," starring Spike Milligan, Peter Sellers, and Harry Secombe. It is available today on record and cassette, and still has aficionados, a quarter of a century after it finished. It was remarkable for a range of massively implausible characters—Major Bloodnock of the fifth Foot and Mouth, the terminally stupid Neddy Seagoon, a sort of schoolboy called Bluebottle—each with an extremely exaggerated voice, a set of catchphrases, and a set of nonsensical situations such as floating Dartmoor Prison across the Atlantic to the Goonited States. Its elaborate sound effects were a much appreciated feature of the show.

Finally, a show which is in some respects the apogee of radio comedy, "Hancock's Half Hour" (also still available on record). All the preceding shows depended in large measure on repeated catchphrases, rapid puns, nonsense, etc., and consisted of short, independent sections with musical breaks in between. "Hancock's Half Hour," starting in 1954, was 30 minutes of nonstop monologue and dialogue with no breaks, no catchphrases, no nonsense and puns: it was entirely a comedy of character, based on the mishaps and misdeeds of a lower-middle-class egomaniac incapable of appreciating that the universe does not revolve entirely around himself.

In these more sophisticated shows of the postwar period lay the seeds of the comic form that currently dominates British comedy broadcasting: the situation comedy, or sitcom, a form which is particularly suitable for broadcasting. Sitcom is conventionally distinguished from variety in these terms: variety consists of a series of unrelated episodes, but sitcom is a miniature comic drama in which a recurrent series of characters in recurrent relations to each other act out a continuous narrative throughout the broadcast. It is a form of comedy which is not unique to Britain—it was pioneered by American radio during the 1930s—but it has probably been more widely exploited in Britain than elsewhere: the British Film Institute's *Sitcom Dossier* lists 159 sitcom *series* between August 1980 and August 1982 alone. Sitcom is also the only category of TV fiction where Britain scarcely imports from the United States at all, and exports massively to the rest of the world: "Fawlty Towers" (by common consent one of the best TV sitcoms, if not the best) was the BBC's most successful export in 1977–78, selling to 45 stations in 17 countries (Wilmut, 1980, p. 17). To this extent sitcom may be considered a peculiarly British product.

This is not to suggest that the transition from radio to TV was unproblematic. The attempt to transplant individual shows direct was on the whole unsuccessful: there was a TV version of "The Goons," which was by common consent far inferior to the radio version. Nonetheless, the move in radio comedy toward comedy of situation and comedy of character, rather than total reliance on gags, nonsense, and catchphrases, etc., proved good preparation for TV comedy.

At this point we enter a period of comic production in the mass media which is relatively homogeneous. The preceding pages have tried to demonstrate how the major institutions of British humor have come to have their characteristic modern profiles, and especially to show how, from being on the disreputable fringe of culture, humor has moved to its heart. In this process, two features were central: first, the possibility of controlling comedy's subversive potential; second, the need for popular entertainment broadcasting during World War II.

Humor in the Literary and Performing Arts

In the early twentieth century, literary farce has been respresented by Ben Travers's plays, notably *A Cuckoo in the Nest*, and in the novel by P. G. Wodehouse, whose stories about the aristocratic cretin Bertie Wooster and his resourceful manservant Jeeves were among the most popular novels of the interwar years. Typical also of this period is the wit of Noel Coward.

Most postwar farce has been in film and television, with some theatrical successes, but mention should be made of the Doctor novels of Richard Gordon, notably *Doctor in the House* (1952); they were turned into successful comedy films in the early 1960s.

The greatest comic novelist of the interwar years was undoubtedly Evelyn Waugh, whose acerbic satires on the follies and immorality of the British equivalent of the Jazz Age are as hilarious as they are biting. In *Decline and Fall* (1928) a would-be young clergyman is sent down from Oxford for indecent behavior, becomes a schoolmaster at an appalling public school, nearly marries a pupil's millionaire mother who gets him sent to prison to cover up her white slaving, then bribes the authorities to change his identity; he returns to Oxford to read theology: in a world of charlatans, hypocrites, and confidence tricksters, the harmless eccentricity of useless learning is at least an innocent refuge.

In the postwar era Angus Wilson continued this tradition of the satiric comedy of manners, in various novels and collections of short stories. More recently, Kingsley Amis has produced novels with a nicely acid touch, especially *Lucky Jim* (1954), a satirical portrait of university life; Malcolm Bradbury has mined the same vein, especially in *The History Man* (1975), a scurrilous and hilarious account of a radical sociologist at a new university.

The postwar era has also seen one of the greatest of modern political satires: George Orwell's *Animal Farm* (1945), in which the animals decide to take over the farm and run it for the benefit of all animals equally. However, the pigs use their superior intelligence and organization to run it for their own benefit on the grounds that they are "more equal than the others."

Less directly political than *Animal Farm* but equally notworthy is a satire of provincial manners by the Welsh poet Dylan Thomas: *Under Milk Wood* (1954). Originally a radio play, also published in book form and as a record, it is a malicious portrait of a small community seething with every kind of repressed desire, described in a language that tends all the time toward lyric poetry.

Postwar English novelists tend in general to write in the traditional novel of manners form, which readily lends itself to comic moments; such are to be found easily in writers such as Ivy Compton-Burnett, T. F. Powys, Muriel Spark, Fay Weldon, and Anthony Powell. Keith Waterhouse's *Billy Liar* (1959) is a genuinely comic creation: a young man with fantasies of power caught forever in the backwater whose awfulness engenders these fantasies in the first place.

CONTEMPORARY HUMOR AND TRENDS

Themes in Contemporary British Humor

One would expect it to be exceptionally difficult to generalize about this topic in a society as riddled by class, gender, and racial differences as Britain is today. In practice, recent BBC audience research shows that comedy audiences cross the class and gender boundaries (there are no data for ethnic divisions):

The profile of audiences to BBC comedy shows on average reflected the proportions of middle and working class people in the population. . . . In contrast audiences to ITV comedies were disproportionately working class, in line with profiles for ITV in general (BBC, 1984).

However, examination of the report's statistical tables reveals that the differences between BBC and ITV audiences are not massive. A report on the audience for situation comedy comes to essentially the same conclusion, except that audiences for ITV sitcoms are disproportionately female, elderly, and working class; this is explained by the general tendency of this section of the population to be heavy TV viewers (BBC, 1984).

These data should be handled with caution. In the first place, although they include a quantitative representation of audience appreciation—i.e., how much each section of the audience enjoyed, or said they enjoyed, the shows in question—statistical data cannot tell us much about what it was in the show that the audience liked or disliked: only aesthetic or psychological analysis can do that. In the second place, BBC audience research is designed to serve as a practical guideline for a public corporation whose aim is to please the population as a whole, and thus its policy is deliberately designed to achieve representative audiences. These figures reveal that on the whole they have succeeded, by carefully tailoring shows to the middle ground of taste and opinion: how far this taste is a reflection of what people like in nonbroadcast humor is open to question, for it is well-known that there are many jokes which are told in informal contexts and in clubs which cannot be put on the air. Nonetheless, despite these caveats, the audience research demonstrates that humor crosses class and gender boundaries, thus allowing certain generalizations to be made.

Undoubtedly the commonest topics of humor are sex and punning, and of course their combination. Humor about sexuality in Britain is probably not significantly different from elsewhere in the industrial west: it consists largely of the juvenile form of innuendo, or humorous delight in breaking the taboos of mentioning the unmentionable—at one time underwear was known as "unmentionables," in itself a joke at the time. In common with other countries that have developed a gay movement and a women's movement, sexual humor has become politicized, at least in some quarters: there is an awareness that the traditional dirty joke is often an insult to womanhood, and humor about homosexuality is seen as similarly insulting to gays. One should beware of exaggerating the impact of these considerations since both topics are as common as ever, and even where they have had an impact they do not lessen delight in sexual humor. I was recently at the wedding of some actors, whose friends put on a cabaret for them. One of the sketches consisted of the compere standing up and saying: "Look, Maxine, John knows you've had plenty of boyfriends, and of course he doesn't mind, do you, John? And I expect some of them are here, still good friends, aren't you? Well, look fellers, that's okay, but let's do the decent thing, eh, and give her back her keys—which you won't be needing any more, right?" And the audience howled with laughter as something like 25 sets of keys were thrown onstage!

Punning is often said to be a peculiarly Anglo-Saxon form of humor. Puns are common in other languages too, of course, but it is perhaps the English-speaking races that have traditionally taken most delight in rapid-fire puns and verbal nonsense: Edward Lear's nonsense poetry, the Marx Brothers, "ITMA," the Goons, etc. It is also a tradition that extends into canonical literature, in writers such as Joyce and Beckett. Verbal and conceptual nonsense has been an increasingly popular feature of English humor; for example: "What is yellow and highly dangerous?"—"Shark-infested custard."

In common with other Western countries, jokes about stupidity and foreigners or ethnic minorities are commonplace in Britain. As Christie Davies (1982) has shown, these jokes are international, but are aimed at different groups of people in different countries: in France or Holland, at the Belgians; in the United States, Poles; in Britain, the Irish. Whether these jokes are to be seen as an act of aggression against the communities in question or whether, being jokes, they are not to be taken seriously is an open-ended debate (Palmer, 1987). In Britain, such jokes have probably had an extra edge to them, over the last decade and a half, thanks to the Troubles in Ulster. In general, jokes about race have become politicized, in a period of racial tension, in the same way as jokes about sex; in such contexts humor is a political weapon as well as a form of entertainment, and is the more entertaining the more it is politically barbed, and vice versa.

One further feature of British humor nowadays needs extended commentary. As we have seen, the dominant form of popular humor in the late nineteenth century, the music hall, excluded disrespect for the established order, an exclusion which continued throughout the first half of this century through the censorship of cinema and broadcasting. Of course there was a subterranean tradition of antiestablishment humor, some of it politically motivated: it has been in part recuperated in the *Big Red Joke Book*, a collection of left-wing jokes; but political control of public performance ensured that it stayed subterranean. In this respect the situation changed dramatically in the post-war period and especially in the 1960s, with the rapid growth and enormous popularity of satire. In the 1950s, radio comedy broke new ground by satirizing, usually rather gently, current events and institutions, but in the early 1960s a new sort of entertainer appeared: the university satirist.

Autumn 1960 saw the London opening of a show called *Beyond the Fringe*, a series of revue sketches performed by members of the Cambridge Footlights Club. They included a savage denunciation of the government's nuclear defense policy and an aggressive portrayal of the Church of England as a complacent irrelevancy. Its enormous success—it ran until 1966, transferring to Broadway in 1962—spawned an entire industry: the magazine *Private Eye*, a satire nightclub called The Establishment, and—crucially—a weekly TV show called "That Was The Week That Was," abbreviated to TWTWTW, or TW3, presented by an unknown Cambridge man called David Frost. Launched in November 1962, it lasted five months, during which time its audience rose from 2.5 million to 12.5 million; it attracted an enormous postbag and drew its audience from across the entire social spectrum; it was also massively detested by conservatives, who saw everything they believed in treated with total irreverence.

This irreverence was an integral part of the general cultural revolution of the 1960s. Within the mass media it spawned an entire generation of satire shows, which still compose a significant proportion of broadcast output. Recent and current TV shows such as "Carrot's Lib," "The Young Ones," "Not the Nine O'Clock News," and "Whoops Apocalypse" are in a tradition that stems directly from TW3 and the university satire of the 1960s. This style of humor also extends far beyond the boundaries of the mass media, by featuring prominently in cabaret performances—usually in a less censored version than is normal on TV—and by profoundly influencing the general sense of humor of an entire generation.

Since the 1960s English humor has also been marked by the impact of sick humor. Originally an import from the United States, this style of humor rapidly became naturalized. Although it is effectively banned from broadcasting, it flourishes in everyday life and in collections of jokes distributed in book form. When applied to the topics of satire it becomes a particularly savage lampoon. The IRA bomb which nearly killed the British government at the Tory party conference in October 1984 seriously injured Norman Tebbit, one of Mrs. Thatcher's most hard-line supporters in the cabinet, who was famous (or infamous, depending on your politics) for saying to the unemployed: "On your bike!" (i.e., go out and get a job), a phrase which suggested considerably less than sympathy. A few days after the bomb someone wrote in to my local station: "On your crutches, Tebbit!"

Finally, alternative comedy. In the late 1970s a new generation of young comedians developed a style of comedy that was significantly different from its predecessors. Their inspirations were the raw energy of the punk movement and a vitriolic hatred of the Conservative government. In their political motivation they owed something to the university satirists of the 1960s and 1970s, but they were also much cruder and more aggressive. Their style can be defined negatively by their refusal to make racist or sexist jokes, positively by four features: their favorite butts (Conservatives, pretentiousness, the fashionable young middle classes); a range of humorous topics that was much more extended than usual—for example, a monologue on the habits of hedgehogs in the grass verges of motorways; a preference for extended character-based monologue rather than the sequence of fast one-liners and gags preferred by traditional comics in the Bob Hope style; and a deliberate attempt to engage in dialogue with the audience.

This style was born in a small club in London's Soho, the Comedy Store (now regrettably defunct), and its style was defined as much by the forms of interaction with the audience, made possible by the atmosphere of a small club, as by the political commitment of the comedians. It is still a style that is more successful in clubs and similar venues than on radio and television, though many of its performers also write for broadcast shows. In London there are currently around a dozen such clubs (listed in the magazines *Time Out* and *City Limits*), and the performers are regularly to be found at provincial arts centers and colleges, occasionally in provincial clubs. In the last few years, this style seems to have lost some of its cutting edge: it is far less directly political, and the performers appear more prepared to regard themselves as "pure entertainers." It is a style that so far has rarely been able to find a mass audience: the only large-scale successes so far are the TV show "The Young Ones," which made Rik Mayall a household name for anyone under 25 and was largely regarded with blank incomprehension by anyone over 30; and the solo performances of Alexei Sayle, whose audiences seem to be drawn largely from the people he attacks the most. However, continuing and increased broadcasting exposure may yet turn this style into the new orthodoxy.

Last, alternative comedy is responsible for the appearance on the stage and on TV of both black comedians (Lenny Henry has had a series of one-man TV shows) and comediennes (notably Victoria Woods); despite the long tradition of excellent comic actresses in this country and of female comic singers in the music halls, joke telling in public has been dominated by men.

Humor in the Mass Media

Specialized Newspapers

There are two specialized newspapers, both weekly, for humor in Britain: *Punch* and *Private Eye*. They are very different in tone, *Punch* being an old, established paper (founded in 1841) which is relatively genteel—though nonetheless hard-hitting on occasion—whereas *Private Eye* was founded during the antiestablishment satire boom of the early sixties and has a reputation both for childishness and scurrilousness. It attacks on leading public figures have many times landed it in court for libel, sued, for instance, by the financier Sir James Goldsmith, who was one of its favorite targets, known to the paper as Goldenballs, which gives a good indication of its style of humor. Somehow, despite massive fines, it has survived; despite the childishness it is often genuinely witty; and many of its personal attacks are no doubt thoroughly deserved.

To these should be added the mass of comics for children. While much of their material is nonhumorous, consisting of adventure stories and so forth, much of course is humorous. Since the 1960s there have been many occasional comic-strip publications for adults too, most of them reprints of American publications such as *Fritz the Cat*.

National Daily Newspapers

All British daily newspapers include cartoons, usually several. Certain of these are directly political, Most make reference to current affairs in some form or other, but some portray only general humorous situations. In general, the tendency is for quality newspapers' cartoons to be more concerned with current affairs, and for the tabloids to include more less-specific humor. The *Guardian*, a prominent quality daily, publishes three cartoons daily: a political strip called

If, a raucous anarchistic send-up of current affairs and politicians featuring, inter alia, Mrs. Thatcher machine-gunning members of her government, President Reagan revealing that he is actually made of wood, a left-wing Falklands penguin, assorted drunken journalists, etc.; the American import *Doonesbury*; and a single-frame whimsical commentary on minor events by Marc. It also regularly, but not daily, publishes a political cartoon by Gabbard, and frequently reprints American political cartoons; it also frequently enlivens feature pages with occasional single-frame cartoons relevant to the subject in question. Finally, once a week, on Mondays, it prints a large-scale strip cartoon, a quarter of a page, by Posy, whose affectionately satirized characters are drawn predominantly from intellectual middle-class families: lectures, advertising people, and their punk or student children; these cartoons are also available in book form, which argues for their popularity. Posy's absence is one of the few gaps in the paper which draws howls of protest from a large number of readers.

A typical example in this respect of the tabloids, the *Daily Mirror* publishes a daily Laughter Column, of between three and five single-column cartoons on general subjects, and five strip cartoons, of which four are continuous stories carried over from day to day and one is a single-day gag line. Of these five, one—*Andy Cap*—is sufficiently famous to be considered a national institution. The paper gets a lot of mail about cartoons and many requests from readers for original copies. The cartoon page is often demanded by advertisers, which testifies to its popularity. Only the daily political cartoon is directly linked to current affairs.

Probably the most famous English cartoonist is Giles, published weekly by the *Sunday Express*; a selection of his cartoons is published annually in book form and is a popular Christmas present.

As well as cartoons, most newspapers carry occasional humorous pieces of writing and like to include pieces of news which are humorous, to enliven their pages. The *Guardian*, for instance, has a daily irreverent look at Parliament by Michael White.

Cinema

The Golden Age of the English cinema was the 1930s. However, Britain continued after the war to successfully produce films with perculiarly British subjects, and prime topics were the wartime experience and comedy; the earlier style of comedy, starring already established music hall and variety stars, declined rapidly in popularity after the war. Noteworthy postwar comic successes were the series of films starring Alec Guiness (especially *The Ladykillers* and *Kind Hearts and Coronets*), a gentle, affectionate comedy starring a vintage car (*Genevieve*), and an adaption of Oscar Wilde's play *The Importance of Being Ernest*. The brief renaissance of British film in the late fifties and early sixties produced several first-rate comedies, of which one at least is famous: *Morgan, A Suitable Case for Treatment* stars David Warner as a Trotskyite painter married to society girl Vanessa Redgrave; as his eccentricities and fantasies move toward breakdown, his actions become more and more bizarre and hilarious, albeit with a serious and bleak undertone. Other successful comedy films of this period were *Billy Liar* and *Tom Jones*.

This period also saw the birth of a series of comedies by the same team, the *Carry On* films, which rely heavily on obvious sexual innuendo, chamber pots, spoofs of homosexuality, etc. The members of this team—especially Sid James, Kenneth Williams, and Barbara Windsor—are among the best-known actors and actresses in Britain, and are genuinely household names. Despite—or rather because of—its crudity, this series is among the most enduringly popular of the last three decades; it is frequently recycled on TV, recently largely in the form of excerpts. There is a direct continuity, both of style and personnel, between these films and the successful radio shows of the fifties and early sixties. The seventies also saw the series of successful *Pink Panther* films, starring Peter Sellers of the Goons as the terminally stupid and clumsy Inspector Clouseau.

As elsewhere in the industrial world, British cinema has been hit by the expansion of TV, in the area of comedy as much as in other genres. But the impact is not entirely one way: successful TV series have spawned feature films, notably the films by the Monty Python team: *And Now for Something Completely Different* (largely a compilation of TV sketches), *Monty Python and the Holy Grail*, *The Life of Brian*, and *The Meaning of Life*.

The last three or four years have seen another modest renaissance of British cinema, due in large measure to the increased availability of state funding. Some of this has produced cinematic comedy, though the overwhelming tendency has been toward serious cinema. Directors Bill Forsyth and Richard Eyres have produced (respectively) *Local Hero*, *Gregory's Girl*, and *Comfort and Joy*; and *Loose Connections* and *Laughter House*. A send-up of the Bulldog Drummond thrillers, *Bullshot*, is currently in production. The tone of the Forsyth and Eyres films is predominantly gentle satire and comedy of character: the zanier side of British comedy is well represented in the cinema by the Monty Python films.

Records and Audiocassettes

In the period of music hall, the comic song was a staple of the entertainment. In a period where the music industry is dominated by rock and its derivatives, the comic song in its traditional form is largely a thing of the past on record. However, certain successful rock bands prominently feature comic words; the two most noteworthy recent examples are Ian Dury and the Blockheads, and Chas and Dave, whose comic song "Rabbit" was briefly in the hit parade. Ian Dury's album *New Boots and Panties* contains one song, "Billericay Dickie" (pronounced so that the words rhyme), which is among the finest examples of scatological ingenuity and verbal inventiveness for years.

There are of course recordings of traditional comic opera, such as Gilbert and Sullivan, but a more recent innovation has been the availability of recordings of recent broadcast comedy. Classic BBC radio shows such as "The Goons" and "Hancock's Half Hour" are available in this format, as well as many more recent shows such as "Round the Horne" (a traditional show relying heavily on puns and sexual innuendo), "I'm Sorry I'll Read That Again" and "The Grumbleweeds." The BBC also issues audio recordings of the sound tracks of successful TV comedies such as "Fawlty Towers" and "Not the Nine O'Clock News."

Occasionally recordings of other comedians are made by record companies, but by and large the majority of audio comedy is off-air rather than original material.

Radio Comedy

The 1968 reorganization of the BBC to combat nonstop pop music broadcasting by the private radio stations entailed a certain downgrading of the spoken word, and concomitant budgetary reductions, as two of the four channels became nearly exclusively devoted to music, and a third, half devoted to it. The amount of nonmusical light entertainment available on the BBC was reduced, and the Golden Age of radio comedy was at an end.

This does not mean that there is no good radio comedy anymore, but it tends to be less elaborate than before and to rely on lesser-known performers, which it easily loses to TV as they become established: "To the Manor Born," a recent successful and much-repeated TV sitcom, was originally planned as a radio comedy. Radio comedy now tends to rely heavily on adaptations of TV sitcoms, but it has produced pacemaking shows such as "I'm Sorry, I'll Read That Again," a forerunner of successful TV satire shows such as "Not the Nine O'Clock News."

Television Comedy

As the main medium of popular entertainment, television is also the main purveyor of comedy in contemporary Britain. Television comedy largely falls into two categories: variety and situation comedies (sitcom), both of which are staples of TV programming, with perhaps somewhat more emphasis on sitcom than on variety. It is now a rare day that does not have two sitcoms in the schedules. However, while sitcom is a staple of programming and undoubtedly popular, it is not well regarded; this judgment by Sir Denis Foreman, chairman of Granada Television, is typical:

Comedy has found its own television forms in *Monty Python* and *Not the Nine O'Clock News*, but there is still a stodgy wedge of what is quaintly called situation comedy around, which is not much more than the extended music hall sketch. This form only rises to the sublime when it (rarely) becomes a comedy of character as in *Fawlty Towers* and *Porridge*.

Sir Denis's preference for "Monty Python's Flying Circus" is very common as it was one of the most successful TV shows of the 1970s. It was a very specifically televisual show both in its use of graphics and in its regular scheduling and recurrent performers, most of whom have continued to perform in other shows or in film. Each weekly episode consisted of a series of sketches, mostly unrelated to each other despite some recurrent characters and situations. Its success was founded on an impeccably calculated sense of the bizarre; witness the famous scene involving a shopkeeper, an irate customer, and a parrot that might be Norwegian Blue, or just plain dead.

Variety represents a smaller percentage of TV time than sitcom; perhaps it is more difficult to produce successfully than sitcom, as it depends more heavily on the personality of the individual comedian. When it is successful it is very successful indeed, and the most popular variety shows have among the highest audience figures for all television fiction. Variety's basic formula derives from the music hall, with only a significant reduction in the role of music to distinguish it: comedians with well-developed public personae telling jokes, brief comic sketches, and a little music. The most successful and innovative recent ones are "The Morecombe and Wise Show"—now finished due to the early death of Eric Morecombe—and "The Two Ronnies," Ronnie Barker and Ronnie Corbett. Others featuring comedians such as Les Dawson and Benny Hilll tend to rely heavily on more traditional comic material. Recently some variety shows have begun to return to the more satirical material typical of sixties shows such as TW3: both "Not the Nine O'Clock News" and "Carrot's Lib" include direct and sometimes savage attacks on public figures and policies.

The chief characteristic of sitcom is that each series takes a situation which is in some way plausible in everyday terms and uses this as the framework within which comedy can be developed: a witty unemployed graduate ("Shelley"), a middle-class ecological dropout and his wife who decide to live by subsistence farming on their suburban garden ("The Good Life"), a hotel with an incompetent aggressive owner who thinks he is the incarnation of professional and cultural perfection ("Fawlty Towers"), Britain's Civil Defense force in World War II ("Dad's Army"), an "agony aunt" on a woman's magazine whose own personal life leaves something to be desired ("Agony"). As each episode is a continuous narrative, this enables the comedy to deal with situations that the audience will recognize as plausible, in much the same way as the traditional literary comedy of manners by Goldsmith, Beaumarchais, and others (this comparison is not intended to imply any comparison of aesthetic standards). Sitcoms thus deal with matters that are equally the stuff of serious fiction or of social or philosophical commentary: "The Good Life" deals with the contradiction in attitudes toward material success and the price that it demands, the urge for authenticity, etc., that has been a feature of both public debates and popular experience over the last two decades; "Fawlty Towers" (arguably the best sitcom ever produced) rises to real heights of psychological exploration in its farcical exaggeration of the near paranoia of its eponymous hero. This serious side of sticom has been the subject of recent extended critical treatment by the British Film Institute in the *BFI Sitcom Dossier*.

One of the features of British sitcom which appears to distinguish it from other countries' humorous plays is its focus upon national types. That is to say, the central characters of each sitcom, instead of referring to some universal feature of "the British character," or some universal feature of human nature, tend to refer instead to some social type: the unemployed university graduate, the middle-class dropout, the working-class thief, etc. However, it is clear that the primary purpose of sitcom is to entertain by creating mirth, and thus sitcoms refer to plausible real-life situations in order to provide a peg on which to hang joke situations. As a result, the manner in which the serious situations in question are referred to inevitably alters our perceptions of them: they are evoked "in the comic mode," and what is said about them in a sitcom cannot be reduced to a noncomic way of treating them; they are, in fact, "not to be taken seriously" (Palmer, 1987).

Selected episodes of certain sitcoms are available for hire from the British Film Institute Film and Video Library. Videocassettes of many popular comedy programs are also commercially available.

Working Men's Clubs

In Britain the stand-up comic (the man—or occasionally woman—who simply stands in front of an audience and tells jokes) is still well-known. Television tends to prefer the more elaborate forms of variety and sitcom, although there have been occasional series of shows featuring stand-up comics: the best-known is Granada Television's "The Comedians," which consists entirely of jokes told straight to camera. Stand-up comics also find work in variety shows on TV and in the theatre—nowadays mostly confined to summer shows at the seaside and the single surviving London variety theatre, the Palladium.

However, the standard venue for the stand-up comic is the working men's club, a long-established British institution. In the mid-nineteenth century moral reformers were convinced that the moral improvement of the British working class depended on weaning them away from the pub, and one of the many ways proposed was the establishment of a network of clubs for working men, serving nonalcoholic refreshments and offering "rational entertainment," i.e., educational and cultural activities. The institution has survived, although nowadays the entertainment the clubs offer does not differ substantially from that offered anywhere else: rock music, strip tease, mild gambling, comedians, etc. Because these institutions are clubs, performances are less censored than broadcast ones, and the style of comedy tends to be considerably broader. These clubs form a more important part of public life in the north of England than in the south.

Theatre

It is now relatively rare for theatres to be used for solo comic performances, or for cabaret or variety—with the exception of London's surviving variety theatre, the Palladium. Recent exceptions include a cabaret in benefit of Amnesty International starring many of the most famous TV satirists, called *The Secret Policeman's Ball*, and the frequent one-man shows by alternative comedian Alexei Sayle; variety shows starring major comedians also appear in the theatre at Christmas and at seaside resorts in the summer. With cabaret and variety otherwise relegated to TV and the clubs, theatre concentrates on full-length comic drama. The state theatre companies such as the National Theatre and the Royal Shakespeare Company tend to concentrate on classical comedy, with occasional modern works; they have also revived nineteenth-century farce, by writers such as Feydeau, with considerable success. Noteworthy modern comic playwrights are the late Joe Orton, whose *Loot* and a *A Day in the Death of Joe Egg* are famous as mixed tragedy and farce, and Peter Shaffer. John Osborne's plays contain good comic moments. Trevor Griffith's *Comedians* uses the figure of the stand-up comic as a metaphor for the position of culture in class warfare, and on the way deals impeccably with the ambiguities of comedy that is excessive. Totally unserious in its implications was *The Rocky Horror Show*, about a high camp Dr. Frankenstein, now a film.

Farce is well represented on the London stage, with numerous productions at any one time. This includes the play which claims to be the longest-running comedy in the world, *No Sex Please, We're British*, which is currently (1984) in its fourteenth year of continuous performance. In recent years, comedy—including musical comedy—has tended to dominate the London stage.

Provincial theatres in England can rarely generate long-running performances and tend to be organized on the repertory system in which plays either run for a week before being replaced or alternate day by day for a short season. Few have permanent companies of actors or directors, and this makes it difficult to generalize about what is performed in them: however, it is safe to say that comedy—but not variety—is a staple of this programming.

UNIVERSAL FUNCTIONS OF HUMOR AND THE NATIONAL MANIFESTATIONS

This writer wishes to enter the caveat that the notion of universal functions of humor appears to him to be extremely dubious, for reasons explored in his own publications on the subject (Palmer, 1987). However, there is good reason to believe that in the modern industrial world, in societies with essentially similar social structures and very similar cultures, the functions of humor may be remarkably similar, perhaps to the point of universality within these social and geographical boundaries.

Aggressive Humor

Jokes about stupidity, at the expense of ethnic subgroups, have already been discussed. Other traditional scapegoats have been the supposed meanness of the Scots and the Jews, the supposed greed of the Jews, the supposed stupidity of northerners and country people, and the supposed charlatanism of the learned professions, especially doctors. Many of these topics have become significantly less popular in recent years, it is my impression: whereas it was formerly easy to raise a laugh just by imitating a country or northern accent (in the south—perhaps the reverse was true in the north), nowadays this is unlikely. Current scapegoats are more likely to be character types or professions (the medical profession still seems to be high on the list). It is my impression that in recent years British humor has grown increasingly aggressive.

Sexual Humor

Sexuality is probably the commonest topic of humor in Great Britain. Much of it is intensely scatological. Homosexuality, chiefly male, is a favorite topic, though it is difficult to say whether this is sexual humor or aggressive humor or both. Similarly, feminists insist that most conventional sexual humor is in fact an act of aggression against women. Public sexual humor is invariably much more restrained than the version that circulates privately.

Social Humor

A sense of humor is a highly valued trait in Great Britain: ''not to have a sense of humor'' is a deep criticism of any one in this country. It is a popular myth here that certain nations do not have a sense of humor, notably the Germans; to some extent they are being supplanted in popular mythology by Russians. The recent resurgence in satire has been discussed already, as has the decreasing use of humor as a political weapon, compared with the last century: if politicians use humor today, it is probably for the same reason that teachers do—to give a good impression and to be remembered.

Humor as a Defense Mechanism

Gallows humor is not common in Great Britain, unless one includes sick humor in this category. However, sick humor is often intensely aggressive rather than defensive. In general, British humor tends to be aggressive toward perceived deviant or other out-groups rather than self-disparaging. For instance, drunkenness is a popular topic of humor, but although it is not necessarily aimed at any particular group within society (sometimes at the Irish or the Scots), the implication is always that drunkenness is an unusual form of behavior.

Intellectual Humor

Nonsense, absurdity, and punning are among the most popular forms of humor in this country. Periodically, crops of absurd jokes with a common theme rampage across the country, as for instance the elephant jokes of the sixties:

Why do elephants paint their toenails red?
So they can hide in cherry trees.

REFERENCES

Agee, J. (1969) "Comedy's Greatest Era." In *Agee on Film*, vol. 1. New York: Putnam.

Aldgate, T. (1981) *British Cinema in the 1930's*. London: Open University (U203).

Apter, M. J. (1982) *The Experience of Motivation*. New York: Academic Press.

Apter, M. J., and Smith, K. C. P. (1977) "Humor and the Theory of Psychological Reversals." In *It's a Funny Thing, Humor*. Ed. A. J. Chapman and H. C. Foot. London: Pergamon Press.

BBC Audience Research Department (1984) *Comedy Shows and Situation Comedies*. London: BBC Publications.

BFI Sitcom Group (1982) *Television Sitcom*. London: British Film Institute.

Davis, C. (1982) "Ethnic Jokes, Moral Values and Social Boundaries." *British Journal of Sociology* 33: 383–403.

Doran, J. (1858) *History of Court Fools*. London: Eyre Methuen.

Durgnat, R. (1969) *The Crazy Mirror*. London: Faber.

Everson, W. K. (1970) *The Films of Laurel and Hardy*. London: Citadel Press.

George, M. D. (1967) *Hogarth to Cruikshank*. London: Allen Lane.

Gurewitch, M. (1975) *Comedy, The Irrational Vision*. Ithaca, N. Y.: Cornell University Press.

Handleman, D., and Kapferer, B. (1972) "Forms of Joking Activity: A Comparative Approach." *American Anthropologist* 74: 484–517.

Jefferson G. (1979) "A Technique for Inviting Laughter and Its Subsequent Acceptance Delineation." In *Everyday Language*. Ed. G. Psathas. New York: Irvington Publishers.

Langer, S. (1977) *Feeling and Form*. New York: Macmillan.

Malcolmson, R. (1973) *Popular Recreations in English Society 1700–1850*. N. Y.: Cambridge University Press.

Mander, F. and Mitchenson, B. (1965) *British Music Hall*. London: Studio vista.

Mast, G. (1974) "The Comic Mind: Comedy and the Movies" In *Film Theory and Criticism*. Ed. G. Mast and M. Cohn. Oxford: Oxford University Press, 458–68.

Nichol, A. (1963) *The World of Harlequin*. Cambridge University Press.

Orwell, G. (1961) "The Art of Donald McGill." In *Collected Essays*. London: Heinemann, Mercury Books.

Palmer, J. (1987) *The Logic of the Absurd*. London: British Film Institute.

Pepys, S. (1919) *The Diary*. London: G. Bell.

Richardson, H. (1961) *Mediaeval Fairs and Markets of York*. London: Borthwick Institute of Historical Research, St. Anthony Hall Publications, No. 20.

Scannel, P., and Cardiff, D. (1981) *Radio in World War Two*. London: Open University (U203).

Schaeffer, N. (1981) *The Art of Laughter*. New York: Columbia University Press.

Schutz, C. E. (1976) *Political Humor*. London: Fairleigh Dickenson.

Seidman, S (1981) *Comedian Comedy*. London: Bowker, UMI Research.

Swain, B. (1932) *Fools and Folly*. New York: Columbia University Press.

Took, B. (1976) *Laughter in the Air*. London: Robson Books.

Torrance, R. (1978) *The Comic Hero*. Cambridge, Mass.: Harvard University Press.

Vicinus, M. (1974) *The Industrial Muse*. London: Croom Helm.

Waites, B. (1981) *The Music Hall*. London: Popular Culture, Open University (U203).

Wilmut, R. (1980) *From Fringe to Flying Circus*. London: Eyre Methuen.

Wilson, C. P. (1979) *Jokes: Form, Content, Use and Function*. New York: Academic Press.

Humor in Israel

BACKGROUND

Israel, the homeland of the Jewish people, has a unique history as well as a unique present. This is the only country in the world which has only a minority of its people as citizens (there are about 14 million Jews in the world; only 4 million live in Israel). It has a language, Hebrew, not spoken by the majority of its people. While modern Israel is a new country, it has a very ancient history, and in order to understand Israeli humor, one has to understand something about Jewish life and culture.

Hebrew is a language which for two millennia was not used in daily life. In Israel in a short lapse of time it became anew a spoken and lively language with all the modern technical terminology and a lively slang. During their history, in addition to Hebrew, Jews developed two other languages used exclusively by them: Yiddish (in Europe and later in other parts of the world) and Ladino (in certain parts of Europe and the Middle East). During almost two thousand years Jews lived in the Diaspora, and most of them used three languages: Hebrew for the study of the sacred writings, Yiddish or Ladino to communicate among themselves, and the language of the host country to communicate with their neighbors. This richness of language is probably one of the main reasons for the development of Jewish humor. In addition, Jews, being a persecuted minority all along their history, tried to destory the terrible realities they had to live in, with the only weapon they had at their disposal: by changing and distorting it, so that for a while it didn't look so terrible; the proof: it can make you laugh. Laughing at the absurdity of reality as well as at themselves is an old tradition with Jews. Being the chosen people and living in the worst possible conditions, victims of pogroms and targets of hatred from their fellow human beings, seemed some kind of divine irony. One way of dealing with it was to adopt irony and use it to deal with reality.

In order to understand Israeli humor, one has to understand its cultural roots, I shall present only the parts of Jewish humor developed by Jews and addressed only to Jews. That is humor created only in languages understood by Jews exclusively (Hebrew or Yiddish). Therefore, Jewish humor in America or Europe will be considered in this chapter only when it was produced for Jews exclusively. First let us look into the most ancient Hebrew writings, since humor can already be found in them.

TRADITIONAL FORMS AND EXPRESSIONS OF HUMOR

Historical Roots in Antiquity: The Bible and the Talmud

The Bible is at the same time a compilation of sacred writings and a book of history, describing what happened to the Jewish people after Adam and Eve. The Talmud is a work done during twelve centuries (from the fifth century B.C. to the eighth century A.D.). It is the collective work of rabbis and sages commenting on and explaining the Bible. Both the Bible and the Talmud are considered sacred writings.

Since *humor* is a word with Latin origin, it does not appear in the Bible. However, *laughter* is mentioned many times. As research shows, laughter appears 50 times and conveys many different intentions. As modern research shows, laughter can have different meanings, and this was already clear in the Bible. For those reading the Bible in a different language, frequently instead of *laughter* they find terms given by the translators for its meaning as they understood it. In the English translation the following words are used for *tzehok* (laughter in Hebrew): play, enjoy, insults, mock, fondle, rejoice, scoff, and even laugh. In addition to the relative frequency of laughter, many examples of humor appear in the Bible. Irony is evident and brilliant in the question people asked Moses after he took them out of Egypt: "Because there was no grave in Egypt have you taken us away, to die in the wilderness" (Exodus 14:11). The same ironic touch is seen when Joseph's brothers, who did not like him and his dreams, decided to kill him: "we will say some evil beast devoured him and we shall see what will become of his dreams'' (Genesis 37:20). Or Eliahu talking sarcastically about a pagan god: ''Cry aloud for he is a god, either he is talking or he is pursuing or he is on a journey or peradventure he sleeps and must be awakened'' (1 Kings 18:27). Self-irony and laughter are expressed by Sarah: ''Therefore Sarah laughed within herself saying, After I am waxed old shall I have pleasure, my lord being old also?'' (Genesis 18:12). Her son was named Isaac (Yitzhak, he shall laugh).

Laughter can be a form of social punishment, as Henri Bergson (1911) explained in his theory. This view was also expressed in the Bible: ''But now they that are younger than I have me in derision . . . '' (Job 30:1) (in Hebrew the word laugh is translated here as derision). Even God's laughter can be seen as punishment: ''But you O Lord, shall laugh at them and shall have all nations in derision'' (Psalms 59:18).

Many references to laughter, humorous tales, and rules about joking appear in the Talmud. It seems that Talmudic sages were able to differentiate between ''laughing at'' and ''laughing with.'' While formal prohibitions to laugh at are frequently mentioned, other views, where the accent is on ''laughing with,'' are encouraged. There is an explicit Talmudic dictum: ''Rabbi Nachman says, all joking is prohibited except jokes about idol worship'' (Sanhedrin, p. 36). Here, unmistakably, the point is to ''laugh at,'' what in modern terms would be considered aggressive humor. But laughter was also considered positive; ''tears of sadness are bad, tears of laughter are beautiful'' (Shabat, 151). The firt book of research relating humor to education was written in 1979 in France (Ziv, 1979). It demonstrated what appeared already in the Talmud: ''Before starting to teach, Rabah joked and pupils laughed, afterwards he started seriously teaching Halacha'' (Masechet Tephachim, 23, 117).

But more important than direct references about laughter and joking is the way of thinking that the learning of the Talmud encouraged. Since the first century, education for Jewish boys was compulsory from age four. They studied by examining things from all angles, speculated, and were encouraged to find contradictions. The passing from concrete to abstract and vice versa, asking all possible questions to clarify a point, and finding the most subtle answers to complex problems were appreciated. This way of thinking, in which endless argumentation, sometimes for its own sake, could lead anywhere. This kind of scholastic discussion is called *pilpul* and was highly valued. It is considered by some literary critics as one of the bases of Jewish literature of all times (Stora Sandor, 1984). The tendency to look for a solution to even simple problems only after turning around all possible (and sometimes impossible) speculations is one of the mental traits encouraged by generations of students of the Talmud. Since Talmudic studies existed at all age levels and were encouraged in all Jewish communities, even the poorest ones, many generations passed it on, influencing even those who nowadays are far from Talmudic studies. This way of thinking, seeing the contradictions and incongruities and finding surprising solutions, is an important ingredient in any humor creation. This is probably one of the reasons for the great number of Jewish humorists in most countries where Jews lived.

Popular Forms

The religious tradition and the study of the Bible and the Talmud were the main intellectual occupations of Jews in the Diaspora. Humor and satire are generally antagonistic approaches to accepted values, and this could not be permitted in the study of religious writing. However, because humorous relief was needed, some liberties were admitted and even encouraged. Once a year, it was permissible not to be serious, and drinking was highly recommended. The gaiety found its expression in the Purim spiel. Purim is a holiday in which Jews celebrate their escape from annihilation by their enemies in Persia, thanks to Queen Esther. During Purim festivities everybody is supposed to disguise, drink, and be merry.

During the Middle Ages, a Purim rabbi was chosen, his behavior being a caricature of the real rabbi. He gave illogical and funny "rabbinical decisions" to the great delight of his listeners, including the rabbi. However, this was for a day only; immediately afterwards, the congregation got back again to serious studies, till next Purim.

Slowly, Jews enriched their Talmudic folklore and stories by adopting popular European folk stories (Ausubel, 1948). Many of these stories responded to the psychological need to mock someone weaker than oneself, a need particularly keen in people who felt at the bottom of the social ladder, as Jews felt in most parts of the world. They created stories about simple-minded people who seemed to do the dumbest things. These new "heroes" gave a momentary feeling of superiority to a community of persecuted people.

Famous Humorous Folkloric Figures

The Hasidic movement, which started in Eastern Europe in the middle of the eighteenth century, saw the relations with God a joyful one, and they loved to laugh sing and dance. This was a serious departure from the traditional forms of Jewish worship. Hasidic sages often used irony and wit to illustrate many points, and this certainly added to their popularity. Some rabbis had court jesters, and Hershele Ostropoler (1770–1810) fulfilled this role in Rabbi Baruch of Miedziborz (Southern Russia). The rabbi was suffering from acute depression and as a defense mechanism promulgated the principle "It is sinful to be sad." As legend has it, Hershele was called to cure the rabbi of depressive moods, by making him laugh. Hershele was a simpleton only on the surface; he frequently expressed deep truths in a humorous way. Many Yiddish penny books were written about Hershele, who delighted the simple people by his jokes and satires against religious hypocrites, rich misers, and pompous people (Bloch, 1921). Hershele is still a popular figure in many children's jokes in Israel today.

Motke Khabad was a jester to Yudel Opatov of Vilna, and Reb Yossifel, the spiritual leader of Chelm, became a folk hero. Chelm was for the Jews what Abdera was for the Greeks, Gotham for the English, and Schilda for the Germans: a place populated by naive, much-talking and not very bright people. One classic example of Chelm stories is one about the old shammes (sexton) who complained that he was too old and tired to make the round of all Jewish homes banging on the shutters to wake people up for the midnight services. The wise men of Chelm discussed in a specially called assembly the solution of the problem. And they finally found it: all shutters would be brought to one place, near the shammes's home and then he could bang on all of them without having to make the tiresome trip around the shtetel. They always found a theoretically perfect solution having only one disadvantage: it is not practical. But why should one worry about the practical aspects of a problem? Great intellects should be involved in intellectual solutions!

Many Jewish writers told stories about Chelm, among them Shalom Aleichem and Itzik Manger. In modern Hebrew slang *Chelmai* (one from Chelm) is still largely used.

The *magiddim* were itinerant preachers who from Talmudic times told stories which frequently had a humorous flavor (Newman, 1962). While trying to enlarge the comprehension of Jewish law and tradition, they introduced many humorous stories, knowing that they would be easily comprehended and even enjoyed by their listeners. They were active and very popular during the Middle Ages and before emancipation. The most famous among them was Jacob ben Wolf Krantz from Dubnow (the Dubnow Maggid, ca. 1740–1804). In his preachings, he frequently used humor, bringing insight to his listeners on higher values of Jewish life (Heinemann, 1963).

The *Badchonim* (jokesters) were the merrymakers at Jewish weddings, which were happy events not only for the family but for the entire community in the shtetel. Frequently, they lasted for many days and became a sort of carnival with music, joking, and dancing. Here probably one can find the beginning of the stand-up comic, made so popular by Jews in the United States. Mel Brooks in one of his movies, *The Mad History of the World*, played the role of a comedian in ancient Rome. When asked about his profession, he answered ''stand-up philosopher.'' The badchonim role was somewhat similar. They talked about married life, about what happens in the community, and about Jewish life in general, using humor and making people happy. A new type of Jewish folklore appeared in which the confrontation with the Gentiles produced the occasion to demonstrate how clever Jews are, obtaining therefore easy victories in an imaginary way. Humor here fulfilled one of its main functions: imaginary superiority. In addition, a new humorist appeared in Jewish humor: the rabbi. In Hasidic humor, rabbis made jokes about people's little failings, generally with a didactic flavor (Kohn, 1915).

Humor in the Literary and Performing Arts

There were two great epochs in Jewish literature during the Diaspora in Europe. The first lasted through the Middle Ages in Spain, in Southern France, and in

Italy. Jewish writers wrote in Hebrew, and many used humor as their means of expression. Satire and parody were extremely popular among those who knew how to read Hebrew.

The second epoch followed the French Revolution, when Jews were for the first time in their history in the Diaspora granted citizenship rights. It developed during the nineteenth and early twentieth century, mainly in Eastern Europe (Liptzin, 1971). There, the main language of expression was Yiddish, a language which developed among Jews in Germany around the eleventh century. It is an extremely rich language, a mixture of the many languages learned by Jews who had to wander from one nation to another and learn the local language. As Rosten notes: "In the course of twenty-four hours, a son of Yudah, speaking Yiddish today, may, without being aware of it, raid over two dozen other languages" (Rosten, 1977, p. 24). The change to Yiddish in Jewish literature came with the realization that Hebrew was a language used only by intellectuals, while Yiddish was the popular language. In order to have greater influence, most Jewish writers started to write in Yiddish, while some continued to use both languages.

The Middle Ages

In Spain under Arab conquerors, Jews knew a period of great development, known as the Golden Age (Israel, 1958). Among the many writers who dealt with religious and secular things, humorists and satirists were greatly appreciated. Among them, Abraham Ibn Ezra, who lived in the twelfth century, used sophisticated, self-disparaging humor. In "Out of luck" he writes about his misfortune:

The heavenly sphere and the constellations strayed from their path when I was born. If my business were in candles, the sun would not set until I died! However I struggle, I cannot succeed, for my stars have ruined me: if I were a dealer in shrouds, no one would die as long as I lived (quoted in Carmi 1981, p. 353).

This can be considered as the ancestor of the antihero, the schlemiel, a typical figure in Jewish humor (Wisse, 1971), who when meeting hardships and disaster, instead of crying and lamenting, is able to see the laughter in the situation. Bernard Malamud in *The Fixer* made his hero Yakov Bok recite this little poem by Ibn Ezra. Taking one's distance from one's unhappiness, looking at it with irony, is a way of coping with it, an attitude which later became the hallmark of many Jewish humorists.

Alharizi, Yehuda Ben Solomon Ben Hophni (1170–1235), was one of the great poets of medieval Hebrew literature. he introduced the "Mosaic style" in which he used partial quotations from the Bible and the Talmud completely out of context, thus creating humorous effects. This style was to be used by many Jewish humorists from Shalom Aleichem to Joseph Heller. Many writers during this period used humor in their Hebrew writings.

Emancipation and the Beginnings of Modern Jewish Humor

After the French Revolution, on September 27, 1791, the National Assembly in France granted the Jews the right to take an oath of citizenship. This was known as Emancipation, which was followed by similar decisions in most countries of Western Europe a century later.

The new opportunities offered to Jews created different sets of problems in Western and Eastern Europe. While Emancipation in Western Europe created great opportunities for Jews to integrate into the dominant culture, a strong ambivalence was created for those who wanted to integrate and stay Jewish at the same time. Some, such as Heine, decided to convert, but Heine's lack of satisfaction was evident in the use of self-irony even against conversion: "I wouldn't trust the sincerity of a Jew who convered to Christianity; no Jew can truly believe in the holiness of another Jew.

Two new cultural movements emerged in the Jewish world. The first, called Haskalah (enlightenment in Hebrew), developed first in Western Europe, and the second, the Hasidic (followers) movement, started in Eastern Europe. The Haskalah wanted to modernize Jewish thought, open it to sciences and humanism, change behavior, discard traditional clothes, and learn only the sacred writings. The Hasidim believed in loving God through joyful worship and emotional expression. Great rabbis held courts and were the uncontested leaders of the community.

A great flight developed between the two schools of thought. However, unlike most other religious battles, this was an intellectual one. The lively battle between the two currents was conducted by writers, who used mostly humorous satire as a weapon against the ideological enemy. The fact that satire was the main weapon is an additional affirmation of the importance of humor in Jewish life.

Two main currents can be identified in the satirical writings encouraged by the Haskalah movement. The first was virulent, sometimes even vitriolic, satire, in which tradition and the "unhealthy and unproductive" life of the Jews were attacked. This approach can be considered as "fighting satire." The second, written mainly in Yiddish, was a kind of recognition that the wonderful ideas of the Haskalah would not easily change Jewish fate, and the traditional life in the shtetel was viewed in a loving way, in which satire appeared side by side with mild criticism. This approach was "loving satire" (Ziv, 1987).

The Period of Fighting Satire

Among the many writers of this period, one should be particularly mentioned: Shlome Ettinger (1840's playwright), who wrote the comedy *Serkele*, in which a Jewish woman, because of the traditional role forcing her to work and battle with economic problems while her husband studies, becomes a ruthless businesswoman rising to affluence. Ettinger also wrote clever moralistic fables. In one, wanting to point out that it is better to overlook little misfortunes than to provoke great tragedies, he wrote the story of the rooster. Since one morning the farmer forgot to feed him, he decided not to crow on the following morning. The farmer, deciding that the rooster is no longer of use as a timekeeper, slaughters it. "Don't make waves," a slogan of carefulness learned by Jews in their long history of being persecuted, is nicely expressed in this fable. The slogan is made fun of in one of the classic Jewish jokes of self-disparagement:

Three Jews are sentenced to death. They are put in front of a firing squad. The officer turns to the first condemned man.

"Do you want a blindfold?"

"Yes, sir."

He asks the second one the same question.

"Yes, sir."

He asks the third.

"No, I don't want anything from you awful people."

The second man turns to him and whispers:

"Moishe, don't make trouble now."

Self-disparagement was considered by Freud as one of the main characteristics of Jewish humor. He wrote: "I do not know whether there are many other instances of a people making fun to such a degree of its own character" (Freud, 1962, p. 126).

The Period of Loving Satire

"Loving satire" is an original Jewish approach to satire. While satire is directed "against" persons, institutions, or concepts, Jewish satire of the shtetel is a kind of critical identification with the people. While they are laughable, the little people (*Kleine mentchele*) are understood, loved, and even admired—not for their life-style but for their inner qualities. The tragedies and the hardships of these little people are encountered with an understanding smile. "Laughing through tears" is the main weapon of the little people and those identifying with them. The Jewish writers of the nineteenth century made this laughter an admirable art which is part of the continuing Jewish heritage of fighting adversity with humor.

One of the greatest turn-of-the-century Yiddish writers, innovating the language considered "the outcast daughter of my people," was Shalem Yakob Abramowitcz, better known as Mendele Mocher Sefarim (Mendele the Bookseller). Mendele's humor was a mixture of satire, irony with identification and love, and understanding for the little people who, in spite of the difficult life they led, had some nobility, dreamed of higher ideals, and were always proud to be Jews.

Shalom Aleichem, born as Sholem Rabinowitz, was the greatest humorist writer of Jewish literature. His immortal characters, living in Kasrilevka (a fictional but typical small Jewish town), and mostly his attitude of looking at sad things with humor, made him probably the best-loved and most popular writer. His irony is bittersweet, and his characters, in spite of their naive schlemielish behavior are always lovable. Shalom Aleichem does not laugh at them but causes the reader to laugh with them.

Aleichem expressed his philosophy on humor as a way of fighting human suffering in a letter addressed to a friend. In it he wrote: "I tell you, it is an ugly and mean world, and only to spite it we mustn't weep. If you want to know, this is the constant source of my good spirit, of my, what is called 'humor.' Not to cry, out of spite. Only to laugh out of spite, only to laugh'' (Priger 1961, p. 154). His heroes lead a difficult life, but they know how to smile at adversity and always keep up hope. His best character is Tevye the milkman, the wise but naive Jew, honest and hardworking, talking with God, in whom he believes with fervor, but questions concerning the ways He deals with His chosen people. When in trouble, and this happens to Tevye most of the time, he finds solace in quoting (incorrectly and out of context) the Bible and the Talmud. In Aleichem's writings one can find time and again one of the main characters of Jewish humor as a way of coping: twisting around and giving an original interpretation of a traumatic experience.

Yiddish theatre also started to flourish at the end of the nineteenth century. Since the Russians banished Yiddish theatre, fearing that it would encourage revolutionary sentiment, it developed in other European countries, and later in the United States. Abraham Goldfaben (1840–1908) is considered the father of the Yiddish theatre. Before him, with the exception of amateur Purim spiels, the Jewish stage was nonexistent.

Humor in the Visual Arts

While Jewish humor flourished in literature, folklore, and theatre, nothing humorous was created in the visual arts. This was probably due to the fact that painting or drawing human images is prohibited by Jewish tradition. Jewish cartoonists were latecomers to the humor scene.

DEVELOPMENT OF HUMOR IN THE TWENTIETH CENTURY

At the end of the nineteenth century, as a result of terrible persecutions, pogroms, and poverty, massive emigration from Eastern Europe ended a chapter of Jewish life and humor. The great majority chose "the land of opportunities," but a small idealistic minority chose "the promised land." Jewish life, as well as Jewish humor, developed in different ways in the two countries.

Israeli Humor

Israeli humor developed from the rich tradition of Jewish humor. However, in the beginning years of Israel some new characteristics appeared, reflecting the change in the Israelis' views of themselves. As Jews in Israel changed their ideals, behavior, and self-perception, they also changed their humor. Israeli humor did not in the beginning follow the tradition of Jewish humor of the Diaspora.

The extreme seriousness of the pioneers, wanting to build not only a "new homeland" but also a "new Jew," did not leave much place for self-disparagement. A real hero cannnot accept seeing himself as a schlumiel, and believe with fervor, almost with fanaticism, in the realization of a national ideal does not induce one to see oneself as funny. Slowly, with maturity, Israeli character seems to change, and with it, the humor of the Israelis, who are no longer so enchanted with themselves and are even able to see the ridiculous in their life and behavior. It is not as easy to forget almost two millennia of cultural background in the Diaspora, as the founders of modern Israel wanted to.

The relatively short history of modern Israel can be divided into four parts. Unfortunately, reflecting life conditions in Israel, the signposts separating these periods are wars. The four periods are

1. Before independence
2. From independence to the Six Day War (1948–1967)
3. From the Six-Day War to Lebanon (1967–1982)
4. After Lebanon.

Let us look at the development of humor in these four different periods.

Before Independence

Jewish presence in Israel never ceased. While Palestine, as it was called, was under different dominations, Jewish communities continued to exist. During Roman rule Jews were tolerated and had religious freedom. With Christianity, anti-Jewish legislation appeared, and it was continued by the Byzantine rulers. Nevertheless, Jewish culture continued, and sacred writings continued to be produced. Arab rulers, the Crusaders, and the Turkish rulers all had to deal with the stubborn Jewish population which never gave up its religion and values.

The first wave of massive immigration, which came at the end of the nineteenth century, was ideologically motivated. They came to Palestine in order to re-create a Jewish homeland based on different values from those held by Jews in the Diaspora. They also wanted to rebuild themselves, to create a Jew as different as possible from the "Galut" type.

Jews from Europe brought with them the tradition of Jewish humor, and satirical theatres and humorist newspapers flourished. This is extremely remarkable when one remembers that the papers were written in Hebrew and that the plays were interpreted by actors who generally did not know the language very well. And let us remember that the Hebrew-speaking population was a rather small one.

Humorous newspapers in Hebrew appeared in the 1920s when the Jewish population in Palestine numbered about a quarter of a million. The first satirical newsletter was published by Avigdor Ha-Meiri, who also founded the first satirical theatre in Palestine. The newsletter, called *Lev Hadash* (A New Heart), was published in only eight issues. The first humor newspaper, *Leyehudim* (For the Jews), was published in 1924 by a few journalists. Many others appeared for short periods, and some enjoyed a real popularity: *Egel Hazahav* (The Golden Calf), which appeared in 1939, and *Sikot* (Needles), which was the translation of the name of a famous Polish humor newspaper. The weekly *Kantoniada*, based on the idea of having Eretz Israel divided in cantons, had a short life, like many other publications which appeared mostly around Purim.

Cartoonists started to publish their work in these journals as well as in a few daily newspapers. Their work reflected different aspects of life in the Yishuv (the Jewish settlement), but most cartoons were political in nature. This tendency to accept political cartoons, but not cartoons depicting and making fun of life in general, is still very much alive in Israel today. Most of the nonpolitical cartoons appearing in Israeli newspapers are reproduced from American or European publications. Bas, Navon, and Nardi were the best-known cartoonists of the period before independence.

Satirical theatre in Hebrew started on May 1, 1927, and was animated by Avigdor Ha-Meiri. The theatre was called "Hakumkum" (The Kettle), and its main intention was to "scald the Yishuv, with the Kettle's steam." Indeed, satire made fun of various Jewish organizations in a gentle way, and many asked by what right the actors did so. The second satirical theatre, Ha-Matateh (The Broom), which started in 1928, mostly used to mock the British rulers, in spite of their censorship. The theatre was extremely popular, but it decided to close down not long after the departure of the British. The decision was made because they felt that one cannot make fun of the independent homeland, which for most of the actors, newcomers from Europe, was the realization of a dream, too exquisite to be taken as a target for satire.

Israeli humor in this period followed the tradition of Jewish humor, so well-known on the Europen scene. However, one new form of humor reflected the new image the Israelis wanted for themselves. This humor was created by the new Israeli generation, which was the backbone of the army. The Hagana, the unofficial Israeli army, was founded in 1920, and in it, the Palmach (shock troops) was considered the elite. The humor they created reflected their life, gently making fun of the inner problems of the army and of course of the British. The jokes were of the tall-story kind, rather long, in which popular figures, which later become legends, did their tricks. These stories, published in the fifties but created in the forties, were collected in a book called *Yalkut Hakezavim* (Bag of Lies). *Kazab* is an Arab word meaning *lie* or *exaggeration*. The fact that an Arab word was chosen to create a new Hebrew word, probably reflected the wish to be considered assimilated in the new Middle Eastern environment.

In *Yalkut*, the heroes were manly, making fun of everything, stealing from the kibbutz, doing fantastic exaggerations and being certain that they were the supermen representing the new Yishuv. Everything was gay, not a single joke about suffering or being in difficulty. Difficulties were easily solved by the naive-but-wise heroes. They were capable of getting the best of the English mandatory troops, who were caricatured as dumb and credulous. The heroes had Arab names or mostly first names and nicknames like Moshe Hashamen (Moshe the fat man). The stories were mild satire with kind humor, accepting and admiring the little foibles of the heroes. It was clear that for the writers those Palmach kids were the best, the most noble, and the real elite of the new Jewish society in Palestine. The popularity of the book was probably due to the understanding of the mythical heroes and the admiration to which they were entitled, since they were at least theoretically military heroes. They were at the same time naive and clever, pure and shrewd. They seemed to live in a world where everything was fun, and no political, economic, or other kind of trouble existed. They were a bunch of "grown up eternal adolescents," just having a good time. The main characteristics of the *chizbat* were as follows: a rather long story, told to a group around the fire, the hero being a person known to all, in which there is always a kernel of truth. Many Arab words were used, almost no Yiddish or European languages. This was in order to underline the "local flavor" of Hebrew and Arab vocabulary, which stressed involvement in what is going on "here and now." While the punch line was not very original, it created an atmosphere of group cohesiveness and a folklore on "private jokes" enjoyed by those who belong.

In European Jewish folklore, schnorers, scholars, rabbis, merchants, and schlemiels were the heroes; in the *chizbat*, soldiers, *shomrim* (guards), and mostly kibbutzniks took their place. The main victim was the greenhorn (*hatzanhan*, the paratrooper), emphasizing probably the idea that the newcomers are not really "in." In a land based on immigration this kind of joking probably helped to create a kind of "Mayflower elite." Even in today's Israeli humor the term *WASP* is used to describe *Vatik* (not a newcomer), *Askhenazi* (most members of the Palmach and the old power structure were from Eastern Europe), *Socialist* (the prevailing ideology of the times), and *Palmach*.

Oring, who did brilliant anthropological research on the beginnings of Israeli humor, has a very poor opinion of the originality of the jokes of the Palmach. He wrote: "The most important aspect of the chizbat's uniqueness is that the Palmach felt it was unique" (Oring, 1981, p. 123). He might be right about some of the contents of the jokes, but he was certainly wrong about the techniques they used. They reflected a new way of life, introducing in most Israelis' lives, a folklore of life in the army which was as unknown to the Jews as the army itself. To this day, many Israelis know about the way of life of the beginning of Israel's army from *Yalkut Hakezavim*, which created a few popular figures having a great nostalgic value.

From Independence to the Six-Day War

Although the folklore of the Palmach was created before the independence war, *Yalkut Hakezavim* was published after the war, in 1952, creating a wave of nostalgia. The creation of the State of Israel was accompanied by the rise of a bureaucracy and the slow disappearance of the great idealistic values. Proud of their accomplishments, Israelis developed behavioral characteristics as different as possible from the "Galuth image." Being tough, serious, and proud of every bit of what was going on in Israel was the order of the day. George Mikes, the famous British-Jewish humorist (of Hungarian origin), wrote very astute observations about the Israelis in his book *Milk and Honey*. Among his perceptions is one typical of Jewish irony: "If you want to get on with the Israelis, praise them. It is silly to praise people behind their backs. Not very manly either. Tell them openly to their faces that you think they are wonderful. Have the courage to insist that they are admirable, brave, brilliant, efficient, noble and inimitable. At first, I thought such statements might embarrass them. But not at all. They do not mind them, They can face the truth. They say it themselves" (Mikes, 1951, p. 34).

An atmosphere of self-importance, putting forward self-assurance, doesn't encourage humor. In spite of this atmosphere, humor developed, a kind of humor which was a stranger to the characteristics of Eastern European humor. The roots of the new humor were mostly aggressive, and negative stereotypes came alive with each wave of emigration. Rumanians were the butt of jokes about "thieving"; Moroccans, for using their knives too easily; Germans, for not understanding quickly enough, and so on. All this underlines the "scapegoat principle," which describes the need people have to find others to consider laughable in order to feel superior. Jews, who for long generations were the targets for others' mocking, had to find victims, and they found their victims among themselves. Perhaps the most cruel joke was the use of the term *soap* (spineless), still used in today's slang but whose origins are fortunately forgotten. The expression *soap* designated those who let themselves be slaughtered in Europe and made into soap by Nazis, without fighting.

Jokes about immigrants' difficulties in adopting the new ways flourished:

A line of workers at a construction site passes a bucket from one worker to another. Every passage is accompanied by a few words from each worker: "Bitte, Herr Doktor." "Danke, Herr Doktor."

Still wondering about the creation of the new state, in which such unknown characters as Jewish thieves and Jewish policemen were real, many jokes appeared in which policemen behaved apologetically and thieves discussed the human side of their profession, convincing the policemen that thieves were *mentch* (human beings) too.

However, the new bureaucrats and politicians rapidly became the favorite target. It was a gradual passage from great admiration of the leaders to a more critical view. For the young Israelis, the practical aspect of the realization of their ideals proved to be an unpalatable cup of tea. Pioneering asceticism was replaced by a desire for personal gains and luxuries. Equalitarian ideology was considered a thing of the past, and instead of wanting to be an exemplary state for a special people or a light for non-Jews, most Israelis, especially the young ones, wanted to be "just like other nations," normal, not better than others, and certainly not worse.

The Sinai War with its tremendous military victory greatly bolstered Israelis' self-confidence and, let us say it, their arrogance. The tough guy, who never talks about emotions or weaknesses, was reinforced even more. Humor was rather pale and a rare occurrence on Israeli radio (television was not yet introduced) or in newspapers. One humorous radio program was extremely popular. Called "Three in a Boat," it enjoyed a long-lasting fame. It consisted of a roundtable where humorists were asked questions which they supposedly answered spontaneously. The programs were enjoyed by almost everybody, included little political satire, and were mostly humor for humor's sake. Two books which became best-sellers were published, including some of the radio programs.

In the fifties humorous columns started to be published in the daily newspapers. The humor of this period was mostly the result of the work of newcomers from Europe, especially the Hungarians. The most important among them, and certainly Israel's greatest humorist, was and still is Ephraim Kishon. A new immigrant from Hungary, he did not know a word of Hebrew when he arrived. In a short time, he had not only learned the language but wrote humorous columns which became rapidly famous. His mastery of Hebrew was such that he introduced many innovations, rapidly picked up by his readers (i.e., practically everybody). His versatility was and still is quite extraordinary. Not only did he have a daily column in the most popular daily in Israel, but he wrote a few comedies successfully presented to full houses in Israel and in most countries around the world. *His Name Precedes Him* was a satire in which the new bureaucracy with its *protekzia* was gently made fun of. He also wrote most of the material for one of the most popular army entertainment groups, and later for one of the most successful theatre companies, the Green Onion. He wrote and directed the best comedy films ever produced in Israel, which won him international recognition (*The Policeman* was nominated for an Oscar as best foreign movie). Kishon's satire was mild and loving; the people he attacked were more like schlemiels than cruel and bad people. Rather similar was the style of Tomi Lapid, who in addition to his humorous columns and material for radio, wrote a comedy in which he satirized many aspects of Israeli society. Lapid's satire, like Kishon's was mild and understanding, in the tradition of "loving satire." In the world of cartoons, Dosh (who created the image of the little Israeli who became the symbol of Israel in the same way Uncle Sam is the symbol of the United States) and *Zeev*, both also *olim* (newcomers) from Hungary, enriched the humorous look at Israelis, without harsh criticism. Most humor of this period was created by *olim* from Eastern Europe who brought with them the tradition of Jewish humor prevalent there.

From the Six-Day War to Lebanon

The Six-Day War was not only a great military victory. It also changed the self-image of most Israelis and probably of many Jews around the world. Suddenly the little David slaughtered Goliath anew, and then he started to believe that he was some kind of superman. Israelis became conquerors, having acquired huge territories and maintaining more than one million Arabs under military rule. That Jewish military governors now ruled over powerless minorities had a strong ironic touch for those who had not forgotten the Jewish heritage of the Diaspora.

The general euphoria did not completely silence some dissidents who started asking questions about the morality of being a conqueror. The first satirical play after the Six Day War, called *Malkat Hambatia* (The Queen of the Bathroom), vigorously attacked the Israeli political establishment and its policies concerning the occupied territories. Hanoch Levin, the author of the play, was so much against the general consensus that his play was represented only 19 times and was abandoned due to the public outcry.

However, Levin's satire was followed by other funny, critical looks at Israeli realities. The new medium of television brought lively satire into everybody's home. The weekly program "Head Cleaning" (Nikui Rosh) was written by the new generation of humorists. Israeli-born, they did not look at the country as a miracle but as a fact which can be criticized, a reality having good and bad aspects. The leaders make mistakes, and politicians are not motivated only by "the good of country." The television program made quite a furor not only in the general public but among politicians as well. After almost each weekly show of the satirical program, the main topic of discussion in the Knesset (Parliament) was the program, which was considered by some politicians (mostly those who were the targets of the last show) as "attacking the morale of the country." Humor was never accepted by Israeli politicians as a normal part of the country's life. Because most of Israeli humor during this period was political, the politicians appeared as liars and cheaters wanting only to hold on to power. The new generation of humorists, B. Michael, Ephraim Sidon, Yonathan Gefen, all sabras (born in Israel), used virulent, savage satire against the government and its policies. Cabaret satire, presented onstage, became popular, and what Levin had dared to present in his first satirical plays was now accepted and enjoyed an immense popularity. Some old-timers from the Palmach days, like Dan Ben Amotz (one of the writers of *Yalkut Hakezavim*) and Amos Kenan, joined the ranks. Seeing themselves as keepers of the first idealistic views, destroyed by politicians, they helped keep up a kind of constant satirical attack against the political establishment.

The Yom Kippur War was a hard shock for most Israelis, who were convinced of their military superiority. The surprise attack, the great dangers, and the huge number of losses again did something to the Israeli self-image. It had a sobering effect, and although it ended with a military victory, it certainly was not a political one. The continuing domination of a huge Arab population, with no peaceful solution in sight, created a lot of uneasiness. The elections in 1976 changed for the first time the political dominance of the Socialist party, and the right came into power. A political shock followed the military one, and Israelis had to adjust to the new realities.

Political humor and virulent satire were mobilized to attack those in power. Since the power was on the right side of the political spectrum, most satire came from the left. While Levin's first satirical play was rejected by the majority of Israelis, his other plays not only were accepted but had a huge success. For the first time, Israel, its policies, and its feeling of always being right were satirized in a savage way. Yehoshua Sobol, one of Israel's most prolific playwrights, wrote a few satirical reviews ferociously attacking the political leadership. Hanoch Levin continued his satirical work, and violent satire became ''in.'' Contrary to the older generation of humorists, who saw in political and bureaucratic manipulations a kind of schlemieli way of dealing with Israeli realities, the new generation showed politicians as vicious liars, ready to cheat and even to start wars in order to gain or retain power.

However, this satirical overkill became boring in the long run, for satirists just kept repeating themselves. Some of them—B. Michael, Ephraim Sidon, Kobi Niv, and Dudu Geva—started writing absurd humor. This is possibly a renewal of traditional Jewish humor: if you cannot fight a cruel reality, change it by distorting it. If you can laugh at it, it just shows that it is not so terrible. A book entitled *Zoo Aretz Zoo* (a wordplay on ''In this a country?'' or ''a zoo country'') became a cult book for many Israeli youngsters fed up with politics. Absurd and even sexual humor (a great novelty in Israeli humor) and a new modern style of cartoons, comic strips, brought a new wind into Israeli humor. However, political satire was still dominant by far.

Israeli literature did not produce a single comic novel, and S. Y. Agnon, a virtuous user of irony, who received the Nobel Prize for literature, had his writing so deeply rooted in old Jewish tradition that few saw him representing the mainstream of Israeli spirit.

AFTER LEBANON: CONTEMPORARY HUMOR AND TRENDS

This Lebanon war, the first on which the Israeli consensus was broken, created an even stronger satirical outcry. But since they were the same satirists attacking the same targets, the public and finally the satirists themselves got a bit tired. New forms of humor appeared on the Israeli scene, some of them relating to the more traditional themes of Jewish humor. For the first time, the Israeli schlemiel appeared in some sketches: a soldier, a bit confused, doing his best to keep alive and get home in one piece, keeping his morale by using some self-disparaging humor. This was something entirely new, the Israelis seeing their soldiers either as heroes or as apprentice philosophers talking about the cruelty of war.

Some nostalgic looks at Diaspora Jewish humor appeared. A theatrical version of Dan Greenburg's *How To Be a Jewish Mother* had a long career and great success. A new generation of Israeli humorists, in their twenties, started a new style of humor in which absurdity in a kind of modern Marx Brothers style, presented on the army radio, became a cult among youngsters. The daily program they created and presented was entitled "What's happening?" (*Ma Yiesh*). Satire, nonsense, and self-disparagement were having a feast and helping to create a healthy humorous atmosphere. Many daily newspapers started a weekly humor supplement, the most famous being *Another Thing* (*Davar Acher*), which appears in the socialist party's daily *Davar*. Every week on its frontispiece it has the official motto of socialism starting with "Proletarians of the world . . ." (officially it ends with "unite"). It is followed by such truths as "didn't we tell you?" or "calm down!" or even "take five." When a political party's journal makes fun of the party's own historical slogan, self-disparagement is not dead.

What is the future direction of Israeli humor? A humorist explained: "Jewish humor developed in Eastern Europe as a defense mechanism. Jews were living in small shtetels, surrounded by a huge majority of Christians who hated them and tried many times to destroy them. Today everything has changed: Jews live in a small state surrounded by a huge majority of Arabs who hate them and have tried many times to destroy them. So, don't worry, we still need Jewish humor for survival."

UNIVERSAL FUNCTIONS OF HUMOR AND NATIONAL MANIFESTATIONS

Aggressive humor is probably the main characteristic of Israeli humor. This is an important change from traditional Jewish humor, which was mostly characterized by "loving satire" and self-disparagement. The reasons for this development should be clear from the description of the evolution of Jewish humor in Israel. Aggressiveness is probably one of the main characteristics of Israelis in general, and this is perhaps understandable in a people living in conditions that include a war every decade.

The division between the aggressive humorists and those who use mainly the traditional "loving satire" is very clear. The humorists of the loving satire came from Europe and brought with them the main elements of Jewish humor. The more aggressive ones are Israeli-born, and they represent in their writings the temporary changes in Jewish mentality resulting from the special conditions of life in Israel.

Sexual humor is very rare in Israeli culture. This might be due to the fact that Hebrew, a sacred language for thousands of years, has no terms to deal with profanities. Most sexual or scatological curse words are of Russian, Yiddish, or Arabic origin. Hebrew slang had not yet developed such terms of its own. Sexual cartoons are extremely rare and almost never obscene. Jewish humor, even before the new state of Israel, was never sex-minded.

Social humor is the most prominent function of humor in Israel. In a country with 23 political parties and people coming from 86 different nations where they had always been a part of a minority, the experience of being in a majority, with a government which can be criticized without fear, is probably a feast. The traditional forms of Jewish humor, irony and satire, flourish.

Humor as defense mechanism is more and more the hallmark of Israeli humor. Together with aggressive humor, irony and national self-disparagement seem to be characteristic of Israeli humor in recent years. While on a personal level Israelis do not make fun of themselves, as a collectivity they certainly do.

Intellectual humor is a modern, flourishing trend. While wordplay was always a characteristic of Jews who were bilingual or trilingual in the Diaspora, the great task in Israel was to learn a language common for all. As Kishon once wrote: "Israel is the only country in the world where parents learn the mother tongue from their children." However, as Hebrew slang becomes richer, many jokes are created around it. Lately, absurdity has become more popular among humorists.

INFORMATION SOURCES

There is no national society or organization dealing with humor in Israel, and the country also lacks a humor journal. The one exception is the *Journal of Irreproducible Research Results*, published in English and addressed to the international academic community, where it is highly appreciated. Israel recently started to study its own humor, both contemporary and historical. Two international conferences on Jewish humor, both under the auspices of Tel Aviv University, were held in 1984 in Israel and in 1986 in the United States.

REFERENCES

Ausubel, N. (1948) *Treasury of Jewish Folklore*. New York: Crown.
Bloch, C. (1921) *Hersh Ostropoler*. Vienna: B. Harz.
Carmi, T., ed. (1981) *Hebrew Verse*. London: Allen Lane.
Freud, S. (1962) *The Joke and Its Relation to Unconsciousness* (originally published in 1905). New York: Morrow.
Heinemann, B. (1963) *The Maggid of Dubno and His Parables*. New York: Philip Feldheim.

Israel, I. (1958) *Jewish Life in the Middle Ages*. New York: Meridian Books.

Kohn, Y. P. (1915) *Rabbi's Humor, Then and Now*. Berlin: Kaupter.

Liptzin, S. (1971) *A History of Yiddish Literature*. New York: Johnathan David.

Mikes, G. (1951) *Milk and Honey*. London: Andre Deutch.

Newman, L. I. (1962) *Maggidim and Hasidim: Their Wisdom*. New York: Bloch.

Oring, E. (1981) *Israeli Humor: The Content and Structure of the Chizbat of the Palmach*. Albany: State University of New York Press.

Priger, S. (1961) *Shalom Aleichem's Life*. Jerusalem: Stern.

Rosten, L. (1977) *Treasury of Jewish Quotations*. New York: Bantam.

Stora Sandor, J. (1984) *L'Humour juif dans la littérature: de Job a Woody Allen*. Paris: PUF.

Wisse, R. R. (1971) *The Schlemiel as Modern Hero*. Chicago: Chicago University Press.

Ziv, A. (1979) *L'humour en education: approche psychologique* (Humor in Education: A Psychological Approach). Paris: E. S. F.

———. (1987) "Jewish Humor." In *Encyclopedia Judaica*, vol. 12.

Studies on Humor in Israel (*all books are in Hebrew*)

Bergson, H. (1911) *Laughter: An Essay on the Meaning of the Comic*. New York: Macmillan.

Alexander, D. (1985) *The Jester and the King: Political Satire in Israel: A Temporary Summary 1948–1984*. Tel Aviv: Sifriat Hapoalim.

Friedlender, Y. (1984) *Bemisterei Hasatira: Hebrew Satire in Europe in the 19th Century*. Ramat Gan: Bar Ilan University.

Ziv, A. (1981) *The Psychology of Humor*. Tel Aviv: Yahdav.

———. (1984) *Jewish Humor*. Tel Aviv: Papyrus.

———. (1984) *Humor and Personality*. Tel Aviv: Papyrus.

STAFFORDSHIRE
POLYTECHNIC
LIBRARY

Humor in Italy

BACKGROUND

A full study of Italian humor is also in many ways a study of the Italian way of life, a task beyond the scope of this chapter. Here the reader will find only an exposition of perhaps a little schematic for such a vibrant and dynamic topic. What follows should be considered merely as guidelines which the reader can use for further exploration of the rich field of Italian humor.

What are the origins of Italian humor? The humorists of today speak in a language that contains dialectical modulations, and many actually express themselves in the local dialect of their native district. This is a result of the political and cultural history of Italy. Before the political unification of Italy in 1870, the country for centuries had consisted of a number of small states, each with its own traditions and naturally its unique sense of humor. These cultures still survive and today combine together to constitute Italian culture. Dealing with Italian humor, one has to keep in mind that a Sicilian, Milanese, Napolitan, Roman, etc., has his own specific humor. Italian humor evolved from this harmonious melting pot of statehoods and therefore has a cosmopolitan flavor.

The Italian people, split into small states for centuries, have been conquered, exhausted, and impoverished of their natural and artistic resources many times throughout history. It seems that the only weapon that was left to this powerless people conquered by foreign armies was the weapon of humor. Not even Mussolini's dreams of grandeur succeeded in turning the Italians into an aggressive and "serious" nation.

This state of affairs stands out especially in the underdeveloped zones of Italy, where one finds people who, although they suffered more at the hands of historical events, seem to know more than others how to enjoy life, to laugh, and in turn to make others laugh with them. The image of the Italian who enjoys friends, food, love, and humor is not a baseless stereotype but rather a recognition of the way the Italian has dealt with the unending hardships of living under tyrants. One would not be wrong in assuming that the Italian people learned the art of making-do, of surviving. Taking a stroll through the streets of modern Naples will be enough to make one realize that the many surrealistic figures that appear in Italian humor are not comic fantasies from a playful imagination but are rather taken from real life.

Before proceeding, we should keep in mind another useful generalization that will be of help in understanding the nature of Italian humor. Italy has traditionally been a nation with a split personality or Janus-like nature in which two opposite souls live within the same peninsula, both with strong subconscious roots.

First, there is the pagan soul who loves to rejoice without inhibitions in all of life's manifestation, a pure hedonistic soul. It springs from the roots of the ancient Roman Empire, of satyrs and the comedies of Plautus, Oratius's poetry, and the *Satyricon* of Petronius. It is also alive throughout the country's feasts and carnivals that have survived down through the centuries.

The other soul is a Catholic one which is also deeply rooted in Italy. This second soul is a moralizer and a disciplinarian and is rather inhibited. Its temporal institute, the Church, has in the past considered the subject of unbridled humor as unfitting and amoral. On the other hand, this second soul has been a rare and ready target as well as a great stimulus for the mocking spirit of the pagan soul, fighting for freedom and against prejudices (of course, with prejudices of its own).

There is also the fundamental nature of humor, which likes to reduce pompousness at every occasion and has caused a great deal of pain to the Catholic soul by creating dogmatical and ideological problems for all political powers. Often, the two opposing souls were at war, and the field of battle was a fertile ground for the growth of Italian humor. New factors, such as the secularization of society in the twentieth century, have brought other paradigms to Italian humor, mainly political and social ones. The Church is no longer the main target of humor, and sexual and political humor have become major categories. However, they do not completely shadow the humor of every man in his daily life as witnessed by the hundreds of characters that populate the history of Italian humor.

TRADITIONAL FORMS AND EXPRESSIONS OF HUMOR BEFORE THE TWENTIETH CENTURY

Popular Forms

As in other countries, at a certain time the humor of the circus and of the caravans of nomadic comic actors was legitimized by its appearance upon the stage. Of course, clowns and jugglers continued to entertain in the streets up until recent years, and the circus is still alive (one can see a glimpse of the circus clown's life in Fellini's film *The Clowns*).

Looking back at history, we see that in the beginning there was chaos of all regional humor which only later would become typically Italian. All these regional forms owe much to their Latin ancestors: the love for improvisations in the streets and onstage, the gusto for farce with its paradoxes and sexual allusions, survived through the Middle Ages till today. The origins of the satirical comedies of Trentius and Plautus are religious and popular. The first public representations were held during the pagan rites of Bacchus (the Greek Dionysus transformed by Romans). These particular collective rites show the importance for the peninsula's people to find ways of freely expressing their urges. So, theatre can be considered to have been in Italy the principal vehicle of humor through the ages: of the common people in the streets during the carnival and in the particular feasts of each Italian village, commemorating the *patrono*, the saint protector of the village. The theatres in the courts of kings and nobles, performed by jesters and itinerary companies of clowns on the roads, were the predecessors of the modern Italian theatre.

Popular humor gave free rein to the energy accumulated frustrations and energies of people in days of poverty, exploitation, and trouble. For the power, from the Roman emperors on, the confusions of the masquerades had always been better than riots. These manifestations were therefore always permitted and even encouraged. The Church, almost against its will, made the carnival an institution, followed naturally by periods of restraints or *quaresima,* having thus some rewards in the acceptance of pagan entertainment. During the Middle Ages, every lord was proud of having a man of letters in his court: poet or novelist, and sometimes a cultured humorist such as Boccaccio, Pietro Aretino, or the poet Cecco Angilorieri. It appears that Italy has seen humor products being celebrated as artistic masterpieces. This was greatly helped by the rich Latin literature preceding it.

As in other countries in Europe, April Fools' Day was and still is a widely enjoyed feast. It is not a collective occasion of mockery; it is for the individual the permitted occasion to perpetrate the wicked jokes he has not the courage to do during the year.

Concerning regional humor, its most flourishing place was Tuscany, with

Florence as capital; the best-known popular humor in Italy comes from Naples, Rome, and their environments, while the center of the art of cabaret has been Milan.

Humor in the Literary and Performing Arts

The Italian language is a natural outgrowth of Latin. Its development was gradual, and Italian was recognized as a new language only around 915. The Latin heritage is part of the Italian one, and it is important to show in a few lines how rich Latin theatre and literature were in humor.

Theatre: Titus Maccius Plautus (ca. 254–186 B.C.) wrote many plays; actually 130 have been attributed to him.He wrote many comedies, among them *Amphitrion*, a hilarious play of mistaken identity, dealing with Zeus's love affair. The immortality of the play can best be understood by looking at the many adaptations written by such greats as Molière, Dryden, Kleist, and Giraudoux. *I Captive* (The Captives) is a comedy filled with comic irony; *Mercator* (The Merchant), an excellent farce; and *Casin*, a rather sexy comedy, are among his most famous works.

Terence (ca. 185–159 B.C.) was another comedy writer, whose *Eunuchus* (The Eunuch), a most amusing play sometimes condemned as immoral, influenced Shakespeare's *Taming of the Shrew*. Lucilius (180–102 B.C.) is considered the originator of satire as a separate genre. Of his 30 books of satires, few are extant, but their billiance still shines. He greatly influenced Horace (65–5 B.C.), who wrote *Satires* poking fun at many aspects of Romans' lives.

Ovid (43 B.C.–A.D. 17), the great epic poet, lyricist, and dramatist, left works still popular today in many languages. The best known is *Ars Amatoria* (The Art of Love), about which Dimsdale wrote 19 centuries later: "it is a monument of wit and delicate tapestry, prompted by deviltry and restricted by no reluctance to shock" (Dimsdale, 1935, p. 306).

Among the other great satirists, one must mention Petronius (ca. A.D. 24–65), who left us his *Satyricon*; Artial (ca. A.D. 40–102); and Juvenal (ca. A.D. 60–97).

Italian theatre has its origins in the circus and the nomadic actors and jesters who played in the streets. In the eighteenth century some of the actors left the streets and started appearing onstage, thus laying the foundations of modern theatre. The Italian modern theatre was officially born, with humor as its mid-wide, in the eighteenth century. The Venetian plawright Carlo Goldoni (1702–1792) presented beautiful comedies, using at times the masks of the carnival to present the life of the middleclass. Goldoni employed the local dialect of Venice and showed people's lives and problems without being didactic. He analyzed with humor and wit the customs and desires of the people of his time. Goldoni is considered the forerunner of the classical theatrical style called Commedia dell'Arte which also influenced wide circles outside Italy in later years, such as Molière, Meyerhold, Reinhardt, and Copeau. The roots of Commedia dell'Arte go back to the Roman comedies of Plautus and Terentius (second century B.C.), the typical characters of which were adapted in the sixteenth century by Commedia dell'Arte. The cast included, among others, the Pedant, the Boastful Soldier, the Sly, and the Foolish Servants, with new ones taken from common life joining them later.

The comic actors of Commedia dell'Arte were professionals who improvised on a plot given by the author, called a *canovaccio* (dishcloth), and some of them, being very skillful acrobats, even identified physically with their fantastic characters. At the beginning with the Paduan Ruzzante the form was rougher, but 200 years later with Goldoni, it rose to a higher and more realistic level, and the comedies finally became fully structured theatre. The history of all modern Western comedy in the threatre derives from the Commedia dell'Arte.

It is easy to find in any part of Italy a theatrical company appearing onstage with one of Goldoni's works: if you are lucky, then you might catch the Piccolo Teatro di Milano's version of *Arlecchino, Servitore di due Padroni* (The Servant of Two Masters), which is one of Goldoni's better comedies.

Literature: Humor has been a fundamental part of Italian literature since its beginnings in the fourteenth century. In an account of those writers who were "purely" humorous one must start with Giovanni Boccaccio (1313–1375). Boccaccio's collection of 100 humorous short stories under the title *Decameron* has become a great classic in world literature. These tales of an imaginary Florence in the Middle Ages are full of a sublte and mocking eroticism and humor that spring out of the cunning and cleverness of the characters. In Italy *Decameron* is still read with delight and was cast as a movie by Pier Paolo Pasolini in 1971. It is rather singular but symptomatic that the masterpiece of one of the earliest Italian classicists (together with Petrarch and Dante Alighieri) is a work of humor.

Inspired by Boccaccio, Matteo Bandello (1485–1561) is considered the greatest writer of witty stories in the Renaissance. His tales, perhaps not masterpieces, have a very realistic substance, giving an extremely lively picture of his time. Pietro Aretino is another typical figure of the Renaissance. He was one of the *poligrafi*, an intellectual with multiple interests typical of that period's intellectual atmosphere. Aretino was an expert in the arts, a political observer, an eclectic, a writer, and author of five lovely comedies. In his comedies he reflects the free, sarcastic, and exciting spirit of the Renaissance.

During the age of "Controriforma," in the middle of the sixteenth century, the Santo Uffizio court imposed a limit on free expression. The intellectual life, public humor included, was crushed by ideological conformism. The conscience of harmony between man and nature, the faith in his creative potential, so typical of the Renaissance, was almost destroyed by bigotry. In addition, the Spanish occupation of the country during the sixteenth century, with its violent barbarianism, added an additional blow to Italian intellectualism, including humor. Some notable figures appeared in spite of the difficulty of the times. Alessandro Tassoni (1565–1635) wrote an epic parody about the Spanish conquerors and their ignorant and vicious style of life. The best-known popular writer of the period was Giulio Cesare Croce (1550–1609), who created two immortal characters in his books: Bertoldo and Bertoldino. Bertoldo, with his popular wisdom, brings to the corrupted court of King Alboino, love, cunning, and a sense of human dignity. Between the dialect writers, the greatest of this time was the Napolitan Gianbatista Basile, a writer with a rare richness of imagination. In the same century, the leadership of Tuscan dialect in literature (the proto-Italian of Dante and Boccaccio) came to an end, and a diffusion of works in other dialects appeared expressing a refusal of the classic models of the previous century.

In the eighteenth century, with the new atmosphere brought by the development of science and the birth of the Enlightenment, the theatre became the place where humor reached its highest with Goldoni and the new Commedia dell'Arte. The nineteenth century, the century of romanticism and positivism, did not create a valid and structured humorous prose; instead, the glory of the dialectical and popular culture continued to grow. The best-known examples are the Milanese Carlo Porta (1775–1821) and the Roman Giuseppe Belli (1791–1803). Social and political problems of the times find their expression in their witty, humoristic poems.

Humor in the Visual Arts

Caricature is word of Italian origin. Some consider it a term used in homage of Annibale Carracci, the father of modern caricature. Others believe that the word reflects simply its Italian origin, from *caricare* meaning "to load" or "to surcharge." Many of the greatest Italian painters included caricatures in their work. Paolo Uccello in the fifteenth century painted his battle scenes, turning over perspectives, regarding the armies with irony, showing blue fields and red towns, sacrificing reality to his smile. The great Leonardo da Vinci left many sketches of human caricatures, grotesque and funny; some can be admired at the Uffizi Museum in Florence. A great ancestor of caricature has been the painter Giuseppe Arcimboldi (1527–1593); bizarre artist, he became famous for his fantastic heads formed by fruits, animals, fishes, trees, vegetables, and flowers. His famous painting *L'ortolano* (the vegetable dealer) if seen upside down is a wonderful basket of vegetables; turned around it is the dealer itself. Carracci's followers, Pier Leone Ghezzi (1674–1755) and Adriano Cecconi (1838–1886), were considered among the most brilliant European caricaturists. Cecconi was a sculptor and a painter, leader and main theorist of the Machiaoli group of antiacademic artists in Florence. He was one of the rare artists to work in comic sculpture. His 1880 exhibition in Rome was a huge success.

Carlo Pellegrini (1838–1889), better known by his pseudonym Ape, was famous for his work in *Vanity Fair*. His caricature of Disraeli was the first lithograph to appear in the magazine. He lived in England part of his life and was considered by Max Beerbohm as "the only true caricaturist in England." Part of his work is preserved in the Royal Library at Windsor.

Leonetto Cappiello (1875–1942) became famous at age 19 when he published a book of caricatures entitled *Lanterna Magica*. Then, he lived in France where he became extemely popular, publishing his caricatures in *Le Rire*, *Le Figaro*, and many other prestigious journals. He is considered one of the greatest poster artists, a field in which he became famous after ceasing to draw caricatures in 1905.

Not many remember that Enrico Caruso (1873–1921), the great tenor, was also an accomplished caricaturist. His sketches of fellow artists, musicians, and statesmen were regularly published in *La Follia*, the Italian newspaper in New York. Pulitzer offered him $50,000 a year for a monthly caricature, but he refused. When Pulitzer asked him how much *La Follia* paid him, he answered, "Nothing" (Feaver, 1981).

DEVELOPMENT OF HUMOR IN THE TWENTIETH CENTURY

Popular Forms

While popular forms of humor still exist and carnivals are celebrated in Italy in different places on special occasions, more modern forms of entertainment have largely taken their place. Popular humor has been rediscovered in the last 20 years, after a long period in which the media threatened the folkloristic and provincial expression of the arts. The renewed interest in popular art started with the contestation movement in 1968 by youth who wanted something instead of the values of a capitalistic society. Traditional arts like pantomime, puppet shows, and street theatre became popular again, not only as artistic expression but also as a way of getting in touch with national and personal roots. The new passion for the popular forms of art, both artistic and archeological, served to reinforce regional traditions and rich cultural dimensions in many cities great and small. A good example is the fantastic Carnival of Venice, which for some years has returned with its beauty, its mess, and its grandiose tradition. Practically every Italian city has its own tradition of popular art, from which humor is rarely missing, to show tourists and culture lovers.

Humor in the Literary and Performing Arts

There are three major figures who as author-actors at the beginning of this century were most influential in the renewal of comedy on the stage. The first, Ettore Petrolini, was born in Rome in 1886. With a very personal and grotesque touch, he performed numerous characters of his invention, like the famous satire of the viveur in Gastone, parodies of well-known figures such as Hamlet and Faust, original satirical "pastiches" as Nerone, proposed again in a homonymous film in 1934.

Leopoldo Fregoli (1867–1936) was the greatest mime and imitator of his time. He began his career, as the legend goes, performing in front of his captors in

Ethiopia. He was famous for the speed of transforming the characters that he played; he would switch roles as much as 60 times in one performance, thus becoming a legend among audiences throughout Europe. In some ways his legacy is carried on today by Gigi Proietti, an extremely professional actor, who has studied Petrolini thoroughly. Two others who are impersonators also were born in Rome: Carlo Verdone and Enrico Montesano. Montesano mimics politicians of all parties and persons of all races and sexes.

The third great comedian is Eduardo Scarpetta (1853–1925), a classicist of the Napolitan farce. As actor and playwright he invented the modern masque of Felice Sciosciammocca, and his humorous plays, with their paradoxical but realistic protagonists, have been a source of inspiration for many Napolitan artists.

Among them is Eduardo de Filippo, who is considered by many to be the greatest since the forties. He is an author and both a dramatic and comic actor. He began his career on the stage with Scarpetta's company. In 1945 he established his own company and reaped tremendous success throughout the world as well as in Italy. His play *Sabato, domenica, lunedi* (Saturday, Sunday, Monday) was performed in 1973 by Laurence Olivier in the National Theatre in London. Until his death in 1984 at the age of 84, de Filippo was the "Master" of the theatre in Italy.

De Filippo's comedies are about a cruel but comical Naples, "secret" in his words, more authentic than the classic stereotype of the Napolitan who sings with his heart held in his hand. It is a Naples of poverty and ordinary people, nameless and forgotten. De Filippo's universe is concentrated on married life and family, and his characters, usually of a poor background, fight against a cruel and painful existence. The fundamental humor in many of his plays enhances the psychological complexity of the characters; the implicit social indictment is just an element in the staging of the carefully balanced personality of the individual. De Filippo is already considered a classic, and some of his best works are *Filomena Marturano* (1946), *Il sindaco del rione Sanita* (The Major of the Holiness District, 1961), and *Gli esami non finiscono mai* (Exams Never End, 1983).

In addition to de Filippo, there are at least three playwrights worth mentioning. Dario Fo (b. 1926), who lives and works in Milan, has brilliant plays that are high-spirited and characterized by a profound social satire. In the sixties, with comedies such as *La Signora e Da Buttare* (The Lady Is To Be Thrown Out, 1967) Dario Fo provoked the anger of bigots and conservatives as well as clerics for directing his satire at them. Since the early seventies he has written scripts with strong political content, expressing ideas similar to those of the extraparliamentary left. Fo uses clownish humor to vindicate the proletariat in plays often set in the Middle Ages, in an allegory on present social problems. His work is founded on the concept of the collective theatre and carries a revolutionary message that denotes a professional and coherent attitude even to those that do not share his ideology. Only recently has television opened its doors to Fo showing *Mistero Buffo* (Funny Mystery, 1969) and *Morte Accidentale di un Anarchico* (Accidental Death of an Anarchist, 1970).

Ennio Flaiano (1910–1972), journalist, film and theatre critic, author of novels, and one of the most preferred scriptwriters of Federico Fellini (*La Dolce Vita, La Strada, I Vitelloni*), has also written comedies that wittily and ironically describe contemporary life. The image left by Flaiano is that of a fine inventor of jokes, *calembours* (word play), and puns. Among his best books of fantasy and aphorisms are *Autobiografia del blu di Prussia* (Autobiography of the Prussian Blue, 1974) and *Le notti bianche* (The White Nights, 1972). The playwright Flaiano liked best was Oscar Wilde, with whom he has in common a delicate and subtle humor. His comedies like *Un marziano a Roma* (A Martian in Rome), performed by the Vittorio Gassman company in 1960, have often met with mixed reactions in spite of their undoubted qualities. Rome is the real protagonist of his plays: Flaiano defined the capital of Italy as a "motherly and implacable" city in which "to live is to throw part of life away." In *La conversazione continuamente interrotta* (The Conversation Continuously Interrupted, 1969), he describes with humor the daily life of an intellectual in crisis while an endless telephone call is the counterpart to the false and grotesque world of the Roman intelligentsia. Flaiano is still a little-known figure waiting for discovery by a wider audience.

Umberto Simonetta has in recent years drawn attention for the good, humorous plays he has created. He has been successful with his plays which were first cast in the Teatro Girolamo in Milan, the theatre that Simonetta was manager of. He recently presented the actor Maurizio Micheli, who has been very popular on Italian television. With Micheli, Simonetta wrote *Mi voleva Strehler* (Strehler Wanted Me, 1981), a funny monologue based on the world of the theatre and showing the troubles an unknown actor has trying to emerge from obscurity. Certainly, one of the greatest figures in Italian playwriting was Luigi Pirandello (1867–1936), the Sicilian writer who won the Nobel Prize for literature in 1934. Ancestor of the theatre of the absurd, Prandello wrote plays like *Sei personaggi in cerca d'autore* (Six characters in Search of an Author, 1921), *Enrico IV* (1922), and *Come tu mi vuoi* (As You Want Me, 1930), which are still played all over the world. In his plays he approached with sensitivity and black humor the existential crisis of modern man, struggling in the world, confused between reality and appearances. His best-known novel, *Il Fu Mattia Pascal* (1904), and the story *La Giara* (The Jug), recently made into a film, are masterpieces of humor.

Intellectual humor, written to be read and not performed, has in Italian literature an undisputed master, Achille Campanile, who for a period of 50 years until 1976, dominated this form of *vis comica*. Campanile is a universal writer: in his novels, stories, and plays he does not deal with a specific environment in a peculiar dialectical language, as customary in Italy. On the contrary, he shows the individual, the animal or thing without name as ageless, from any town or any country. What sets campanile apart from others is his fantasy. He fulfilled, as the critic Carlo Bo wrote, "the most paradoxical of the investigations that has been ever conducted on reality." Campanile plays a game of creating a crisis in any type of world or logical system that the human mind is able to create.

The fact that Campanile is universal but also typically Italian, literary but also with a wide popular appeal, is demonstrated by the large number of his gags that are transformed into the best Italian jokes told by persons in all walks of life from executives to common servants. Umberto Eco stated that through careful study of Campanile's works it would be possible to write an essay containing all the mechanisms of humor. It would not be an exaggeration to say that Campanile is one of the few Italian writers who have managed to get thoroughly into the mainstream of daily life. The reason may be that he has been one of its most careful observers. Campanile has also given a particular touch to Italian humor and demonstrated the simultaneous use of more than one kind of comic effect.

Campanile devoted himself to theatre too, although unsuccessfully to begin with, apparently as a result of taking his singular comedies too far away from the traditional boundaries of comedy. During his lifetime he was neglected by reviewers, and only in his last years and after his death did Campanile receive the acclaim that he so richly deserved. Among his plays *Se la luna mi porta fortuna* (If the Moon Brings Me Luck, 1927) stands out, as does the collection of stories *Manuale di conversazione* (Manual of Conversation, 1973). The seekers of Campanile's treasurers would be well advised to look up the series of articles he wrote in the TV review column in the weekly magazine *L'Europeo*, they are one-page masterpieces. It is worth noting that the amusing reviews that Sergio Saviane writes for *L'Espresso* and those by Beniamino Placido for *La Republica* are similar in their close analysis of the Italian media.

Humor in the Visual Arts

At the beginning of the century, weekly magazines such as *L'Asino* (The donkey), a satirical paper of socialist leanings, were a great hit. Through cartoons, articles, accounts, and interviews *L'Asino* analyzed the political life of the period with clever irony. The fans of this type of humor would appreciate the collections of the former editor Feltrinelli, which were recently published.

Futurism, founded by Tommaso Marinetti, exploded in Italy with painters such as Umberto Boccioni, Gino Severini, and Giacomo Balla and poets such as Aldo Palzzeschi. The movement wanted to break all accepted artistic rules and used many forms of absurd humor "pour épater les bourgeois." The movement unfortunately degenerated in something linked with fascism. Marinetti's "Zang! Tum! Tumb!," an onomatopoetic poem on a battle, remains famous. After World War I the satirical newspapers *Pasquino* and *Il Becco Giallo* appeared. The first was established a century ago, for a short period and reappeared in 1918—the second was born and died fighting fascism. Leo Longanesi (1905–1957), journalist, writer, publisher, and an intelligent and clever caricaturist, used his magazines for social and literary polemics. The drawings of the painter Giuseppe Novello (b. 1897) are wonderful, subtly ironic descriptions of the Italian middle class of the thirties, forties, and fifties, with their manias and myths. In 1921, Vito De Bellis founded with Oberdan Cotone the weekly *Marc'Aurelio*, which in a few years sold more than 300,000 copies. This magazine lived alongside fascism, in spite of the irony of its articles and cartoons on daily life. The new *Marc'Aurelio* helped create a genre of surrealistic humor that prompted Eugene Ionesco to affirm that his comedies could not have existed without the inspiration of Italian humor.

After the long winter of fascist censorship, political satire came out of its silence and broke out with many magazines dedicated to political satire. *Il Travaso* lasted for 20 years and became the first step in the career of the cartoonists of today's middle-aged generation. *Il Candido*, from 1945 to 1961 a fiercely anticommunist satirical magazine, mirrored that period of wild opposition between those who voted for the leftist parties and those that did not. The content of the magazine, however, was not exclusively political but also included cartoons and articles on daily customs and living by various young humorists without political leanings.

Giovanni Guareschi, who with Giovanni Mosca founded *Candido*, created a character still very popular in the Italy: Don Camillo, a pugnacious priest of the Parmisan countryside, who was the protagonist of Guareschi's fiction. Don Camillo has an opponent-friend, the communist mayor of the town, Peppone. From the book series came a few motion pictures with the French comedian Fernandel and the Italian Gino Cervi.

Public or Specialized Places for Humorous Expression

Humor in Italian theatres, outside of the established playhouses, is found in the cabarets. The peculiar characteristic of a cabaret is a certain amount of aggressiveness on the part of the entertainer. The comedian finds himself often performing all alone in front of an audience in a tiny hall with no space separating him from his audience. If the comedian is not aggressive and pugnacious, he risks losing the audience and being swallowed up by the people who paid to hear him. The cabaret has been for more than twenty years the testing ground and springboard for all aspiring comedians, with the best of them going on to film and stage.

The most celebrated cabaret in Italy is definitely the Derby in Milan. The Derby was home to Cochi and Renato, famous duo of comedians and TV stars during the seventies. Today Cochi Ponzoni is devoted to prose theatre, and Pozzetto has achieved sucess in comic films. His character is usually the young, simple-minded, but principled Milanese worker who is an easy prey of events but manages to pull through by using great determination. One may claim that Rena Pozzetto's definite gifts could be put to use in better ways.

The Derby, the temple of cabaret in Milan has also bred comic singers. This is where Giorgio Gaber and Enzo Jannacci launched their successful careers. Gaber, after a period performing light popular muic, became a politically engaged singer. In his crowded theatrical shows, each song alternates with a monologue, all of which is enhanced by his gift for good timing and sharp delivery. Gaber's lyrics deal with such issues as the crisis of marriage, political and social prejudices, and the neurosis of the metropolitan individual. Gaber has a large following, mainly among the younger generation. Enzo Jannacci is a surgeon who in the sixties sang of the grotesque life that existed on the outskirts of Milan. Today he combines jazz with humor, absurdity, and a surrealistic atmosphere with good music.

Others have emerged from the ranks of the Derby, such as Diego Abatantuono, who does a fine impersonation of a classic type: the immigrant from southern Italy, a football fan, who tries at any cost to pass for a Milanese. Massimo Boldi and Teo Teocoli, who together resemble Laurel and Hardy, are also from the Derby. In summary, one may safely claim that the cabaret is the midwife of most great Italian comedians.

Before World War II, the vaudeville theatre in Italy was on its way to being transformed into a more understandable and more pliable form than the old pattern of dialectical farce. The companies of actors were traveling more widely than before throughout Italy, and they had also started to appear in the new "royal courtyard" of the day, the radio. These companies were composed of singers, ballet girls, and their soubrettes, with the support of comic actors. In the years leading up to the fifties, there were two different levels of performance: the sumptuous star-filled variety show in the large theatres, and on the other level, the squalid *avanspettacolo* (before the main show), with performances of low quality held in the dirtiest cinemas of the cities during the breaks between films. The public considered these poor actors more targets for ridicule and insults than entertainers. The *avanspettacolo* played the role of a nursery for many future stars of comedy in films and television.

One comedian more than any other has stayed on in the hearts of generations of Italians: "Toto," (Antonio de Curtis, 1898–1967). He is the model Italian from Naples who knows how to get along in every situation and spends most of his time as a dignified beggar. From 1933 to 1949 he headed a variety company, and from 1937 to 1966 he acted in over 120 films. In spite of the questionable value of most of the films, his *vis comica* has been so strong and peculiar that no Italian dislikes him. Toto's talent is in mimicking the character of the little man, impeded and defenseless, but ready to overcome any obstacle with absurd and surrealistic solutions. This great comedian, with his asymmetrical figure, jutting chin and cheekbones, gave the best of himself in films such as *Napoli Milionaria* (Napoli the Millionaire, 1950) by Eduardo de Filippo, *Guardie e Ladri* (Cops and Thieves, 1951) by Steno (Stefano Vanzina) and Mario Monticelli, *I Solito Ignoti* (The Usually Anonymous, 1958) by Mario Monticelli, and in his last and perhaps best performance, *Uccellacci e Uccellini* (Bad birds and little birds, 1966) by Pier Paolo Pasolini.

Humor in the Mass Media

In Italy, as we shall see, it is quite the rule that a successful comedian appears in radio, TV, and cinema, so that there is no need for a separate analysis for each of these media, even though radio, in spite of the establishment during the seventies of private channels, has evolved into an almost music-and-news-only medium.

The late fifties and early sixties are the times called "the boom years" in Italy. These were the years of the car and television for all, of full confidence in the economic future that coincided with the birth of "Italian comedy" (*comedia all'Italiana*). These brilliant, realistic, and good films are with a little transformation still in good health. Comedy is, depending on the script, the director, and the particular actor, sometimes mixed with drama. The effect is not absurd humor but realistic humor. The actors, coming usually from the *avanspettacolo* and the *riviste* of variety, are slightly paradoxical archetypes of many average Italians.

Renato Rascel and Macario had great success in the fifties impersonating clown characters, or childish dreamers. Later on, the actors Walter Chiari and Gino Bramieri became more famous for their jokes than for their actual virtue in recitation.

The following are a list of still-active actors and comedians (they are actually both), who since those times have played their roles very well. Alberto Sordi, a Roman actor born in 1920, is certainly the most versatile of this generation. Throughout his long career he succeeded in embodying all the characteristic parts in the Italian universe. His roles at the start of his career, in the two Fellini movies *Sceicco Bianco* (The white sheik, 1951) and *I vitelloni* (1953), are still unforgettable. Afterwards Sordi acted in, among others, *Un Americano a Roma* (An American in Rome) as a youngster who wishes to behave like an American. He has portrayed many roles in films: the Roman swaggerer, the constable, the immigrant, the rich parvenu, and so forth. After this period, Sordi played more dramatic roles in *La grande guerra* (The great war, 1961) by Monicelli; as the ambitious physician in *Il medico della mutua* (The physician of National Health, 1968) and as the man arrested by mistake who is submerged in the labyrinth of the Italian justice system in *Detenuto in attesa di giudizio* (Prisoner waiting for judgment, 1971) by Loy. Sordi also had dramatic roles in *Scopone Scientifico* (1972) and *Il marchese del grillo* (The Marquis of Crickets, 1982) by Luigi Comencini. His films awaken mixed feelings of identification, love, and shame, as his characters are examples of real individuals with all their virtues and vices.

Sordi has sometimes directed some of his films, for example, *Il tassinaro* (The misfortunes of a taxi-driver, 1984). A quaint marginal note: since 1938 Sordi has been the Italian voice of Oliver Hardy.

Born in 1921, Nino Manfredi had the same artistic background as Sordi. Manfredi has been starring since the fifties in feature films, and he has appeared in many television shows. Among his films are *La parmigiana* (The Girl from

Parma, 1962); *Nell'ano del Signore* (In the Year of the Lord, 1969) by Luigi Magni; *Per grazia ricevuta* (For Grace Received, 1974), his directoral debut; *Cafe express* (1981) by Nanny Loy; and *Sapore di donna* (1982) by Alberto Lattuada. He has acted the average good guy, historical figures, the man with delicate manners, and an innocent fighting a violent reality. In his latest movies Manfredi seems to be attracted to more melodramatic roles.

Ugo Tognazzi, born in 1922 in Cremona, performs with extraordinary refinement usually sarcastic and ironic roles. His films are always directed by experienced people like Dino Risi, Luigi Comencini, and Lina Wertmuller. Outstanding are the films *La grande abbuffata* (The huge eating, 1973) by Marco Ferreri and *Amici miei* (My friends, 1977) by Monicelli, together with the actors Gastoine Moscin, Philippe Noiret, and Renzo Montagnani, in a story about the tricks and rascally deeds of four Florentine friends. This film has almost become in Italy a cult movie. In *Il vizietto* (The little vice, 1978), Tognazzi acts as a sweet homosexual mate of Michel Serrault, and after its great success they filmed a sequal some years later.

Finally, Vittorio Gassman, a great dramatic actor and one of the most celebrated Italian actors, has often revealed his comic talents. Several good examples in film are *L'armata Brancaleone* (The Brancaleone Army, 1966) by Comencini, in which Gassman plays the comic part of a mercenary soldier going to the crusades; *La grande guerra* together with Sordi; *I mostri* (Monsters) and *Profumo di donna* (1974) by Risi. Of course, the humorous wit of Gassman can be easily appreciated also in his theatrical monologues (when he can be a thorough prima donna) as well as in his autobiography, *Un avvenire alle spalle* (A Future Behind Him, 1984).

It is true that audiences of filmgoers prefer high-quality comedies like those of Woody Allen and the Italian humorists who have something valuable to say. However, one must consider the fact that the most successful (financially) films and television shows of the year are often the most dull-witted, with the usual sexual gags and the inevitable coarse language. In that sense, we advise avoiding the shows of comedians such as Lino Banfi and Alvaro Vita. Another actor, Adriano Celentano, who was a well-known pop-song singer in the sixties, acted in several comedies in a way that resembled Jerry Lewis but succeeded in demonstrating a comic talent of his own. He started as a director in his beautiful *Yuppi Du* (1973), a funny and surrealistic story placed in Venice, starring Charlotte Rampling. Unfortunately, after this promising start, Celentano played the role of the cool guy or the Latin lover in many films that were profitable but not very funny. At the same low level stand the Sicilians Franco Franchi and Ciccio Ingrassia: they appeared for 20 years in less than mediocre films (excluding the splendid role Ingrassia played as the foul uncle in Fellini's *Amarcord* and the recent *La Giara*, based on a Pirandello novel, in which parts are played by both Franchi and Ingrassia. Somewhat similar to Abbott and Costello, Franchi and Ingrassia are slightly better in their television show, but their humor is not profound nor very original.

CONTEMPORARY HUMOR AND TRENDS

Cinema and Television

In recent years a new generation of comedians has come into public attention in the various types of entertainment media in Italy. During the seventies Italian humor in film and television survived through those we have mentioned earlier, but no new major creators of comedy arrived on the scene. But in the last five years new figures have started to renew and vitalize Italian humor so that it escapes the confines of its provincialism. The typical comedian of this new generation is about 30 years old and almost invariably started performing in the theatre, in cabarets, and in festivals throughout Italy. They have created new, more mature characters, and each comedian has a unique personality and peculiarities as well as a specific style of humorous speech. They are somehow more sophisticated, and many direct their own work. The results are often films of very high quality.

Carlo Verdone is one example of this new generation. He has risen from the little Roman theatres in the provinces to appearances in radio and television. He acts in and directs his films. He has a gift of mime similar to that of Fregoli. Verdone can transform himself in a few minutes into a young Roman swaggerer, a shy employer and his wife, a priest, an old lady and so on almost without limit. Two of his films are very enjoyable, *Un sacco bello* (A Beautiful Sack, 1979) and *Borotalco* (Talc Powder, 1982).

Beppe Grillo, from Genoa, is endowed with a gift for humor. After a short period of silence he returned triumphantly with his own television series. Though one has to make an effort to follow the fast rhythm of his delivery, which, together with a whining and complaining voice (with an added Genoese modulation), forms the signature of one of the most intelligent comedians performing today in Italy. He has the power to make people laugh at themselves and their problems and involves the audience in his performance. His latest work was a satirical show about Brazil in which he attacked the myth of Brazilian folklore with imitations, interviews, and monologues.

The humor of Francesco Nuti, a young comedian from Florence, is the most delicate. His character is usually the young and shy boy, unable to cause harm, who is always entangled in complicated love stories. Nuti's comical strength is in talking candidly with a childlike and lovable sincerity. In *Sono Contento* (I am glad, 1984, by Porzio) his girlfriend is abandoning him, but he tries to appear happy for her sake although he is underneath it all extremely nervous.

Maurizio Nichetti, the king of pantomime, is both actor in and director of films and television shows. Imagine the spirit of Keaton and Chaplin embodied in a short Milanese who has uncombed hair, rounded glasses, and a flowing mustache. His films have usually only a musical soundtrack; the rest is left to mimicry and images. The effect is inferior to that of the two American comedians and has a somewhat déjà vu quality to it, but good amusement is assured even for those who cannot speak a word of Italian.

The new comedian of Naples is Massimo Troisi. From cabaret he quickly made his way to directing his own films in which he is also the protagonist. He is the young and honest man without means who tries to build his own life in *Ricomincio da Tre* (Try again from three, 1981). There we see him beginning life anew from three, and not from zero as in the Italian expression, because in at least three things he was successful in his life.

I Gatti di Vicolo Miracoli are a trio of popular comedians from Verone. They are fans of Woody Allen, and they are the only comedians who are capable of creating in song, dance, and acting the rhythm of Mack Sennett's Keystone Cops with additional witty gags. One of the trio, Arturo Corso, is a teacher in the Cabaret School at the Derby in Milan, the first school of its kind in Italy.

Alberto Benigni is the most absent-minded modern comedian. He was discovered together with other comedians by Renzo Arbore, who has also directed many TV shows as well as two surrealistic films, *Il Papocchio* (The Muppet, 1981) and *FFSS* (1983), starring Benigni. Benigni's lyrical Tuscan accent adds another dimension to his comedy.

Last is the unique artist Nanni Moretti, who started out as a director and then became an actor, and is one of the most genial figures of this generation. His films are remarkable works, starting with the early 16mm black-and-white *Sono un Autarchico* (1977). His films are beautiful creations, amusing, irreverent X-rays of the youth in Italy as they pass from political engagement to avant-garde, to mystical experience or to integration in the establishment. From *Ecce Bombo* (Here is Bombo, 1980) to *Sogni d'Oro* (Golden Dreams, 1981, acclaimed at the Venice Film Festival) they are easily exportable movies. His latest effort, *Bianca* (1984), is a masterpiece. The hero is a seemingly normal young man who lives normally with only slight manias. His perversions and paranoia are revealed just at the end, when we are convinced that he is an ordinary good guy. Moretti deserves more than a few lines to encompass his talent; in 1986 he won the Silver Bear award at the Berlin Film Festival.

A new phenomenon has conquered Italian televiewers: the huge success (measured by the ratings) of purely humorous shows. One example is "Drive In"; another is the more popular, young, young show where cabaretists alternate in a frenetic rhythm. Between them Ezio Greggio and Gianfrance D'Angelo portray a great number of funny persons, and the program was sold even to networks outside Italy. One show draws the attention of sociologists, philosophers, and politicians (sometimes even Arab Terrorists). In 1985, Renzo Arbore, the most prolific and intelligent talent scout for comedians, created a funny, sharp, and lovely show entitled "Quelli della notte" (People of the Night). This show, in an apartment-like studio with unknown comedians and musicians, has glued millions of Italians to their TV sets every night for months from 10:30 to midnight. This show has become the first sociological phenomenon related to humor that involves the whole country. It has introduced new verbal expressions and idioms into the Italian language. Among other weird characters appearing in the show, one can mention Ferrini, a paradoxical caricature of the stereotyped communist. His saying "non capisco ma mi adeguo" (I don't understand, but I adjust myself) became so popular that it was used even by the prime minister. Pazzaglia is a professor of philosophy who makes laughter with all kinds of existential questions (taken seriously by many academics). Andy Lutto, who performed a funny Arab sheik, has been compelled to stop following the threats on his life by some Arab terrorists.

Contemporary Visual Humor

Among the cultivated public there is a demand for the higher-quality cartoons. There is an annual book called *Humor Graphic* which is a collection of the best works in the field. *Humor Graphic* combines good graphics with a humor that is philosophical and surrealistic. Each issue is presented, together with an exhibition of the original works, in the summer of Milan.

Over the years there have been many independent outlets for humorous cartoons. In the Bordighera Festival a comic strip or a cartoon is chosen for an annual prize. This festival has come down in recent years in quality and organization, leaving only the Marostica Festival in the springtime, which also has a section for international contributors.

There are also the strictly political cartoons appearing in daily newspapers as well as in the weekly magazines. For example, in *La Repubblica* every Wednesday there is a double spread of political cartoons on the major political topic of the week, under the title "Satyricon." The master of this field is Giorgio Forattini, who has a daily cartoon in *La Repubblica* and in *La Stampa*. He has published several collections of his work, and he makes appearances on television where he creates a cartoon before the cameras.

In 1971 the attempt to publish the American *Mad* magazine in Italian, after the success of the French effort, failed after a few years of agony. Obviously nobody enjoyed noninvolved humor, and the youth of Italy were engaged and did not want attention diverted from more serious matters. Moreover, *Mad* magazine was generally judged too "Yankee" in spite of some Italian artists' contributions, while the few fans cried out in protest against the irretrievable loss. In 1977 the quarterly *Help!* was created by the Visual Group, the best cartoonists of that period. Although only a few issues were published, there was a new atmosphere of imagination. Worth mentioning among the monthly collection of cartoons are *Il Mago*, *Linus*, and *Eureka*, the last two of which are still in good health. These monthlies were filed mostly with comic strips patterned after the *Peanuts* series by Charles Schulz. In *Eureka* among the best series are *Stormtruppen* by Bonvi about a hypothetical and ruined German Army, and the adventures of a wily wolf in *Lupo Alberto* by Silver. Another magazine worthy of attention is the monthly *Alan Ford*. Since 1970 its creators, Magnus and Bunker, have produced new missions for the TNT detective agency, the weirdest in New York City, all in a vein of surrealistic humor. The better early issues are still in print.

Among today's caricaturists, Barry Fantoni (b. 1940) is probably one of the best known, his talent being expressed in many media. He is a filmmaker and actor, theatre designer, thriller writer, and musician. His illustrations, cartoons, and caricatures have been regularly published in many European and American journals.

Giuseppe Zaccaris (Zac) is the unique guest artist of the Parisian *Le Canard enchaine*. He describes himself as "new feudal conversative liberatarian anarchist of the extreme left." He is always in opposition, and his humorous drawings have many times shocked the establishment. With *Satirix* he risked prison for "insult to president Pompidou." Some exemplaries of his monthly *L'Anamorfico* were published from 1984 till his death in 1985.

The young Carlo Tullio Altan, with his ironic, socially oriented cartoons in the weekly *Panorama* portrays fathers and sons, husbands and wives, or colleagues at work, showing how funny the lack of communication in our times can be. Tullio Pericoli (b. 1935), with his delicate and dreamy touch, comments in his magazine *L'Esspresso* on the week's main problem. His drawings, resembling those of Saul Steinberg, have been exhibited all over Italy.

Humorous Literature

If one wishes to have a general idea of whims, manias, occurrences, and myths of Italy in the eighties, then the books of Luca Goldoni, written in his uniquely precise style, are both instructive and amusing. They are easily recognizable in bookstores as their titles are typical figures of speech: *D' che ti mando io* (Say I am sending you, 1976), *Cioe* (1977), and *Dipende* (It depends, 1980), to name a few. Goldoni is a journalist for the daily *Corriere della Sera* (The Evening Courier); his analysis of daily life tends to be humorous, but he sometimes seems more like a moralizing schoolteacher than a humorist. In spite of this his books are very amusing; each chapter is like a short story on one theme. In his latest book, *Lei m'insegna* (You teach me, 1984), Goldoni takes a look at the Italians' summer, the army, the family therapies, and the Italian school system, all from the point of view of an open-minded father. He can be classified as a "humorist of the obvious"; he describes reality as it is, stressing that minimal quantity of paradox sufficient to unveil its absurdity. In the books of Paolo Villaggio, a film and television actor and writer, we are told the misfortunes of the average employee, Fantozzi, the unlucky victim of his superiors, colleagues, and of destiny in general (the stories are gloomy and sometimes grotesque). They are not masterpieces, but they were well received and inspired a film starring Villaggio.

Luciano De Crescenzo, an electrical engineer by profession, now a full-time writer, is the author of *Cosi Parlo Bellavista* (So spoke Bellavista, 1977), a candid report on the spirit of Naples today. He has conquered the Italian public and has appeared on television and radio as a chronicler of his city, Naples. De Crescenzo recounts wisely and wittily the prejudices, habits, and state of mind of the people who populate this many-colored city, living on high hopes while collapsing at the same time. In 1984, De Crescenzo published *Storia della Filosofia Antica* (History of Ancient Philosophy), a witty textbook dealing with ancient philosophy, and directed his first film, a fiction based in Naples.

Stefano Bennis is from a new generation of Italian humorists who have been raised on *Il Male* (The Pain). He is without doubt one of today's brightest and most fanciful writers. Benni has a page all to himself in the weekly magazine *Panorama* and contributes to the daily *Il Manifesto*. In one of his first works, the book *Bar Sport* (1976), Benni laughs at the football fanaticism of the simpleminded customers of a typical bar. With the wonderful *Non siamo Stati Noi* (It wasn't us, 1978) and *Spettacoloso* (Spectacular, 1981), Benni demonstrated his talents as a prolific and irreverent commentator of the ''hidden'' vices of people, especially of the younger generation. His first effort at fiction, *Terra* (Earth!, 1984), is a mocking science fiction tale and maybe indicates the arrival of an excellent writer with much to offer in the future.

Humor in Music

There are many singers who employ some humor or irony in their lyrics. Here we will mention only those that are considered specifically humorous.

The musical band called Squallor is a mystery: in their albums there are no credits, and their lyrics are pure nonsense, extremely funny, but sometimes rather vulgar. Many Italians suspect that behind this band are some of the most famous TV celebrities from Rome and Naples.

Skiantos is an odd band from Bologna and the musicians play rock music with nonsense lyrics. In 1977 they established the genre of Insane Rock (*rock dimenziale*), with a strong punk and blues influence. The results are savegely funny; their humor is based on the use of teenage slang and familiar places, which they then take to extremes, to the point of madness. The Skiantos band's concerts were once a legend for the happenings during performances. Now the members of the group concentrate mostly on their music.

UNIVERSAL FUNCTIONS OF HUMOR AND THE NATIONAL MANIFESTATIONS

Aggressive Humor

The development of cabaret humor created a need for the comic to interact with the public. Sometimes the easiest way was to attack the audience, and a certain dialogue developed. Many TV comics adopted the style, and the weapon of humor was well accepted. Aggressive humor is getting more sophisticated; cream pies are not so enjoyable anymore. In order to pass a message avoiding drama and anguish, humor can be, and often is, used in an aggressive way.

However, as we mentioned, the aggression is coated in a sophisticated message, so that laughter seems to be its main objective.

The best-known form of aggressive humor is the ethnic one. Since Italians are in general rather tolerant people, there is little ethnic humor directed against Jews, blacks, or Scottish people, the main targets of much European humor. Mostly, Italian ethnic humor is directed from one Italian group to another, the degree of aggression being therefore rather benign. For instance, the Genovese are targets of humor about stinginess; Sicilians, about "family honor" or the Mafia; Romans, about feasts; Napolitans, about the art of making a living; and the women of Bologna, about "special sex services." A special trait of these innerethnic jokes is that sometimes they are told by the "victim" group itself, making the aggression self-directed.

One professional category is the favorite target of aggresive humor (in addition to the usual ones, politicians, priests, and academics): the carabinieri, the police under the responsibility of the Minister of the Interior. There is a long tradition of humor directed against them, and the stereotype of the carabinieri as dumb jerks has made them the laughingstock of popular entertainment from puppet shows to the movies.

Sexual Humor

Sex is a frequent topic of popular humor. One can speak about sex in Italy, where in spite of the deep Catholicism, there is no puritanism. A special sexual humor is devoted to the south of the country where the family *onore* (honor) is sacred. In many jokes, stories, and even movies the figure of the *cornuto* (betrayed husband) and the situation of adultery are considered extremely funny. Scatological jokes are also rather popular, and they are used among contemporaries; a dirty joke would never be told by a nephew to his grandfather, who would be scandalized. In common conversations, during parties, no matter the social group, sexual jokes, even the most embarrassing, are rather popular.

Social Humor

Political satire in Italy has been one of the most widespread forms of humor in the postwar period: it is understandable, for during the fascist regime (1924–1945) any criticism, epecially humorous, was censored and persecuted. By the 1960s the number of political cartoonists and satirical writers was almost exhausted. This was a result also of the cooling down of the political atmosphere. This stagnation of political satire (but not of social humor) lasted until the years of the youth protests from 1968 to 1975. In this period, with the help of stencil machines and minimal financing, there were a number of new efforts at political satire. On the other hand, the intense political atmosphere seemed to make people ignore non-political forms of humor and satire, whose creators were called "indifferents." Not many in Italy subscribed to the slogan written on the walls of the Sorbonne University in Paris in May of 1968: "I am a Marxist, Groucho oriented." In 1968 only six editions of the delicious *Allucinogeno* (Hallucinogen) and the 1971 short-lived effort *Ca Balla* (Dance Street) succeeded in presenting a large concentration of good left-oriented political humor. Cartoons and humorous articles appear in many newspapers, but one cannot find one magazine that has managed to assemble them together.

In 1978 an offset pamphlet called *Wow* was published by a group calling itself the Metropolitan Indians. Funny young people dressed and painted as redskins, they invaded the streets of boredom created by a serious approach to policy. The Metropolitan Indians howled and laughed at the young political leaders, at the pale students of the middle class, at terrorists and bureaucrats, in short at all who took themselves too seriously. They established the Fifth International, the International of nonsense and mockery.

In the same year, a successful weekly magazine of political and social satirical cartoons was born in Rome. Young people with a flippant tongue and new ideas wrote and drew for the issues of this magazine, which was called *Il Male* (the evil). The articles, jokes, and gags were stamped with a black humor, without euphemisms, that mocked and bantered both figures and events of political and criminal life, show business, and other, more mundane walks of life. Sometimes *Il Male* created political "affairs" and had many complaints lodged against its staff. All the same, it held on to an image of being congenial to all views, and for some years it enjoyed a large wave of sympathy.

On one occasion, the death of Pope John Paul I, the staff of *Il Male* amused themselves by devoting the whole issue to the Pope and his "mysterious" premature death, presenting some odious and most wicked hypotheses. Among the many clever ideas and masterpeits of *Il Male* are the wonderful counterfeits of prestigious newspaper headlines. There was quite a panic when *Il Male* was published as *Corriere della Sera* (the largest circulation in Italy), announcing the outbreak of World War III, or when as *La Repubblica* it announced a steep rise in petrol prices which resulted in a rush by thousands of unsuspecting readers to the gas stations.

Il Male was closed in 1982, and the staff split up and went to many other publications. The major offspring was a new monthly review called *Frigidaire*. This is a magazine of visual and musical avant-garde edited by Vincenzo Sparagna. It is more professional than its predecessor in its use of articles and photographs from all over the world. The same old irony remains, mixed with a look to postmodernism and the new wave in art and music. The cartoons are reminiscent of video-music clips, among which Rank-Xerox is the most impressive one.

Humor as a Defense Mechanism

Italians in general are rather critical of themselves. As a consequence, self-disparaging humor is flourishing. In spite of the regional differences, Italy is a united country, everyone feeling proud of being Italian (with a few exceptions, however: some South Tirolers who'd rather be Austrian and the Sardinians who don't appreciate the carelessness of the government concerning their specific problems).

With the exception of the fascism interlude, Italians do not percieve themselves as fighters, and during their history they were more often the conquered than the victors. They accept their faults and are ready to laugh at themselves. Two of the greatest film comedians, Nuti and Troisi, represent characters that become autocritical just when they face the worst conditions. The public loves them.

The use of the many regional dialects in humor brings a perspective of loving self-identification.

Intellectual Humor

With the long tradition of sophisticated humor from Boccaccio to Pirandello, one should not be surprised at the popularity of intellectual humor in Italy. Italian humor is considered by many European scholars to be the avant-garde of absurd humor (as noted by Ionesco). In the mass media, intellectual humor is more and more appreciated, and today's comedians study the work of humorists abroad. Woody Allen, the Marx Brothers, and Neil Simon are adored but not directly imitated. They are seen as people with the same passion and the same sense of humor as the Italians.

The nonsense intellectual humor has a great "king of comedy" in today's Italy: Roberto Benigni. The son of a manual worker, he had his first success in nonsense humor in a little town in the province of Tuscany. Later, Benigni became famous on TV, mocking a film reviewer.

CONCLUSION

Analyzing humor is similar to explaining a joke: the result remains always disappointing, and the risk is in not taking into consideration important pieces of the puzzle that is humor. The aim of this chapter is not to exhaust the phenomenon of humor in Italy, and therefore for further reading we recommend the following works. The list is short, but it seems that this is a result of Italians' preference for enjoying humor rather than dealing with it academically. No matter the reason, there is still no systematic study of Italian humor.

HUMOR JOURNALS IN ITALY (IN PARENTHESES THEIR YEAR OF FIRST PUBLICATION)

Frigidaire monthly (1982)

Frizzer monthly (1984)

Humor Graphic annual (1960)

Mad monthly (1971–1973) new release since 1985

Satyricon—each Wednesday (since 1963) in the daily *La Repubblica*

Tango (1986)—each Monday in the daily *L'Unita*

Tempi Supplementari monthly (1984)

There are no national societies or organizations focused on humor.

REFERENCES

Altieri Biagi, M. L. (1980) *La lingua in scena* (Language on scene). Bologna: Zanichelli.

Bartoli, F. (1976) *I comici italiani* (The Italian comedians). Rome: Instituto Enciclopedica Italiano.

———. (1978) *Notizie istoriche de' comici italiani* (Historical notes on Italian comedians). Firenze: Forni.

Bertolucci, A. (1960) *Umoristi dell'Ottocento* (The humorists of the eighteenth century. Milan: Garzanti.

———. (1967) *Umoristi del Novencento* (The humorists of the nineteenth century). Milan: Garzanti.

Bisicchia, A. (1978) *Aspetti de teatro comico del Novecento* (Aspects of the comic theatre in the nineteenth century). Milan: Ghiosoni.

Branca, V., and Mangini, N. (1980) *Studi goldoniani*. (Studies on Goldoni). Venice and Rome: Instituto Collectivo di Cultura.

Calvesi, M. (1967) *Il futurismo* (Futurism). In *Arte Moderni*, vol. 5 Milan: Fabri.

Campanile, A. (1964) *Trattato delle barzellette. Repertiorio, divisione per materie, enciclopedia alafabetica e storica* (The book of jokes. Repertory, subjects, alphabetical and historical encyclopedia). Milan: Unicolpi.

Cicita, A. (1984) *Teorie di comico* (Theories of comedy). Milan: Unicolpi.

Coffey, M. (1976) *Roman Satire*. London: Macmillan.

Colangeli, M. (1982) *Carnevale: luoghi, maschere, riti e protagonisti* (Carnival: places, masks, rites and protagonists). Rome: Laoside.

Cosimi, M., and Cosimi, S. (1985) *Ottant'anni di umorismo in Italia* (Eighty years of humor in Italy). Milan: Spada.

De Castris, L. A. (1962) *Storia di Pirandello* (The story of Pirandello). Bari: Laterza.

Deroblia, M., and Guerrier, V. (1929) *Le rire dans le soleil: les humoristes Italiens* (Laughter in the sun: the Italian humorists). Paris: Baudiniere.

Di Giammateo, F. (1954) *I filmi comici italiani* (The Italian comic films). Milan: Rivista del cinema Italiano, no. 3.

Dimsdale, M. S. (1935) *A History of Latin Literature*. New York: Appleton.

Dorigo, F. (1960) *La commedia all'italiana* (Italian comedy). Rome: Rivista del cinematografo, no. 3.

Fanciulli, G. (1913) *L'umorismo. Note di estetica psicologica* (Humor—notes of aesthetic psychology). Firenze: Cultura Filosofica.

Feaver, W., ed. (1981) *Masters of Caricature*. New York: Alfred A. Knopf.

Ferrante, L. (1961) *I comici goldoniani 1721–1960* (The Goldonian comics). Capelli: Rocca S. Casciano.

Ferroni, G. (1974) *Il comico nelle teorie contemporanee* (The comic in contemporary theory). Rome: Bulzoni.

Getto, G. (1972) *Vita di forme e forme di vita nel Decameron* (Life and forms of life in Decameron). Torino: Petrini.

Gianeri, E., and Isca, E. (1977) *Professione unmorista* (Profession: humorist). Milan: Visual.

Goldsterin, J. H., and McGhee, P. E. (1976) *Psicologia dello humor: prospettive teoriche e quastioni empiriche* (Psychology of humor: theoretical outlooks and empirical questions). Milan: Angeli.

Grotjahn, M. (1981) *Saper ridere: psicologia dell'umorismo* (Know how to laugh: psychology of humor). Milan: Longanesi.

Levi, E. (1958) *Il comico* (The comic). Genoa: Formiggini.

Manzoni, C. (1964) *Gli ani verdi del Bertoldo* (Bertoldo's green years). Milan: Rizzoli.

Marconi, E. (1975) *Problematica generale del' comico' a teatro* (The general problem of the comic in theatre). Milan: Vita e Pensiero.

Marroti, F. (1978) *Comedia e comici nel Seicento* (Comedy and comedians in the sixteenth century). Rome: Bulzoni.

Massarani, T. (1911) *Storia e fisiologia dell'arte del ridere* (History and physiology of the art of laughter). Firenze: Le Monnier.

Maturanzo, S. (1957) *Tradizioni de Napoli* (Napolitan traditions). Naples: Cassella.

Montanelli, I. (1985) *Leo Longanesi*, Milan: Longanesi.

Mosca, G. (1966) *Umoristi Italiani* (Italian humorists). Milan: Editalia.

Musacchio, E. (1985) *Il riso nelle poetiche rinasciameali* (Laughter of Renaissance poets). Bologna: Cappelli.

Musco, A. (1982) *Il cinema comico meridionale* (The comic meridional movies). Mari: Dedalo.

Napolitano, R. (1986) *Comedia all'italiana* (Italian comedy). Rome: Gangemi.

Nicastro, G. (1966) *Goldone et il teatro del Settecento* (Goldoni and the sevententh century theatre). Bari: Laterza.

Olbrechts-Tyetca, L. (1977) *Il comico del discorso* (The comic speech). Milan: La Scuola.

Olivieri, A. (1946) *Fragmmenti della comedia greca e del mimo in Sicilia e nell Magna Grecia* (Fragments of Greek comedy and mime in Sicily and greater Greece). Naples:Libreria Scientifica.

Pandolfi, V. (1958) *La commedia dell'arte*. Firenze: Sansoni.

Pirandello, L. (1974) *On Humor*. London: Chapel Hill.

Ratano, F. (1976) *La satira italiana nel dopoguerra* (Italian satire after the war). Firenze: Sansoni.

Spalding, H. D. (1980) *Treasure of Italian Folklore and Humor*. New York: Grover.

Valeri, M., and Genovesi, G. (1973) *Comico, creativita, educazione* (The comic, creativity and education). Rimini: Guaraldi.

Verdone, M. (1950) *Umanesime del comico* (Humanism of the comic). Rome: Sequenze.

Volpi, D. (1983) *Didattica dell'umorismo* (Didactics of humor). Milan: Scuola.

Zanotto, P. (1959) *Il comico nel cinema italiato dai "muti" di Polidor e Cretinetti ai "parlati" di Toto e Rascel* (The comic in the Italian cinema from the "silents" of Polidor and Cretinetti to the "talkies" of Toto and Rascel). Milan: Primi Piani.

Ziv, A. (1981) *Perche no l'umorismo? La sua funzione nello sviluppo del pensiero e dei rapporti umani* (Why not humor? Its function in the development of thought and humor relations). Milan: Emme.

7   DON L. F. NILSEN AND
ALLEEN PACE NILSEN
WITH KEN DONELSON*

Humor in the United States

BACKGROUND

Pictographs left on stone walls, anthropological evidence of games and play, and stories handed down orally all indicate that the one million native Americans living on the North American continent in what is now the United States had a sense of play and humor. But for practical reasons, this account will begin in the 1600s when settlers from the Old World came to establish colonies in the New World.

These early immigrants had little to smile about. In 1607 (about the same time Shakespeare was writing *Macbeth*), 105 Englishmen came to Jamestown, Virginia. Conditions were so bad that at the end of the first year only 36 were still alive. Further north in Plymouth, only 50 of the 102 who arrived on the *Mayflower* survived the winter. Spanish settlers were somewhat more successful in the

*Ken Donelson, professor of English at Arizona State University, selected the motion pictures, plays, and television shows to be included.

Southwest, Florida, and California. In the next decades, Dutch traders, Puritans, Swedes, Finns, and Frenchmen came so that in 1690, 214,000 settlers lived in America. By 1770 this number had increased tenfold to 2,205,000, with the French controlling a huge fur-trading empire in the middle of the continent. The following characteristics of American humor can be traced directly back to influences from these early circumstances.

An anti-intellectual bent: The settlers found that book learning was not enough to save them from starvation, inclement weather, and diseases. To keep from perishing took a healthy dose of good luck combined with creative problem solving and hard work. Out of their experiences and those of their descendants, grew a strong feeling for "Yankee ingenuity" and the "great American work ethic." These attitudes made it fair game to make fun of the newcomer, the greenhorn, the poor fellow who arrived with book learning but no common sense, the one that Benjamin Franklin described as "so learned that he could name a horse in nine languages. So ignorant, that he bought a cow to ride on" (Blair and McDavid, 1978, p. xii).

A heavy use of exaggeration: The size of the American continent, its diversity, and unusual geographic features inspired awe in those who came to visit. In spite of the hardships they had to endure, its explorers and settlers were caught up in optimistic dreams about their new country and what it had to offer. Generations followed the example of the early Spaniards who reported seeing cities of gold, fountains of youth, and mountains of treasure. Partly out of defensiveness, the people who chose to come to America felt an obligation to prove their superiority. They were like Benjamin Franklin, who, when British critics claimed that the colonies could not produce enough wool to provide each inhabitant with a pair of stockings, replied:

The very Tails of the American Sheep are so laden with Wool, that each has a little Car or Waggon on four little wheels, to support and keep it from trailing on the ground. (Cohen, 1978, p. 250)

Making fun of ethnic minorities: Folklore has always been filled with stories about noodleheads, simpletons, and foolish Jacks. In many cultures such stories have been attributed to people from a specified geographical area, but in America this trend is exaggerated. One reason is that the lack of a firmly established class system means that all individuals can aspire to rise in the social structure. However, climbing the ladder of success means passing other people. Joke tellers lift themselves up by putting others down whether on the basis of racial or geographical origin, religion, or occupation.

The emphasis on racial origins goes back to the very beginning when settlers from Europe came and took away the Indians' lands and thereby their means of earning a livelihood. The settlers salved their consciences by thinking of the Indians as less than human. Thinking of people of color as not having souls was a convenient rationalization for taking advantage not only of "red men" but also of "blacks" brought from Africa to be slaves and of the "yellow men" brought from Asia to wash the "white man's" clothes and build his railroads.

Racist humor has been popular because it makes the joke teller feel smart and therefore superior. For the majority, it relieves tensions and fears over whether the newcomers will compete for the best housing and jobs. In some ways it keeps these dreaded events from occurring because by passing on the prejudices of one generation to another it keeps minorities "in their place."

Dialect as deliciously funny: During the early years of the United States, British visitors would go home predicting the sure death of the Queen's English. Settlers came to English-speaking America with their own languages: French, Spanish, Danish, German, Norwegian, Swedish, Dutch, Yiddish, Russian, or one of a dozen other languages. Never had there been such a mass conversion to a new language, but such conformity did not come about without some accompanying stress. As Walter Blair and Raven McDavid point out, in the 1800s "school marms and dictionary makers were stuffy and stern about spelling, elegant diction, and grammar; therefore, assaults on all three seemed both naughty and funny" (1983, p. xxiii). The result was that the common folk in the 1800s latched onto unlearned speech for their literary pleasure, taking pride in its creativity and its distinctive American, as opposed to British, flavor.

Wit as a way of enforcing social norms: Immigrants came from countries where their behavior had been controlled not only by laws but by rigid class structures, state religions, centuries of tradition, and pervasive economic conditions. They came to the New World in search of freedom, but there is an inherent contradiction between the idea of personal freedom and the blending into a unified society of millions of people coming from countries as different as Finland, China, England, and Armenia. When the behavior of groups or individuals clashed too strongly with the rest of the society, humor was often used as the sandpaper to smooth edges and round off the sharp corners.

For example, in 1846, when members of the newly founded Mormon church went west to Utah and began practicing polygamy, people throughout the rest of the country gave their leader, Brigham Young, such contemptuous nicknames as Bigamy Young, King Brigham, the Sultan of the Wasatch, the Mormon Bull, the Incestuous Saint, the Puissant Procreator, and the husband to a multitude and father to a nation. The purpose of such humor was to intimidate and censure through mockery. Artemus Ward said that Brigham Young "loved not wisely, but two-hundred well," "The pretty girls in Utah mostly marry Young," "Brigham's religion is singular and his wives are plural," and "Out in Utah they practice Bigamy, Trigamy, and Brighamy" (Robertson and Hingston, p. 130).

In 1896, when polygamy was outlawed and Utah became the forty-fifth state in the Union, these jokes lost their sting and faded into historical quaintness because they were no longer needed to enforce social norms (McKay, 1983).

TRADITIONAL FORMS AND EXPRESSIONS IN HUMOR
BEFORE THE TWENTIETH CENTURY

Popular Forms

In New England villages the local tavern became the center of the community, a place where jokes and stories were exchanged. In Boston the first tavern opened in 1634. Toys and dolls were for sale in both Boston and Salem by the mid–1600s, and by the early 1700s the Bowery near New York City had several taverns and theatres. Twenty-five thousand pounds was spent to import rum in 1728. A popular ditty went:

> There's but one Reason I can Think,
> Why People ever cease to drink,
> Sobriety the Cause is not,
> Nor Fear of being deam'd a Sot,
> But if Liquor can't be got.

British soldiers sang a playful song making fun of the Americans. It was about Yankee Doodle Dandy, who with "all the girls was handy. . . . went to town, riding on a pony, stuck a feather in his cap and called it macaroni." When American troops adopted it as a marching tune, it lost its satirical sting and was played when the British troops surrendered at Yorktown.

In 1774, partly as an austerity measure and partly out of religious objections, the Continental Congress banned horse racing, cockfighting, gambling, and theatrical performances. The attitude that drama was wicked or at least frivolous lasted long after the war, but in 1787 *The Contrast* by Bostonian Royall Tyler opened at John Street Theater in New York City. An immediate success, this first American comedy ridiculed aristocratic values while extolling the rustic virtues of its Yankee hero.

In 1790 Benjamin Franklin died, and 20,000 people, the largest crowd ever to gather in what was now the United States, came to Christ's Church in Philadelphia for Franklin's funeral. Much of his popularity was due to the wit and humor of his almanacs, which for 25 years had been providing such witty advice as the following:

Experience keeps a dear school, yet Fools will learn in no other.
Where there's marriage without love, there will be love without marriage.

In 1818 Washington Irving's story *Rip Van Winkle* mentioned the bowling of pins as a popular pastime. The game had probably been popular for some time. In the 1820s football developed in American colleges, first as a form of hazing in which the freshmen kicked the ball around and the sophomores kicked the freshmen around. But by 1873 football was so well established that President

White of Cornell University went down in history when he refused permission for a game by saying that he would not permit 30 men to travel 400 miles to agitate a bag of wind.''

In 1823 the first American minstrel show was performed. Actor Edwin Forrest blackened his face to play the part of Negro Ruban in *Tailor in Distress*, a farce by Sol Smith. Minstrel shows in which white actors pretended to be black actors, singers, and dancers were popular for the next several decades.

Laughing at blacks and at other ''foreigners'' was probably reassuring to many Americans because even though they or their parents were immigrants who spoke with accents, they weren't as ''foreign'' as those being laughed at. One of the most popular jokes of the 1890s was about a Chinese man who, when he saw the cable cars that replaced the horse-drawn trolleys in San Francisco, said ''No pushee, no pullee, but goee like hellee allee samee.''

In 1895 occurred a little-noticed event that would influence humor all over the world. The first movies were made with the first public showing taking place on April 23, 1896, at Koster and Bial's Music Hall in New York. The film included a humorous fight between a tall, thin boxer and a short, fat boxer. The *New York Times* acclaimed the exhibition ''all wonderfully real and singularly exhilarating.''

Humor in the Literary and Performing Arts

On April 30, 1598, the first theatrical performance was given in America. The play, a Spanish comedy about an expedition of soldiers, was presented near what is today El Paso. Like this play, much of the humor enjoyed by the colonists was imported from England and Europe. But in 1647 a truly amusing American book was published. It was Nathaniel Ward's *The Simple Cobbler of Aggawam*. It was supposed to be the reflections of a humble shoemaker, but it was really an attack on current customs and fashions.

In 1666 New Englanders were shocked by another humorous book, George Alsop's *A Character of the Province of Maryland*, with such statements as ''Herds of deer are as numerous in this province of Maryland as cuckolds can be in London, only their horns are not so well dressed and tipped with silver'' (Carruth, 1979, p. 26).

In 1714 Robert Hunter, governor of New York, published *Androboros*, the first play written in the colonies. It was a political satire lampooning the senate and Hunter's lieutenant governor. No record of its being produced exists, but the written version did amuse readers. In 1725 Nathaniel Ames, a Massachusetts physician, published the *Astronomical Diary and Almanack*. It was extremely popular and is thought to have been the prototype for the almanacs that Benjamin Franklin published between 1732 and 1757. Typical entries by Ames included these bits of advice for winter:

> Ladies, take heed, Lay down your fans,
> And handle well Your warming pans.

> This cold, and uncomfortable weather
> Makes Jack and Jill lie close together.

On December 21, 1767, one of the first tall tales appeared in the *Boston Evening Post*. The closing line of the story was "This is a fact." The editor must have felt that such a line was needed after telling about a hunter who shot three mooses, one being ten feet high and ten feet long. On the way home the man also happened to kill a wildcat.

In 1809 Washington Irving, under the name of Diedrich Knickerbocker, published the first American humorous book to impress Europe and England as literature. It was a tongue-in-cheek history of the Dutch in America entitled *History of New York* and became a best-seller.

Social satire as a comedy form attained new prestige in 1845 when Anna Cora Mowatt's *Fashion* was produced. It was the story of a newly rich man with a social-climbing wife. For contrast, Mowatt included foreign characters, a technique that was followed by other playwrights including Harry Watkins with his 1851 *Nature's Nobleman*, Mrs. Sydney Bateman with her 1857 *The Golden Calf*, and William Henry Hurlbert with his 1858 *Americans in Paris*.

Two major trends characterized American literature of the 1800s. First was the exaggeration of the heroes. Albert Marchwardt and Joseph Dillard explained how in most countries storytellers focused on "the little people," dwarves, elves, fairies, etc. But Americans have been so busy doing big jobs that they have never taken time off to let their minds play with the tiny folk who have magic powers. At the end of a hard day's work the American cowboys or miners or lumberjacks or apple pickers have had their fun out of making up stories about men who could do jobs that could just not be done, and in an impossibly short time with one hand tied behind them. The dreams of American workers, naturally enough, have never been delicate, exquisite, or polite—like most fairy stories. They have been big and powerful, and a strong wind is always blowing behind them (Marckwardt and Dillard, 1980, p. 109).

Paul Bunyan could cut down two trees with a single blow of his double-bladed axe, one with the chop, and the other with the return to his shoulder. Strap Buckner could knock down bulls with one hit of his iron pestle. Mike Fink could jump across rivers. John Henry could carry a bale of cotton under each arm and two on his head, and could drive steel better than a steam-powered machine. But Pecos Bill was best of all. He once dug out the Grand Canyon just to get water to his stock. On his gravestone it reads: "Here lies Pecos Bill. He always lied and always will. He once lied loud. He now lies still."

The second characteristic, according to Blair and McDavid in their collection *The Mirth of a Nation: America's Great Dialect Humor* (1983), is that Americans between 1830 and 1900 savored the writings of dialectal humorists. They read their stories in almanacs, newspapers, and magazines. They pasted them in scrapbooks, mailed them to their friends, and quoted them from memory. During the dark nights of the Civil War, Abraham Lincoln was said to read them to relieve tension. He especially appreciated the writings of David R. Locke, who made political observations through the personna of Petroleum V. Nasby, an uneducated, backwoods preacher. Lincoln increased the prestige of the genre by retelling many of the stories and even adapting their style into his public statements as when in the election campaign of 1864 he cautioned voters against swapping horses while crossing the stream.

British critics questioned the poor taste and the sacrificing of "graver considerations" of the American dialectal writers, but at the same time they credited the stories with being the first truly American contribution to the world's literature. After the Civil War, the best of these authors became fairly prosperous, presenting comic lectures, writing syndicated newspaper columns, and publishing best-selling books.

The most famous, of course, was Mark Twain, who went west looking for gold and instead became a newspaper reporter. When he published "The Celebrated Jumping Frog of Calaveras County" in 1865, he became instantly famous. Four years later he used a tour of Europe and the Near East as subject matter for *Innocents Abroad*, which poked great fun at the Old World and the sentimentalism attached to a trip to Europe. In 1872 he published *Roughing It*, a hilarious collection of tall tales and exaggerations about life among Nevada miners. *The Adventures of Tom Sawyer* was published in 1876 and that same year was banned from the public library in Denver and from the children's room in the Brooklyn Library. *Huckleberry Finn*, published in 1884, was even more controversial and has remained so to this day, partly because of readers' varying reactions to the inclusion of the runaway slave, Jim as a major character.

Blair and McDavid classify the dialectal writers as "Rustic Yankees," who specialized in understatement (Seba Smith, Thomas Chandler Haliburton, James Russell Lowell, and Frances Miriam Whitcher); "Frontier Storytellers," who specialized in exaggeration (Hamilton C. Jones, James Kirke Paulding, Thomas Bangs Thorpe, Henry Clay Lewis, Johnson Jones Hooper, Phillip B. January, John S. Robb, William Tappan Thompson, William C. Hall, William Penn Branan, Harden E. Taliaferro, and George Washington Harris); "Funny Fellows," who would play with words and say anything to attract attention (Charles Farrar Browne; Charles H. Smith; David Ross Locke, who wrote as Petroleum V. Nasby; Henry Wheeler Shaw, who wrote as Josh Billings; and Finley Peter Dunne); and "Local Colorists" who were people- and situation-oriented (Harriet Beecher Stowe, George Washington Cable, Joel Chandler Harris, F. Hopkinson Smith, Mary E. Wilkins Freeman, Charles W. Chesnutt, James Whitcomb Riley, Alfred Henry Lewis, and Edward Noyes Westcott).

American author Bret Harte has credited this nineteenth-century humor—"as distinct and original as the country and civilization in which it was developed"—with first breaking the literary bonds that British writers held over Americans. He described it as presenting not only the speech, but "the habits of thought of a people or locality. . . . By degrees, it developed character with incident, often, in a few lines, gave a striking photograph of a community or a section, but always reached its conclusion without an unnecessary word'' (Blair and Mc-David, 1983, p. ix).

Humor in the Visual Arts

In 1754 rumors of a possible war with France inspired Benjamin Franklin to draw what has been called the first American cartoon. It was a picture of a snake cut into parts, the head labeled New England and the other parts labeled with the initials of the rest of the colonies. The caption was "Unite or Die." Franklin used a picture because many of the colonists could not read. The cartoon, published in the *Pennsylvania Gazette*, became a rallying cry for those wanting a federal government as opposed to independent colonies.

Franklin, a man of many talents, has quite rightly been labeled the father of America's humorous literature. As the country's first postmaster general, he founded a system that enabled publishers to get their magazines and newspapers out to the public. His example of including humor and drawings in his own papers and almanacs was followed by other publishers and continues to this day in the mass media.

Throughout the eighteenth and nineteenth centuries, cartoons were published in almanacs and in satirical newspapers such as *Leslie's Illustrated Weekly* and *Harper's Weekly*. And by the late 1800s following the Civil War, cartoons became an established part of regular newspapers. In the 1884 presidential election cartoons were credited with winning the election for Grover Cleveland. By the early 1900s every major city had its own newspaper, and political cartoons became influential in local as well as national politics.

The most famous political cartoonist of the 1800s was Thomas Nast. His 1871 cartoons about Boss Tweed and the Tammany Hall corruption in New York City so infuriated Tweed that he ordered "Stop them damn pictures! I don't care so much what papers write about me. My constituents can't read. But, damn it, they can see the pictures!" Tweed is said to have offered Nast a half million dollars to "study art in Europe" (Robinson, 1984, p. 20). Nast refused, and ironically it was Tweed who eventually fled to Europe. However, a Spanish official recognized him because of one of Nast's drawings, and Tweed was arrested and sent back to the United States. In a more playful vein, Thomas Nast was the first one to draw the elephant that today stands as the symbol for the Republican party and to draw the American interpretation of Santa Claus (Robinson, 1974, p. 21).

In 1863 Frank Leslie immigrated from England and established the first American graphic humor magazines: *Budget of Fun*, *Comic Monthly*, and *Phunny Phellow*. The *San Francisco Wasp* and *Wild Oats* were soon competing. *Puck* was founded in 1877 by Joseph Keppler, an immigrant from Vienna. *Judge* was founded in 1885 and *Life* in 1883. These publications, along with companies such as Currier and Ives, which printed comic lithographs, provided a medium for such artists as A. B. Frost, C. Jay Taylor, Palmer Cox, E. W. Kemble,

T. S. Sullivant, Walt Kuhn, S. D. Ehrart, Walt McDougall, James Montgomery Flagg, and Charles Dana Gibson.

At the turn of the century a new art form was born in America. It was the comic strip, described by William Laas in the *Saturday Review of Literature* as ''one of the liveliest cultural offshoots of our slam-bang civilization'' (Robinson, 1974, p. 12). Newspaper giants Joseph Pultizer and William Randolph Hearst had a bitter rivalry, and in 1893 Pulitzer bought a color press with which he intended to print great artworks for his Sunday paper. However, the technology was not refined enough for artwork, and the editor encouraged Pulitzer to try using the press for comic art. Pulitzer brought in a relatively unknown artist, R. F. Outcault, who drew *Down in Hogan's Alley*, in a city setting filled with children, animals, and squalor. One of the street urchins was a baldheaded kid dressed in a floppy shirt. In what was almost a printer's accident, the pressman tested out a new ink on the floppy shirt. ''That Sunday, a splash of pure, vivid yellow attracted every eye to Outcault's cartoon. The *Yellow Kid*, as he was soon known, was born and with him an indigenous American art form that is now read by more than 200,000,000 people every day, nearly 75 billion a year, making its authors and graphic artists the most widely read and seen in the world'' (Robinson, 1974, p. 12).

The *Yellow Kid* was such a star attraction that Hearst bribed Outcault away from Pulitzer. Pulitzer offered more money and got him back, and then when he again lost out to Hearst, Pulitzer hired artist George Luks to continue drawing *The Kid*. The *Yellow Kid*'s appearance in both newspapers gave rise to the term ''yellow journalism'' to refer to unscrupulous press practices.

With the success of *The Yellow Kid*, editors began looking for other characters who could be the susbject of a continuing story. Hearst had brought back from Germany Wilhelm Busch's *Max und Moritz*, stories of two young pranksters. A staff artist, Rudolph Dirks, used them as the basis of the *Katzenjammer Kids*, Hans and Fritz, who made their debut in December 1897.

Dirks made his stories revolve around the actions of the characters instead of having them be observers of society as Outcault's were. He added to the humor by giving them German accents, and most importantly he developed the speaking balloon, which gave a feeling of immediacy and enabled him to show the thoughts and speech of characters, inanimate as well as animate.

DEVELOPMENT OF HUMOR IN THE EARLY TWENTIETH CENTURY

Popular Forms

Writing humorous limericks was in vogue at the turn of the century. Newspapers printed hundreds of limericks inspired by:

> There once was a man from Nantucket
> Who kept all his cash in a bucket;

> But his daughter, named Nan,
> Ran away with a man,
> And as for the bucket, Nantucket.

In 1905 "Everybody Works but Father" was a popular song relating to people's fears that with women working there wouldn't be enough jobs to go around. As skirts became shorter, a frequently told joke was about a policeman asking a little lost boy why he didn't keep hold of his mother's skirt. The child's answer: "I cou-cou-couldn't reach it."

Expressions from this period that found their way into American English include Theodore Roosevelt's 1912 way of announcing his candidacy, "My hat is in the ring," statesman Thomas R. Marshall's 1915 comment during a tedious Senate debate "What this country really needs is a good fivecent cigar," and the 1917 expression "Pie in the Sky," which came from a hobo folk song adapted into a labor movement song. In 1923 opponents in Louisiana coined the phrase "It won't be Long now" to combat the political threat of a 30-year-old upstart, Huey Long, who was running for governor. He came in third in the election, but the phrase brought him to the attention of the public and he went on to become a political institution.

Among the songs that are still famous because of their playful lyrics is "Yes, We Have No Bananas" from the 1920s and "Mairzy Doats" (translated into "Mares eat oats") from the 1940s. Best-selling books that were popular at least partially because of their humor include Irving Bacheller's *Eben Holden* (1900), Owen Wister's *The Virginian* (1902), O. Henry's collection of short stories *The Four Million* (1906), Betty Smith's *A Tree Grows in Brooklyn* (1943), and Marion Hargrove's early 1940s *See Here, Private Hargrove*, humorous sketches which sold over two and a half million copies.

Humor in the Literary and Performing Arts

Humor writer Robert C. Benchley died in 1945, but in the 1980s nine of his books were still in print. He made people see the funny side of everyday life. Representative titles include *The Early Worm* (1927) and *My Ten Years in a Quandary* (1936). Ogden Nash, perhaps the most often quoted American poet, began publishing his humorous verse in the 1930s. A classic example: "Candy is dandy / but liquor is quicker." Nash was a frequent contributor to the *New Yorker*, a sophisticated magazine founded in 1925 by Harper & Brothers. Whitney Darrow, Jr., Helen E. Hokinson, William Steig, and Charles Addams are among its well-known cartoonists. E. B. White, James Thurber, and Clarence Day were early contributors of essays. The play *Life with Father* was based on sketches that Day wrote for the *New Yorker*.

An American contribution to the entertainment of the world was the development of the musical comedy, a blending of a humorous play and a light opera, soon adapted to film and shown around the world. Popular early musical comedies included *No! No! Nanette* by Vincent Youmans (1923), *A Connecticut Yankee* by Richard Rodgers and Lorenz Hart (1927), and *Pins and Needles* (1937), produced by a group of garment workers in New York with its most popular song being "Sing Me a Song of Social Significance."

Some of the most successful American plays (comedies, satires, and farces) are listed below:

Early Twentieth Century

Langdon Mitchell, *The New York Idea* (1906)

The Twenties

George S. Kaufman and Edna Ferber, *The Royal Family* (1927)

Ben Hecht and Charles MacArthur, *The Front Page* (1928)

The Thirties

Moss Hart and George S. Kaufman, *You Can't Take It with You* (1936)

Moss Hart and George S. Kaufman, *The Man Who Came to Dinner* (1939)

William Saroyan, *The Time of Your Life* (1939)

The Forties

James Thurber and Elliott Nugent, *The Male Animal* (1940)

Joseph Kesselring, *Arsenic and Old Lace* (1941)

Thornton Wilder, *The Skin of Our Teeth* (1942)

Garson Kanin, *Born Yesterday* (1946)

The Fifties

Jo Swerling and Abe Burrows (music and lyrics by Frank Loesser), *Guys and Dolls* (1950)

John Patrick, *The Teahouse of the August Moon* (1952)

William Inge, *Bus Stop* (1955)

Ira Levin, *No Time for Sergeants* (1955)

George Axelrod, *The Seven Year Itch* (1956)

William Saroyan, *The Cave Dwellers* (1957)

Almost all these plays were made later into successful movies.

Humor in the Visual Arts

By 1900 comic strips were an expected part of every major newspaper, at least on Sundays. Cartoonists had freedom to experiment with styles and subject matter, several drawing more than one strip. In 1902 Outcault created the *Buster Brown* strip, which became even more famous than *The Yellow Kid*, partly because in an entrepreneurial venture he set up a booth at the St. Louis Exposition and sold commercial rights to advertisers.

Common themes in comic strips of the early 1900s were immigrant and racial humor. One of Outcault's experiments was *Lil' Mose* about a black man. Today, it looks terribly prejudicial but for its time was considered a sympathetic portrayal. In 1905 James Swinnerton produced a comic strip about a black man named Sam, who while working in menial positions would end up seeing his "betters" appearing foolish. He would laugh and at the end of each strip be punished, usually kicked or struck, but he continued laughing.

In 1907 *Mutt and Jeff* by Bud Fisher was the first strip to run horizontally across the pages of a newspaper and the first to appear as a true daily, six times a week. Fisher was also the first cartoonist to copyright his characters and the first to become wealthy.

Jerry Robinson (1974, pp. 49–77) says that the golden age of the comic strip was between 1910 and 1919 when *Krazy Kat*, *Toonerville Folks*, *Gasoline Alley*, *Harold Teen*, and *The Gumps* were created. This is also when a young engineer, Rube Goldberg, talked the San Francisco *Chronicle* into hiring him as a sports cartoonist. He became famous for his "Inventions," wildly complicated contraptions designed for the simplest tasks. Today any overly complex item is known as a *Rube Goldberg*, and the National Cartoonist Society's highest award "The Reuben" is named for him. Other 1920s comic creations included *Moon Mullins*, *Little Orphan Annie*, *Buck Rogers*, *Tarzan*, and *Popeye*.

During the Depression years of the 1930s, cartoons took on a new look and a new seriousness with such adventure stories as *Prince Valiant*, *Dick Tracy*, *The Phantom*, *Superman*, and *Batman*, marketed in both comic books and newspapers. The two strips from this era that were truly funny and that influenced other genres of humor were Chic Young's *Blondie*, which is credited with being the model for television's family sitcoms, and Al Capp's *Li'l Abner*, a social satire that set the stage for Walt Kelly's *Pogo* in the 1950s and 1960s and for Gary Trudeau's *Doonesbury* in the 1970s and 1980s.

Cartoonists began experimenting with more "adult" topics, and in 1954 comics came under attack for their violence. In some states, legislation was passed, and nationally the industry made an effort at self-regulation. A 1955 University of California report estimated that in a single year a billion comic books were sold, and that the money spent was four times greater than the total book budget of all U.S. public libraries combined.

Public or Specialized Places for Humorous Expression

Through the late 1800s, vaudeville theatres were a popular place for live entertainment featuring comedians, dancers, and musicians. But near the turn of the century, the managers organized and through a gentleman's agreement conspired to keep wages low. In England performers belonged to a union called the Water Rats. In 1900 American performers organized a similar union, but either in retaliation or simply because they could not make a profit and pay the higher wages, many managers closed their theatres while others began showing motion pictures exclusively. Contrary to their intentions, the White Rats contributed to the demise of live theatre and gave a boost to film as the medium of entertainment for the masses.

American soldiers in World War I found humor in a most unlikely place, on the sides of French railroad boxcars inscribed with "Hommes 40—Chevaux 8," meaning the cars could hold 40 men and 8 horses. Soldiers thought the label so funny that when they returned home and formed a section of the American Legion devoted to fun and practical jokes, they called it the "Forty and Eight Society."

In World War II, American soldiers created their own humor all over the world by writing "Kilroy Was Here!" on fences, walls, rocks, and wherever else they thought someone might see it. Usually it was accompanied by a simple drawing:

Humor in the Mass Media

During the late 1920s and 1930s, radio broadcasting began to include variety shows adapted from a vaudeville format. Eddie Cantor, Ed Wynn, and Edgar Bergen and his puppet Charlie McCarthy were favorite performers. Faithful audiences were attracted to stories told about permanent casts of characters as in "The Rise of the Goldbergs," which debuted in 1929 and was last seen on television in 1954. The most famous was "Amos 'n' Andy," which ran from 1928 to the 1950s. Other programs remembered with nostalgic smiles include "Fibber McGee and Molly," "The Honeymooners," "Henry Aldrich," "The George Burns and Gracie Allen Show," "The Jack Benny Show," "The Red Skelton Show," and Fred Allen's "Allen's Alley."

Comic strips, discussed earlier, provided the most popular form of newspaper humor, but columnists also had a place. In the 1920s and early 1930s, Will Rogers's humorous observations ran in approximately 350 daily newspapers. He also gave radio and live performances, beginning with the often-repeated line, "All I know is what I read in the papers." When in 1935 he was killed in a plane crash near Point Barrow, Alaska, he was mourned as a national hero.

The movies, with such stars as Charlie Chaplin, Buster Keaton, Harold Lloyd, Laurel and Hardy, and the Marx Brothers, deserve considerable credit for the development of an "American sense of humor." What the comic strips were to the newspapers, animated cartoons were to the movies. In 1928 Walt Disney released his first cartoon, *Plane Crazy* starring Mickey Mouse, who immediately became an international favorite.

By the 1940s Hollywood was making some serious films, but the public, international and American, preferred such wildly escapist comedies as those of Bud Abbott and Lou Costello. Listed below are some of the best humorous movies, which are all considered "classics" today, followed by the most humorous television shows, of the early twentieth century:

The Twenties

 The Gold Rush (1925), with Charlie Chaplin

 The Freshman (1925), with Harold Lloyd

 The General (1927), with Buster Keaton

 Big Business (1929), with Laurel and Hardy

The Thirties

 Duck Soup (1933), with the Marx Brothers

 Ruggles of Red Gap (1935), with Charlie Ruggles and Charles Laughton

 A Night at the Opera (1935), with the Marx Brothers

 Modern Times (1936), with Charlie Chaplin

The Forties

 His Girl Friday (1940), with Cary Grant and Rosalind Russell

 The Bank Dick (1940), W. C. Fields's greatest film

 The Ghost Breakers (1940), Bob Hope and Paulette Goddard

 To Be or Not to Be (1942), Jack Benny and Carole Lombard

 Arsenic and Old Lace (1944), Cary Grant and Raymond Massey

 Life with Father (1947), William Powell and Irene Dunne

The Fifties

 Born Yesterday (1950), Judy Holliday and William Holden

 The African Queen (1951), Katharine Hepburn and Humphrey Bogart

 Singin' in the Rain (1952), John Wayne and Maureen O'Hara

 The Trouble with Harry (1956), Shirley MacLaine and John Forsythe

 Some Like It Hot (1959), Jack Lemmon and Tony Curtis

The most famous television sitcoms, comedies, satires, and farces are listed below:

1949—"The Goldbergs"

1951—"The George Burns and Gracie Allen Show"
  "I Love Lucy"

1952—"Mr. Peepers" (with Wally Cox)

1953—"Topper" (with Leo G. Carroll)

1955—"The Honeymooners"
  "The Phil Silvers Show: You'll Never Get Rich"

1957—"Leave It to Beaver"

1959—"The Many Loves of Dobie Gillis"

Contemporary Humor and Trends

Popular Forms

Popular humor in the 1960s included the radio and Broadway performances of a creative new comedy team Mike Nichols and Elaine May, Vaughn Meader's "The First Family" record spoofing the Kennedys, and the Smothers Brothers who in 1969 grabbed headlines by being fired and in turn suing CBS for "mindless censorship" of their jokes. People made up Tom Swifties: "Do you want these pancakes?" she asked flippantly. The play on words was based on the overuse of adverbs in the Tom Swift children's books, popular in the 1930s and 1940s.

Black humor of the period is illustrated by the story about the little boy complaining that he's tired of going around in circles. His mother responds, "Shut up or I'll nail your other foot to the floor!" In the 1970s, lightbulb jokes reflected America's preoccupation with ethnicity, professional affiliations, and the feminist movement. For example:

How many Polacks does it take to change a lightbulb? Three—one to hold the lightbulb and two to turn the ladder around.

How many psychologists does it take to change a lightbulb? Only one, but it really has to want to change.

How many feminists does it take to change a lightbulb? That's not funny!

In the 1980s contemporary folklore became popular as collected in such books as Jan Brunvand's *The Vanishing Hitchhiker: American Urban Legends and Their Meanings* and Paul Dickson and Joseph Goulden's *There Are Alligators in Our Sewers and Other American Credos*. The stories all *could* have happened and are usually told by someone who just heard the story from someone who knows the person that it really happened to. An example is the story of the cement-truck driver who drives by his own house and notices a shiny black Cadillac parked in front. He peeks in the window of his house and when he sees a man talking to his wife is overcome with jealousy. In a fit of rage, he empties his load of cement in the open window of the man's Cadillac, only to find that his wife was going to surprise him with the car for his birthday. The salesman was making final arrangements.

A characteristic in American humor, perhaps in all humor, is for people to make jokes about things they are somewhat nervous about. Learning to work with computers is one such area as shown by the 1980s publication of Rich Tennant and John Barry's *The Unofficial I Hate Computers Book*, Jeffrey Holmes's *Shakespeare Was a Computer Programmer*, Ann Bishop's *Hello, Mr.*

Chips: Computer Jokes and Riddles, and Patty Bell and Doug Myrland's *The Official Silicon Valley Guy Handbook*.

Traveling on airplanes is another area of apprehension, and Americans relieve their fears by making up humorous airline names. For example, they call Cascade *Crashcade*, Mohawk *Slow Hawk*, Allegheny *All Agony*, Air France *Air Chance*, and TWA *Try Walking Across*.

Humor in the Literary and Performing Arts

Authors not mentioned elsewhere but whose work is not only anthologized and analyzed but also enjoyed by contemporary readers include the following listed with a sample title: Richard Armour, *Twisted Tales from Shakespeare*; Saul Bellow, *The Adventures of Augie March*; Ray Allen Billington, *Limericks Historical and Hysterical, Plagiarized, Arranged, Annotated, and Some Written by Ray Allen Billington*; Morris Bishop, *The Best of Bishop*; Richard Brautigan, *Trout Fishing in America*; Bob Elliott and Ray Goulding, *From Approximately Coast to Coast . . . It's the Bob and Ray Show*; Nora Ephron, *Crazy Salad*; Jeff Greenfield, *Book of Books*; Piet Hein, *Grooks*; Jim Henson, *Miss Piggy's Guide to Life*; John Irving, *The World According to Garp*; Ken Kesey, *One Flew Over the Cuckoo's Nest*; Benjamin Lee, *It Can't Be Helped*; David Macaulay, *Motel of the Mysteries*; Don Marquis, *archy and mehitabel*; P. J. O'Rourke, *National Lampoon: Sunday Newspaper Parody*; Michael Palin and Terry Jones, *Ripping Yarns*; Paul Rhymer, *Vic and Sade: The Best Radio Plays of Paul Rhymer*; Jean Shepherd, *Wanda Hickey's Night of Golden Memories and Other Disasters*; Max Shulman, *Barefoot Boy with Cheek*; Fritz Spiegl, *A Small Book of Grave Humor*; Frank Sullivan, *The Night the Old Nostalgia Burned Down*; Kurt Vonnegut, Jr., *Breakfast of Champions*; E. B. White, *The Second Tree from the Corner*; and Leonard Wibberley, *The Mouse That Roared*.

In 1962 Joseph Heller's *Catch–22*, which poked great fun at the military establishment, was so popular that its title came into the language to refer to any situation where no matter what you do, you are in the wrong.

In 1966 the New York Drama Critics Circle gave a special citation to Hal Holbrook for his *Mark Twain Tonight!*, a one-man show in which Holbrook impersonates Mark Twain on his 1800s lecture tours. Holbrook continued with the show, taking it around the country. In the 1980s he was still drawing large and enthusiastic crowds.

Another successful one-man show was *P.D.Q. Bach* in which Professor Peter Schikele does a wonderfully funny musical spoof under the guise of a professor of music giving a lecture.

Humorous plays offered in more traditional settings are listed below.

1960s

Tom Jones (music by Harvey Schmidt), *The Fantastiks* (1960)

Abe Burrows, Jack Weinstock, and Willie Gilbert (lyrics and music by Frank Loesser), *How to Succeed in Business without Really Trying* (1961)

Arthur Kopit, *Oh Dad, Poor Dad, Mamma's Hung You in the Closet, and I'm Feeling So Sad* (1961)

S. J. Perelman, *The Beauty Spot* (1962)

Burt Shevelove and Larry Gelbart (music by Stephen Sondheim), *A Funny Thing Happened on the Way to the Forum* (1962)

Herb Garner, *A Thousand Clowns* (1962)

Neil Simon, *Barefoot in the Park* (1963)

Joseph Stein, *Enter Laughing* (1963)

Jules Feiffer, *Little Murders* (1967)

Clark Gesner, *You're a Good Man, Charlie Brown* (1967)

1970s

George Furth (music by Stephen Sondheim), *Company* (1970)

Bob Randall, *6 RMs RIV VU* (1972)

1980s

Lanford Wilson, *Tally's Folly* (1980)

Neil Simon, *Brighton Beach Memoirs* (1982), *Biloxi Blues* (1984)

An important trend in twentieth-century American humor is that it is becoming a legitimate subject for serious academic study by anthropologists, educators, linguists, mathematicians, doctors, philosophers, psychologists, and scientists, with much of their work being interdisciplinary in nature. Victoria Bricker (1973), Johan Huizinga (1962), Barbara Kirshenblatt-Gimblett (1976), and Mahadev Apte (1985) are all anthropologists who have written books on humor. Courses in humor are offered at many universities. Evan Esar and Willard Espy have done books on wordplay. Linguist Victor Raskin's *Semantic Mechanisms of Humor* (1985) describes humor in terms of linguistic incongruity and resolution. In 1976 Norman Cousins published ''Anatomy of an Illness'' in the *New England Journal of Medicine* and in 1983 *The Healing Heart: Antidotes to Panic and Helplessness*. Raymond Moody (1978), Laurence Peter (1973), Laurence Peter and Bill Dana (1982), and Vera Robinson (1977) have also written books exploring the concept of humor as a healing device. Psychologists writing on humor and mental health include John Y. Greig (1923), Boris Sidis (1933), Edmund Bergler (1956), Martin Grotjahn (1957), William Fry, Jr. (1963), Philip Sterling (1965), Jacob Levine (1969), William Willeford (1969), Harvey Mindess (1971), Jeff Goldstein and Paul McGhee (1972), William Fry, Jr., and Melanie Allen (1975), Seymour Fisher and Rhoda Fisher (1981), Norman Holland (1982), Thomas Kuhlman (1984), and Elliot Oring (1984a and 1984b).

Books investigating the importance of humor in sociological research include Patrick Mahony's *Barbed Wit and Malicious Humor* (1956), Lucille Nahemow,

Kathleen McCluskey, and Paul McGhee's *Humor and Aging* (1985), and Marvin Koller's *Humor: A Sociological Perspective* (1985).

Representative titles in the visual arts include Walter Brasch's *Cartoon Monickers: An Insight Into the Animation Industry* (1983) and Roy Nelson's *Humorous Illustration and Cartooning: A Guide for Editors, Advertisers, and Artists* (1984). In 1983 the University of Minnesota Press published *The Mirth of a Nation: America's Great Dialect Humor*, edited by Blair and McDavid, and *Of Huck and Alice: Humorous Writing in American Literature*, by Neil Schmitz.

Other important books include E. B. and Katharine White's *A Subtreasury of American Humor*, Sarah Blacher Cohen's *Comic Relief: Humor in Contemporary American Literature* (1978), Jessica Milner Davis's *Farce*, and Mordecai Richler's *The Best of Modern Humor*.

Books written about humor in American politics include *From Bussing to Bugging: The Best in Congressional Humor* (Gingras, 1973), *Malice in Blunderland: A Foolproof Guide for the Aspiring Bureaucrat* (Martin, 1973), *So This Is Depravity* (Baker), *Theodore Roosevelt Among the Humorists* (Gibson, 1980), *What's Cooking in Congress?*, vols. 1 and 2 (Barba and Barba, 1979, 1982), and *Who's in Charge Here?* (Gardner, 1984). These representative titles give some indication of the irreverent tone humorists take toward American politics.

Humor in the Visual Arts

In keeping with the hurry-up approach to life in the last half of the twentieth century, comic strips have turned away from the continuing adventure story and back to humorous incidents that can be told in one day's allotment of space. The humor is more sophisticated and in many cases seems to be designed to comfort people's lack of control as they face a modern, complex society. Mort Walker's *Beetle Bailey* satirizes the military. Charles Schulz's *Peanuts* shows an adult world peopled exclusively by children whose psychological and philosophical observations coming "from the mouths of babes" are put into new and funny perspectives. Jim Davis's cat named Garfield gives readers the feeling that he's someone they know well but just can't recognize because he's hiding behind a striped fur coat.

Jules Feiffer's illustrations "of man groping hopelessly in psychological turmoil and neurotic anguish" (Robinson, 1974, p. 203) are syndicated under the heading *Feiffer*, much as a political cartoonist would be. Yet his subject matter, the way he lays it out, and his style keep him from being thought of as a political cartoonist. The same could be said of Gary Trudeau, who uses his *Doonesbury* strip to make political and psychological observations based on current events.

In the introduction to the 1980 edition of *Best Editorial Cartoons of the Year*, Daniel Patrick Moynihan described political cartoons as "a totally relaxed art form which nonetheless nourishes . . . healthy disrespect for pretense and pomposity" (Brooks, 1980, p. 9). The best cartoons sound "a repeated call for civic honesty and set forth an almost instinctual standard against which the behavior of government can be measured'' (Brooks, 1980, p. 10).

Since 1922, the Pulitzer Prize Editorial Board has included the political cartoon as a category, and since 1942 the Sigma Delta Chi journalism honorary society has chosen an outstanding cartoon of the year. Selections are also made for various collections identified as ''the best.'' Among those cartoonists whose names are often seen on honored cartoons are Herb Block, Etta Hulme, Bob Englehart, Jeff MacNelly, and Dick Wellmeyer.

Public or Specialized Places for Humorous Expression

A new place to look for humor is on electronic billboards such as those in sports arenas where a clever computer programmer will make a figure resembling the video game *Pac-Man* move across the screen gobbling up the name of the opposing team. Or when a good play is made the word ''Look'' is written with the *o*'s resembling blinking eyes. This is simply an update of the kind of playful writing of such words as de ↑ our, l♥ve, dollar$ and ¢ents, visi👁n, and s⊕cket. In a rebus, a picture stands for a word, as in this bumper sticker:

America: Get your ♥ in it or your 🫏 out of it.

T-shirts, campaign buttons, and posters are used in similar ways. A slight variation is the individualized license plate. By paying an extra fee, car owners are allowed to make up their own license plate as long as they use a limited number of letters, do not repeat one that someone else already has, and are not obscene. For example, *10S NE1* is asking ''Tennis, anyone?''

A few advertisers use humor on billboards, but it is usually more successful on packages or on restaurant menus which people can read at their leisure. Food and humor seem to go together, with nearly every large American city having at least one comedy supper club, while New York, Chicago, Los Angeles, and Las Vegas have several. Many of today's successful Jewish comedians got their starts by performing during the summers in the Catskill Mountains of upstate New York. They worked in the borscht-belt hotels catering to Jewish families coming from New York City for vacations.

Humor in the Mass Media

Today's television comedy can be divided into two categories: the stand-up hostile kind of humor practiced by Don Rickles, Richard Pryor, Eddie Murphy, and Joan Rivers, and the more gentle sit-down kind of humor practiced by Steve Allen, David Letterman, Johnny Carson, and Ed McMahon. For example, in one of the Carson-McMahon routines, Carson gives an answer like ''Catch–22'' and then Ed opens the envelope to read the question, "What would the Los Angeles Dodgers do if they were hit 100 fly balls?"

Comedy writer Robert Orben explained in an interview with Melvin Helitzer that when he first started in the business in 1945, the put-down humor was a simple kind directed at such traditional topics as mothers-in-law, bad cooking, wives who were bad drivers, etc. Then in the 1950s Alan King began talking about troubles with insurance companies, the airplanes, the problems that hit close to home, to which we therefore respond with vehemence. Toward the end of the 1950s, "tell it like it is" social satire got rolling with Mort Sahl and Lenny Bruce. Dick Gregory came in with a racial viewpoint, so that with the hostile humor of the 1970s nothing was sacred. This was evident in such popular television productions as "The Sonny and Cher Comedy Hour," "Saturday Night Live," and "The Dean Martin Show." Equally popular, but with a gentler kind of humor, were "Candid Camera" and "Laugh-In."

More important on television are the situation comedies as described by Larry Mintz in an article entitled "American Humour and the Spirit of the Times." He quoted John Leonard, who said that in that flabby decade of the fifties "the sitcom proposed as a paradigm the incompetent father, the dizzy mother, the innocent child." The 1960s were similar except that war was shown "as a fun thing" and there were "young women with supernatural powers (witch, genie, magical nanny, flying nun) who could take care of their men and their children, look cute and never leave the house." In the 1970s this cast of characters all sat around "discussing abortion, infidelity, impotence, homosexuality, drug addiction, and death." What has been constant has been "the inability of the American father to lace up the shoes of his own mind without falling off his rocker" (Chapman and Foot, 1977, pp. 17–21). Leonard's statement that this perfectly reflects and perpetuates our cultural expectations is just one of the criticisms leveled at situation comedies. Nevertheless, they are the mainstay of American television. The most successful sitcoms are listed below:

1960—"The Andy Griffith Show"

1961—"Car 54, Where Are You?"
      "The Dick Van Dyke Show"

1964—"The Addams Family"
      "Bewitched"

1966—"Get Smart"

1970—"The Mary Tyler Moore Show"

1971—"All in the Family"

1972—"Sanford and Son"
      "The Bob Newhart Show"
      "M*A*S*H"
      "Maude"

1974—"Rhoda"

1975—''Barney Miller''
       ''Phyllis''
       ''Hot l Baltimore''
1977—''Soap''
1978—''Taxi''
1982—''Bob Newhart''
1983—''Cheers''
1984—''The Bill Cosby Show''

Popular humorous movies are purposely listed here beneath the television shows because even the most popular movies are seen by only a fraction of those who see the most popular television shows. On the other hand, most American comedies are seen all over the world and enjoy great popularity.

The Sixties

A Funny Thing Happened on the Way to the Forum (1960), Zero Mostel and Phil Silvers

Dr. Strangelove, Or, How I Learned to Stop Worrying and Love the Bomb (1964), George C. Scott and Peter Sellers

A Thousand Clowns (1965), Jason Robards and Barbara Harris

The Great Race (1965), Jack Lemmon and Tony Curtis

The Graduate (1967), Dustin Hoffman and Anne Bancroft

You're a Big Boy Now (1967), Peter Kastner and Elizabeth Hartman

The Producers (1968), Zero Mostel and Gene Wilder

The Seventies

Bananas (1971), Woody Allen

M*A*S*H (1971), Elliot Gould and Donald Sutherland

Everything You Always Wanted to Know about Sex (1972), Woody Allen

The Sting (1973), Paul Newman and Robert Redford

Young Frankenstein (1974), Gene Wilder and Madeleine Kahn

Harry and Tonto (1974), Art Carney

Love and Death (1975), Woody Allen

Annie Hall (1977), Woody Allen and Diane Keaton

Movie Movie (1978), George C. Scott and Red Buttons

Manhattan (1979), Woody Allen and Diane Keaton

The Eighties

Airplane (1980), Leslie Nielsen and Robert Stack

Tootsie (1982), Dustin Hoffman and Jessica Lange

My Favorite Year (1982), Peter O'Toole and Joe Bologna

Local Hero (1983), Burt Lancaster and Peter Riegert

Broadway Danny Rose (1984), Mia Farrow and Woody Allen

The Purple Rose of Cairo (1985), Mia Farrow

Back to the Future (1985), Michael J. Fox and Christopher Lloyd

Compromising Positions (1985), Raul Julia and Susan Saradon

The only humor heard on radio is that provided by advertisers in commercials. However, until 1987, until its creator decided to move to Norway, there was one genuinely funny radio program being broadcast by National Public Radio. It was Garrison Keillor's "A Prairie Home Companion" about the fictitious town of Lake Woebegon, Minnesota, "the town that time forgot and the decades cannot improve."

Newspaper humor comes in comic strips, editorial cartoons, and humorous columns. Erma Bombeck is the most famous for close-to-home humor. Her columns have been gathered into books including *Aunt Erma's Cope Book, I Lost Everything in the Post-Natal Depression*, and *If Life Is a Bowl of Cherries, What Am I Doing in the Pits?* Art Buchwald is the best and most famous of the political satirists. His books include *And Then I Told the President, Down the Seine and Up the Potomac, Getting High in Government Circles, I Never Danced at the White House*, and *Washington Is Leaking*. Russell Baker and Andy Rooney are other syndicated columnists who consistently add a light touch to the serious points they make.

UNIVERSAL FUNCTIONS OF HUMOR AND THE NATIONAL MANIFESTATIONS

Aggressive Humor

People use humor to bond themselves with their friends and to exclude outsiders as when children shout "Two's company, three's a crowd, four on the sidewalk is never allowed!" Folklore collector Alvin Schwartz has found that nearly all children use antiteacher humor to relieve their frustrations about being in a subservient role. For example, he has heard children singing, "Row, row, row your boat, Gently down the stream. Throw your teacher overboard, And you will hear her scream." San Francisco children sing "Throw your teacher in the bay. The sharks will eat today" (Nilsen, 1983, p. 198).

Schwartz says that children in southern Ohio tell jokes about Briars, migrants from Appalachia newly moved to Ohio in search of jobs. Montana children joke about North Dakotans, Maine children about French Canadians, and children all over the United States about Poles, Italians, and blacks. During the 1979 political crisis when American hostages were being held in Iran, children jumped rope to "eeny, meeny, miney, mo. Catch Khomeini by the toe. If he hollers make him say, 'I surrender U.S.A.' "

Much of the aggressive humor that adults use relates to sex. An obvious example is the sign on a brothel door: "Out to lunch. Go fuck yourself!" As in this joke, hostile humor is usually aimed at a target, probably someone whose behavior deviates from the norm, as in the following stories about prostitutes, virgins, and homosexuals, respectively.

A woman goes into a bank to cash a fifty-dollar check. The teller returns her check saying, ''I'm sorry, Miss. This man has no account here.''

''Oh, my God!'' screams the woman. ''I've been raped!''

Judging by the large number of jokes told about virgins, their behavior is enough different from the norm to arouse degrees of hostility varying from the belligerent graffito ''To the virgins—thanks for nothing!'' to such playful college folklore as the following. At the University of Wisconsin in Madison the most notable landmark is a statue of Abraham Lincoln sitting atop Bascom Hill. Every time a virgin walks up the hill, Lincoln is said to stand up. Rising from the center of the campus of the University of Northern Iowa in Cedar Falls is a majestic bell tower. Local legend says that every time a virgin graduates a brick falls from the tower. It is in perfect condition. One year at Brigham Young University there was no homecoming parade. The committee cancelled it because all the school's virgins were going to march in it. However, one became ill and the other one did not want to walk alone.

The most hostile jokes are told about homosexuals. When AIDS was first diagnosed as a disease prevalent among homosexuals and Haitians, a popular joke was about a young AIDS victim worrying about how he could convince his mother that he was Haitian.

Sexual Humor

American sexual humor can be classified into at least four categories: an ''innocent'' kind of humor that relies on surprise, sexual innuendo, hostile humor (discussed above), and sex-related humor that is interesting because it reveals and/or teaches cultural attitudes.

The innocent kind of humor expresses surprise at the whole amazing system of human reproduction. For example, the story about the little boy who asks his mother where he came from. After she gives him a lengthy lesson on the birds and the bees, he shrugs and says, ''Oh, I just wondered. Bobby comes from Boston.'' On an adult level, this kind of humor may give listeners an insight, as when Brendan Francis remarked, ''The big difference between sex for money and sex for free is that sex for money usually costs a lot less'' (Evans, 1985, p. 5).

In terms of frequency of use, sexual innuendo is probably the largest category of sex-related humor. It can be used over the airwaves and in public places where nonambiguous humor would be frowned upon. With double entendres, those who would disapprove may not catch on, or if they do they can pretend not to. The long-running television show, ''The Newlywed Game,'' which is a combination interview and game show, gets its humor from the way the writers devise questions so that the respondents are likely to answer in ways that will arouse sensuous thoughts. Television talk shows, especially the late-night ones, are similar. Guests try to be as amusing as comedienne Jeanne Robertson, who in a "Tall Is Beautiful" monologue tells how as a teenager she practiced basketball instead of learning to twirl the baton. She ended up as "the only hooker in the Miss America pageant."

Virtually hundreds of bumper stickers are suggestive because of the double meaning of *it*; for example, "Nurses do it with patience," "Teachers do it with class," "Pilots keep it up longer," "Photographers develop it better," and "Architects plan it better."

An example of humor revealing and perhaps shaping cultural attitudes is that related to differing role expectations for males and females. In the early 1970s as the feminist movement garnered public attention, a popular riddle was about an automobile wreck in which a father was killed and his son rushed to a hospital for emergency care. The surgeon called to the operating table took one look at the patient and said, "I can't operate on this boy. He's my son!"

The joke teller would then ask how this could be. The answer was that the surgeon was the boy's mother. There would have been no surprise, no joke, if listeners hadn't thought that all surgeons were male. Two popular paperbacks making fun of strict sex-role expectations are Bruce Feirstein's *Real Men Don't Eat Quiche* and Joyce Jillson's *Real Women Don't Pump Gas*.

Social Humor

"Men will confess to treason, murder, arson, false teeth, or a wig, but will not own up to a lack of a sense of humor," quipped Frank Morre Colby in the July 4, 1976 edition of the *New York Daily News*. Charles Lindner expressed a similar belief: "A person has two legs and one sense of humor, and if you are faced with the choice, it's better to lose a leg" (Witty, 1983, p. 28).

These succinct statements about the value of humor are similar in form to such popular social rules or observations as Murphy's Law, "If anything can can go wrong, it will, and even if it can't, it might"; O'Toole's corollary, "Murphy was an optimist"; and the Peter Principle, which states that in every hierarchy—government, business, or whatever—each employee tends to rise to a level of incompetence, that is, as long as people are doing well, they will continue to be promoted. The result is that every post is filled by an employee not quite competent to execute the duties. C. Northcote Parkinson apparently founded this kind of humor in 1957 when he published *Parkinson's Law*, e.g., "Officials advance subordinates, not rivals." People like these laws because they are witty, compact, and unequivocal. It is very satisfying to reduce complexity to simple and understandable terms.

Capitalism is one of the complexities that Americans must cope with, and they are grateful for any observations which will help, such as those offered by

Dave Broadfoot at the 1983 convention of the National Speakers Association. He pointed out that frankfurters come twelve to a pack while buns come eight to a pack. In order to make everything come out even, one has to have a minimum of twenty-four guests (Moormon, 1983).

Jere Moorman deals with economics on an even grander scale describing various political systems. Capitalism is when you have two cows and sell one and buy a bull. Communism is when you have two cows and you give them to the government and the government gives you some milk. Fascism is when you have two cows and you keep the cows and give the milk to the government and the government then sells you back some of the milk. New Dealism is when you have two cows and you shoot one and milk the other one and then pour the milk down the drain. Socialism is when you have two cows and you give your neighbor one. And finally, totalitarianism is when you have two cows and the government shoots you and keeps the cows (1983).

Until fairly recently, humor and religion were kept separate, but the SALT (Salvation and Laughter Together) organization now publishes a newsletter named *Light* (Laughter in God, History and Theology), while ISAAC (Institute for Sharing Amusing Anecdotes in Church/Synagogue) publishes a journal *Red Rubber Noses*. In 1974 Conrad Hyers published *Zen and the Comic Spirit* followed in 1981 by *The Comic Vision and the Christian Faith*. Robert Polhemus published *Comic Faith* in 1980, and Cal Samra published *Jesus Put on a Happy Face* in 1985.

Humor as a Defense Mechanism

James Thurber wisely observed that ''Humor is emotional chaos remembered in tranquility.'' This explains why people can look back on traumatic events and laugh about them. It also explains the satisfaction derived from self-disparagement. Americans will take whatever trait makes them feel different from the majority of the population and then by laughing at it, make themselves feel better. They hesitate to joke about such ''real'' flaws as their own alcoholism, dishonesty, or emotional illness. More likely they will joke about things which listeners can identify with in a comfortable way. For example, comedian Jack Benny made himself famous by joking about his own stinginess, Sam Levenson joked about the poverty of his childhood, and Rodney Dangerfield joked about his lack of respect.

Dangerfield's humor is the kind that Derek Evans and Dave Fulwiler used in their book *Who's Nobody in America?* (1981), a spoof on Who's Who books. In it Lyle Davis of Huntsville, Alabama, explains that she applied for a job as a dishwasher and finally got called two and a half years later. The boss asked if she could be there at five o'clock. It was already six-fifteen. *Dare to Be Dull* is another book that's funny as a counterbalance to prevailing expectations. Its author, Joseph Troise, is president of the Dull Men's Club.

Modern politicians use disparaging humor to gain the support of the electorate.

STAFFORDSHIRE
POLYTECHNIC
LIBRARY

Many people distrusted the wealth of the Kennedy family, and so when John F. Kennedy was running for president, he combated this mistrust by announcing that he had just received a telegram from his father saying "Don't buy one vote more than necessary. I'll be damned if I'll pay for a landslide." Kennedy knew that once people have laughed at something, they aren't so afraid of it.

This is why President Ronald Reagan would joke about his age. For example, at a Gridiron Club dinner in Washington, D.C., he noted that the club had been founded in 1885 and then expressed disappointment that he had not been invited to their *first* dinner. Former presidential candidate Morris Udall is writing a book on political humor and has chosen the disparaging title of *We Were Laughing About It This Morning*. When Udall was campaigning in Maine, he poked his head in the door of a barbershop and as a way of introducing himself said, "Mo Udall, running for President," to which the barber replied, "Yeah, we were laughing about it this morning."

Intellectual Humor

Ludwig Wittgenstein, the Austrian philosopher, once remarked that a serious and good philosophical work could be written that would consist entirely of jokes. John Paulos's *I Think, Therefore I Laugh* (1985) is an application of Wittgenstein's theory. Paulos explains:

Open any book on analytic philosophy and you will find clarifying distinctions that, if utilized differently, could be the source of humor. The following pairs of phrases serve as examples of what I mean. "Going on to infinity" versus "going on to Milwaukee"; "honesty compels me" versus "my mother compels me".... The first phrase in each case shares the same grammar as the second phrase, yet the logic (in a broad sense) of the two is quite different. (p. 69)

Richard Aquila (1981) and John Morreall (1983) also look at humor from a philosopher's viewpoint.

Scientist Ralph Lewin, author of *The Biology of Algae and Other Verses*, pointed out that natural scientists are as interested in humor as are psychologists, linguists, and philosophers. He gave as evidence the name *Diogenes rotundus* for an algae found living in a barrel, *Hummbrella hydra* for a parasol-shaped algae named in honor of Professor Humm, and *Didemnum ginantonicum* named in honor of Lou Eldredge's favorite beverage (Lewin, 1983, p. 399).

The *Journal of Irreproducible Results*, edited by Alexander Kohn in Israel but published in the United States, is popular because of the way it satirizes academic jargon and pomposity. Humor allows academics and intellectuals to stand back and take a look at their own foibles. J. Frank Dobie observes that "The average Ph.D. thesis is nothing but the transference of bones from one graveyard to another" (Peter, 1976, p. 128), and William Glasser observes, "There are only two places in our world where time takes precedence over the job to be done, school and prison" (Peter, 1976, p. 126).

Douglas Hofstadter's Pulitzer Prize–winning *Gödel, Escher, Bach: An Eternal Golden Braid* exemplifies another kind of intellectual humor. The book explores visual, oral, and statistical illusions. Hofstadter uses the work of Dutch graphic artist M. C. Escher, who lived from 1902 to 1972, to represent the "eternal braid" in art. For music he considers Johann Sebastian Bach's "Endlessly Rising Canon," for mathematical logic K. Godel's translation of an ancient paradox in philosophy into mathematical terms. The paradox is the statement made by Epimenides, a Cretan, who said "All Cretans are liars" (Hofstadter, 1980, pp. 16–17).

REFERENCES

Apte, M. L. (1985) *Humor and Laughter: An Anthropological Perspective*. Bloomington: Indiana University Press.

Aquila, R. E. (1981) *A Limerick History of Philosophy*. Washington, D.C.: University Press of America.

Baker, R. (1980) *So This Is Depravity*. New York: St. Martin.

Barba, H., and Barba, M., eds. (1979) *What's Cooking in Congress? A Smorgasbord of Congressional Recipes*. Saratoga Springs, N.Y.: Harian Creative Press.

———. (1982) *What's Cooking in Congress?—II: A Second Smorgasbord of Congressional Recipes*. Saratoga Springs, N.Y.: Harian Creative Press.

Bateson, G. (1953), "The Position of Humor in Human Communication." In *Cybernetics*. ed. H. von Foerster. New York: Macy Foundation.

Bell, P. and D. Myrland. (1983) *The Official Silicon Valley Guy Handbook*, New York: Avon.

Bender, E. M. (1985) *Humor in America*. Special Issue of *Open Places*, nos. 38–39, Spring 1985.

Bergler, E. (1956) *Laughter and the Sense of Humor*. New York: Intercontinental Medical Book Corporation.

Bishop, A. (1982) *Hello, Mr. Chips: Computer Jokes and Riddles*, New York: Lodestar Books.

Blair, W., and Hill, H. (1978) *America's Humor: From Poor Richard to Doonesbury*. New York: Oxford University Press.

Blair, W., and McDavid, R. I., eds. (1983) *The Mirth of a Nation: America's Great Dialect Humor*. Minneapolis: University of Minnesota Press.

Bloom, E. A., and Bloom, L. D. (1979) *Satire's Persuasive Voice*. Ithaca, N.Y.: Cornell University Press.

Botkin, B. A. (1944) *A Treasury of American Folklore*. New York: Bantam.

Brack, O. M., ed. (1977) *American Humor*. Tempe, Ariz.: Arete.

Brasch, W. (1983) *Cartoon Monickers: An Insight into the Animation Industry*. Bowling Green, Ohio: Bowling Green State University Press.

Bricker, V. R. (1973) *Ritual Humor in Highland Chiapas*. Austin: University of Texas Press.

Brooks, C. (1980) *Best Editorial Cartoons of the Year, 1980 Edition*. Gretna, Louisiana: Pelican.

Brunvand, J. H. (1981) *The Vanishing Hitchhiker: American Urban Legends and Their Meanings*. New York: W. W. Norton.

Caputi, A. (1978) *Buffo: The Genius of Vulgar Comedy*. Detroit: Wayne State University Press.

Carruth, G. ed. (1979) *The Encyclopedia of American Facts and Dates*. 7th ed. New York: Thomas Y. Crowell.

Chapman, A. J., and Foot, H. C., eds. (1977) *It's a Funny Thing, Humor*. New York: Pergamon Press.

Claire, E. (1984) *What's So Funny?—A Foreign Student's Introduction to American Humor*. 2 vols. Rochelle Park, N.J.: Eardley.

Cohen, S. B. (1978) *Comic Relief: Humor in Contemporary American Literature*. Chicago: University of Illinois Press.

Cousins, N. (1976) "Anatomy of an Illness (As Perceived by the Patient)." *New England Journal of Medicine* 295: 458–63.

———. (1983) *The Healing Heart: Antidotes to Panic and Helplessness*. New York: W. W. Norton.

Davis, J. M. (1978) *Farce*. New York: Methuen.

DeRocher, G. (1979) *Rabelais' Laughers and Joubert's Traite du Ris*. University: University of Alabama Press.

Dickson, P., and Goulden, J. C. (1983) *There Are Alligators in Our Sewers and Other American Credos*. New York: Delacorte Press.

Dundes, A., and Pagter, C. R. (1975) *Work Hard and You Shall Be Rewarded: Urban Folklore from the Paperwork Empire*. Bloomington: Indiana University Press.

Eastman, M. (1921) *The Sense of Humor*. New York: Scribner.

———. (1936) *Enjoyment of Laughter*. New York: Simon and Schuster.

Esar, E. (1952a) *Humorous English*. New York: Horizon.

———. (1952b) *The Humor of Humor*. New York: Horizon.

Espy, W. (1983) *A Children's Almanac of Words at Play*. New York: Crown.

———. (1985) *The Garden of Eloquence: A Rhetorical Bestiary*. New York: Dutton.

———. (1984) *Have a Word on Me: A Celebration of Language*. New York: Simon and Schuster.

———. (1979) *The Life and Works of Mr. Anonymous*. New York: Avon.

———. (1983) *Word Puzzles*. New York: Dunbar Books.

———. (1986) *Words to Rhyme with: A Rhyming Dictionary*. New York: Facts on File.

Evans, D., and Fulwiler, D. (1981) *Who's Nobody in America?* New York: Holt, Rinehart and Winston.

Evans, G. (1985) "Wicked Remarks." *Playboy* 32:2 (February): 5.

Farzan, M. (1973) *Another Way of Laughter*. New York: Dutton.

Fisher, S., and Fisher, R. (1981) *Pretend the World Is Funny and Forever: A Psychological Analysis of Comedians, Clowns, and Actors*. Hillsdale, N.J.: Lawrence Erlbaum.

Freud, S. (1976) *Jokes and Their Relation to the Unconscious*. New York: Penguin.

Fry, W. (1963) *Sweet Madness*. Palo Alto, Calif.: Pacific Books.

Fry, W., and Allen, M. (1975) *Make 'em Laugh: Life Studies of Comedy Writers*. Palo Alto, Calif.: Science and Behavior Books.

Gardner, G. (1984) *Who's in Charge Here?* New York: Bantam.

Gibson, W. M. (1980) *Theodore Roosevelt Among the Humorists—W. D. Howells, Mark Twain, and Mr. Dooley*. Knoxville: University of Tennessee Press.

Gingras, A. T. (1973) *The Best in Congressional Humor*. New York: Acropolis Books.

Goldstein, J. H., and McGhee, P. E., eds. (1972) *The Psychology of Humor*. New York: Academic Press.

Greig, J. Y. T. (1923) *The Psychology of Laughter and Comedy*. New York: Dodd, Mead.

Grotjahn, M. (1957) *Beyond Laughter*. New York: McGraw-Hill.

Gruner, C. R. (1978) *Understanding Laughter: The Workings of Wit and Humor*. Chicago: Nelson-Hall.

Hasser, D. M. (1982) *Comic Tones in Science Fiction: The Art of Compromise with Nature*. Westport, Conn.: Greenwood Press.

Helitzer, M. (1984) *Comedy Techniques for Writers and Performers: The HEARTS Theory of Humor and Writing*. Athens, Ohio: Lawhead Press.

Hertzler, J. O. (1970) *Laughter: A Socio-Scientific Analysis*. New York: Exposition Press.

Hofstadter, D. R. (1980) *Gödel, Escher, Bach: An Eternal Golden Braid*. New York: Vintage.

Holland, N. N. (1982) *Laughing: A Psychology of Humor*. Ithaca, N.Y.: Cornell University Press.

Holmes, J. (1975) *Shakespeare Was a Computer Programmer*. New Brunswick, Canada: Brunswick Press.

Huizinga, J. (1962) *Homo Ludens: A Study of the Play-Element in Culture*. Boston: Beacon Press.

Hyers, C. (1974) *Zen and the Comic Spirit*. Philadelphia: Westminster.

———. (1981) *The Comic Vision and the Christian Faith*. New York: Pilgrim Press.

Inge, M. T. (1982) *American Humor*. New York: AMS Press.

Keller, C., ed. (1981) *Growing Up Laughing: Humorists Look at American Youth*. Englewood Cliffs, N.J.: Prentice-Hall.

Kelly, B. (1985) *Learning with Laughter*. Portland, Maine: J. W. Waleh.

Kiley, F., and Shuttleworth, J. M. (1971) *Satire: From Aesop to Buchwald*. New York: Odyssey/Bobbs-Merrill.

Kirshenblatt-Gimblett, B. (1976) *Speech Play: Research and Resources for Studying Linguistic Creativity*. Philadelphia: University of Pennsylvania Press.

Koller, M. (1985) *Humor: A Sociological Perspective*. Houston: Cap and Gown Press.

Kuhlman, T. L. (1984) *Humor and Psychotherapy*. Homewood, Ill.: Dow Jones-Irwin.

Leacock, S. (1935) *Humor: Its Theory and Technique*. New York: Dodd, Mead.

Legman, G. (1968a) *No Laughing Matter: An Analysis of Sexual Humor*. vol. 1. Bloomington: Indiana University Press.

———. (1968b) *Rationale of the Dirty Joke*. New York: Grove Press.

Leonard, F. M. (1981) *Laughter in the Courts of Love: Comedy in Allegory, from Chaucer to Spenser*. Norman, Okla.: Pilgrim Books.

Levine, J. (1969) *Motivation in Humor*. New York: Atherton.

Lewin, R. A. (1983) "Humor in the Scientific Literature." *WHIMSY* 1: 398–99.

Littmann, J. R. (1979) *A Theory of Humor*. Denver: University of Colorado Press.

McDowell, J. H. (1979) *Children's Riddling*. Bloomington: Indiana University Press.

McGhee, P. E. (1979) *Humor: Its Origin and Development*. San Francisco: Freeman.

McGhee, P. E., and Chapman, A. J., eds. (1980) *Children's Humour*. Chichester, England: Wiley.

McGhee, P. E., and Goldstein, J. H. (1972) *The Psychology of Humor*. New York: Academic Press.

————, eds. (1983) *The Handbook of Humor Research.* 2 vols. New York: Springer-Verlag.

Mahony, P. (1956) *Barbed Wit and Malicious Humor.* New York: Citadel.

McKay, D. R. (1983) "The Puissant Procreator: Comic Ridicule of Brigham Young." *WHIMSY* 1: 128–29.

Marckwardt, A. H., and Dillard, J. L. (1980) *American English.* New York: Oxford University Press.

Martin, T. L. (1973) *Malice in Blunderland: A Foolproof Guide for the Aspiring Bureaucrat.* New York: McGraw-Hill.

Mast, G. (1979) *The Comic Mind: Comedy and the Movies.* Chicago: University of Chicago Press.

Mendel, W., ed. (1970) *A Celebration of Humor.* Los Angeles: Mara Books.

Mikes, G. (1971) *Laughing Matter: Towards a Personal Philosophy of Wit and Humor.* New York: Library Press.

Mindess, H. (1971) *Laughter and Liberation.* Los Angeles: Nash.

Mindess, H., Miller, C., Turek, J., Bender, A., and Corbin, S. (1985) *The Antioch Humor Test: Making Sense of Humor.* New York: Avon.

Mindess, H., and Turek, J., eds. (1980) *The Study of Humor.* Los Angeles: Antioch University.

Mintz, L. (1977) "American Humour and the Spirit of the Times." In *It's a Funny Thing, Humour,* edited by A. J. Chapman and H. C. Foot, 17–21. New York: Pergamon Press.

Mintz, L. E. (1984) *Third International Conference on Humor: Conference Abstracts.* Washington, D.C.: Workshop Library on World Humor, American Humor Studies Association, and Montgomery College.

Moody, R. A. (1978) *Laugh After Laugh.* Jacksonville, Fla.: Headwaters Press.

Moormon, J. (1983) *The Humorous Dictionary of Economics.* San Diego, Calif.: Crane.

Morreall, J. (1981) *Laughter and Humor.* Evanston, Ill.: Northwestern University Press.

————. (1983) *Taking Laughter Seriously.* Albany: State University of New York Press.

Nachman, G. (1983) *Out on a Whim.* New York: Doubleday.

Nahemow, L., McCluskey, K., and McGhee, P. E., eds. (1985) *Humor and Aging.* New York: Academic Press.

Nelson, R. P. (1984) *Humorous Illustration and Cartooning: A Guide for Editors, Advertisers, and Artists.* Englewood Cliffs, N.J.: Prentice-Hall.

The New Yorker: Twenty-Fifth Anniversary Album (1951) New York: Harper Brothers.

Nilsen, D. L. F., and Nilsen, A. P. (1978) *Language Play: An Introduction to Linguistics.* Rowley, Mass.: Newbury House.

Nilsen, A. P., and Nilsen, D. L. F. (1983) "Children's Multiple Uses of Oral Language Play." *Language Arts* 60:2 (February 1983): 194–201.

Nilsen, D. L. F. (1984) "Facets." *English Journal* 73:6 (October): 27.

Oring, E., ed. (1984a) *Humor and the Individual.* Los Angeles: California Folklore Society.

Oring, E. (1984b) *The Jokes of Sigmund Freud.* Philadelphia: University of Pennsylvania Press.

Paulos, J. A. (1980) *Mathematics and Humor.* Chicago: University of Chicago Press.

————. (1985) *I Think, Therefore I Laugh: An Alternative Approach to Philosophy.* New York: Columbia University Press.

Pepicello, W. J., and Green, T. A. (1984) *The Language of Riddles, New Perspectives*. Columbus: Ohio State University Press.

Peter, L. (1973) *The Peter Prescription: How to Make Things to Right*. New York: Bantam.

———. (1976) *The Peter Plan: A Proposal for Survival*. New York: William Morrow.

Peter, L., and Dana, B. (1982) *The Laughter Prescription: How to Achieve Health, Happiness, and Peace of Mind Through Humor*. New York: Ballantine.

Piddington, R. (1963) *The Psychology of Laughter: A Study in Social Adaptation*. New York: Gamut Press.

Pirandello, L. (1974) *On Humor*. Chapel Hill: University of North Carolina Press.

Polhemus, R. M. (1980) *Comic Faith*. Chicago: University of Chicago Press.

Rapp, A. (1951) *The Origins of Wit and Humor*. New York: Dutton.

Raskin, V. (1985) *Semantic Mechanisms of Humor*. Boston: D. Reidel.

Reik, T. (1962) *Jewish Wit*. New York: Gamut Press.

Richler, M. (1983) *The Best of Modern Humor*. New York: Alfred A. Knopf.

Robertson, Jeanne. (1984) "Tall Is Beautiful." Cassette. New York: Nightingale-Conant.

Robertson, T. W., and Hingston, E. P., eds. (1970) *Artemus Ward's Panorama*. New York: G. W. Carleton.

Robinson, J. (1974) *The Comics: An Illustrated History of Comic Strip Art*. New York: G. P. Putnam's Sons.

Robinson, V. M. (1977) *Humor and the Health Professions*. Thorofare, N.J.: Charles B. Slack.

Royot, D. (1980) *L'Humour Américain: Des Puritains aux Yankees*. Lyon, France: Presses Universitaires de Lyon.

Samra, C. (1985) *Jesus Put on a Happy Face*. Kalamazoo, Mich.: Rosejoy.

Schmitz, N. (1983) *Of Huck and Alice: Humorous Writing in American Literature*. Minneapolis: University of Minnesota Press.

Shibles, W. (1978a) *Good and Bad Are Funny Things: Ethics in Rhyme for Children*. Whitewater, Wis.: Language Press.

———. (1978b) *Humor: A Critical Analysis for Young People*. Whitewater, Wis.: Language Press.

Shutz, C. E. (1977) *Political Humor*. Cranbury, N.J.: Associated University Press.

Sidis, B. (1933) *The Psychology of Laughter*. New York: Appleton.

Sloane, D. E. E., ed. (1983) *The Literary Humor of the Urban Northeast: 1830–1890*. Baton Rouge: Louisiana State University Press.

Stearns, F. R. (1972) *Laughing: Physiology, Pathophysiology, Psychology, Pathopsychology, and Development*. Springfield, Ill.: Charles C. Thomas.

Sterling, P. (1965) *Laughing on the Outside*. New York: Grosset and Dunlap.

Sully, J. (1909) *Essay on Laughter*. New York: Longman's.

Sypher, W., ed. (1956) *Comedy*. Garden City, N.Y.: Doubleday.

Tennant, R. and J. Barry. (1984) *The Unofficial I Hate Computers Book*. New York: Hayden.

Tittler, J. (1984) *Narrative Irony in the Contemporary Spanish-American Novel*. Ithaca, N.Y.: Cornell University Press.

Troise, J. L. (1983) *Dare to Be Dull*. New York: Bantam.

True, H. (1980) *Humor Power: How to Get It, Give It, and Gain*. Garden City, N.Y.: Doubleday.

Veron, E., ed. (1976) *Humor in America*. New York: Harcourt Brace Jovanovich.

Weiss, H. S., and Weiss, M. J., eds. (1977) *The American Way of Laughing*. New York: Bantam.

White, E. B., and White, K. (1941) *A Subtreasury of American Humor*. New York: AMS Press.

Wilde, L. (1976) *How the Great Comedy Writers Create Laughter*. New York: Nelson-Hall.

Willeford, W. (1969) *The Fool and His Scepter: A Study in Clowns and Jesters and Their Audience*. Evanston, Ill.: Northwestern University Press.

Williams, K. J., and Duffey, B., eds. (1983) *Chicago's Public Wits: A Chapter in the American Comic Spirit*. Baton Rouge: Louisiana State University Press.

Wilson, C. P. (1979) *Jokes: Form, Content, Use and Function*. New York: Academic Press.

Wilson, J., and Jacobs, H. (1979) *Justin Wilson's Cajun Humor*. Gretna, La.: Pelican.

Witty, S. "The Laugh-Makers" in *Psychology Today*, 17:8 (August): 28.

Wolfenstein, M. (1954) *Children's Humor: A Psychological Analysis*. Glencoe, Ill.: Free Press.

Yacowar, M. (1982) *Loser Take All: The Comic Art of Woody Allen*. New York: Frederick Ungar.

Zimmerman, E. (1983) *Swift's Narrative Satires: Author and Authority*. Ithaca, N.Y.: Cornell University Press.

Ziv, A. (1984) *Personality and Sense of Humor*. New York: Springer.

8   VLADIMIR KOLESARIĆ,
MIRJANA KRIZMANIĆ
AND ANTUN ROHAČEK

Humor in Yugoslavia

HISTORICAL BACKGROUND

The Socialist Federative Republic of Yugoslavia (SFRY) has a population of about 22 million in six republics and two autonomous provinces. The republics are Bosnia and Herzegovina, Croatia, Macedonia, Montenegro, Serbia, and Slovenia. The autonomous provinces of Voyvodina and Kosovo make up part of the Republic of Serbia. The population consists of Croat, Macedonian, Montenegrin, Muslim, Serbian, and Slovenian peoples, who account for about 90 percent of all inhabitants and nationalities, including Albanians, Bulgarians, Germans, Hungarians, Romanies, Rumanians, Turks, and others. The SFRY was established during the Struggle for National Liberation in the course of World War II, on November 29, 1943.

The nations and nationalities who now inhabit the territory of Yugoslavia have

The contributors would like to thank Mira Vlatković for the translation in English, and Vesna Hercigonja, Krešimir Martinčić, Josip Silić and Dubravko Horvatić for their very useful help in the search for information sources.

had a turbulent history because the Balkan Peninsula has always been a sphere of interest of both the major and minor powers. Southern Slavs came to the Balkan Peninsula in the sixth and seventh centuries A.D. They did not form one state, but lived in several smaller ones based on tribal associations. Their territory was threatened from all sides by the Franks, the Byzantines, the Republic of Venice, Hungary, and Bulgaria. After the schism of the Christian Church, Slovenes and Croats came under the influence of the Western Catholic Church, while the Serbs, Montenegrins, and Macedonians were under the influence of the Eastern Orthodox Church. In their new homeland the Slavs were mainly engaged in cultivating land in lowlands, especially in the plains in the north of the country and along rivers; in livestock breeding in the highlands, and fishing and farming in the coastal parts. In the ninth century, after the campaigns by Charles the Great, the northwestern and western parts of the country recognized the rule of the Franks. The area of what today is Slovenia remained under Frank and German rule until after the Middle Ages. In the twelfth century, Croatia united itself with Hungary. One part of the islands and towns of the Adriatic Coast was ruled by Byzantium or Venice, or made part of the Croato-Hungarian state.

The second half of the fourteenth century saw the invasion of the Balkans by the Turks from Asia Minor. By the beginning of the sixteenth century they had conquered Macedonia, Serbia, Bosnia, Herzegovina, Montenegro, and a part of Croatia. The Croato-Hungarian state succumbed to their later invasion in the early sixteenth century. It was then that the parts of Croatia and Hungary not invaded by the Turks joined the Hapsburg Monarchy. Thus, between the sixteenth and eighteenth centuries the Southern Slavonic peoples were ruled by three masters: the Hapsburgs, the Venetians, and the Turks. Slovenia and Croatia remained in the Hapsburg Monarchy, the Austro-Hungarian Empire, until its fall in 1918. Bosnia and Herzegovina were annexed to the empire in 1878 until which time they had been under Turkish rule. The Berlin Congress recognized the independence of Serbia and Montenegro.

Dubrovnik had an exceptional history and enjoyed an exceptional position. Founded in the seventh century A.D., it developed (together with its immediate surroundings) into an independent republic in the fifteenth century and remained so until 1808 when the French annexed it to the Kingdom of Italy. The people of Dubrovnik thrived through diversified trade and highly developed shipping. A particular trait of Dubrovnik is that the rich cultural life developed during the course of its history left a lasting trace both in history of the Yugoslav peoples and in Europe.

The Kingdom of the Serbs, Croats, and Slovenes came into being after the end of World War I, covering the area now roughly corresponding to that of present-day Yugoslavia. However, this interwar formation did not fulfill the strivings of the peoples of Yugoslavia for an independent state community.

This brief survey of the history of the Southern Slavonic peoples shows that the major part of their efforts had to be directed toward maintaining national identity and, in spite of foreign obtrusion, toward the development of their own culture.

TRADITIONAL FORMS AND EXPRESSIONS OF HUMOR

Popular Forms

Humor in Yugoslavia should be viewed above all through folk humor. Folk humor, it goes without saying, is linked to the history of the peoples of Yugoslavia; and historically observed, it is manifested in what might be termed folklore or spoken literature. This aspect of anonymous folk creativity is manifested in poems, stories, tales, fables, short stories, anecdotes, proverbs, drinking songs, mocking rhymes, riddles, and even curses. It shows that folk humor finds its expression in a variety of ways through speech communication. We should add to these the various forms of informally staged expressions of humor and wit, which have nothing to do with either amateur or professional theatre companies.

It is believed that the origins of folk literature can be traced back to very ancient times, even prehistory. Folklore in this country can be dated to the time of the migration of the Slavs to the Balkan Peninsula.

Folk poems and tales make up a part of the regular school curricula. There is ample literature available on their classification, dating, form, and contents. Since there is no bibliography of folk literature, but many books and articles on folk literature with very similar contents, it is not justifiable to cite any particular author. Bearing in mind the fact that each nation and nationality has its own folk literature, besides many translations from other Yugoslav languages, such a task becomes impossible, and that is why only the sources used in the writing of this chapter appear in the references at the end. Humor and wit, however, occur rarely as the subject of special treatises, although there are a certain number of such writings. In the majority of such texts, folk wit and humor are mentioned or dealt with only in passing.

Epic and lyric poetry often reveal humorous traits, or they contain at least an occasional humorous rhyme. There are poems which can be said to be humorous as a whole. These verses usually mock folk heroes, who are otherwise known and lavishly glorified by heroic poetry. Thus, for instance, there are humorous poems about Prince Marko, who is one of the most popular heroes of epic folk poetry.

Up until the first half of this century folk poetry was mainly passed on with an accompaniment by musical instruments such as the fiddle and the tamboura. The tune was mostly a very simple and monotonous chant. Urbanization naturally suppressed this manner of singing. Still, shorter forms of folk poetry have survived (in nonurbanized milieus only); as a rule they are sung to a common folk tune. These tunes differ greatly depending on the region. Consequently, the folk tunes of Slovenia, Hrvatsko Zagroje, Dalmatia, Slavonia, Voyvodina, Bos-

nia and Herzegovina, Montenegro, Serbia, Kosovo, and Macedonia are clearly
differentiated. Very often these are short lyrical songs, basically similar in their
subject (mainly love). Humor comes to the fore in very short verses (almost
without exception sung in couplets). In Srijem and Slavonia they are called
bećarac, a playboy-bachelor's song; in Dalmatinska Zagora they are called,
among other things, *gange*. A light, cheerful tone, mostly ironic and skittish,
is predominant in those short songs, usually a decasyllabic couplet; their subject
is love, their tune very simple but characteristic, e.g.,

> Alaj volim curicu u cicu,
> sto se dade ljubiti po licu
>
> Oh, I love a lass in chintz
> who will let me kiss her cheeks.

or

> U mog strica osam kobasica,
> sedam przi osmu strina drzi
>
> My uncle has eight sausages, he fries seven in a pan
> while the eighth my aunt holds patiently in her hand.

They are usually sung by young people on various occasions such as fairs,
holidays, weddings, or other village entertainments. In urbanized places there
are songs similar to folk songs, but heavily influenced by foreign music and
subject. They are sometimes called "old-city songs." One example is

> Gle mjeseca, al' se nakrivio,
> sram ga billo i on se napio
>
> See the moon, on one side shrunk
> shame on her, she too has got drunk.

Folktales, which may still be passed on by word of mouth, for traditional
reasons, in some less urbanized parts of the country today, often contain a
humorous vein, so that sometimes they are listed as a special kind of folktale.

The target figures of humorous folktales more often than not are secular or
church dignitaries or some typical funny characters. Although in many tales the
characters are not named, they are easily recognizable.

Humorous folktales can refer to general human weaknesses. In such cases,
the tale makes fun of a variety of socially unacceptable behaviors, such as lies,
boasts, laziness, theft, miserliness, avarice, etc., especially on the part of merchants and the well-to-do.

The target of the joke can be neighboring villages, tribes, ethnic groups, or
even nations in general. Such stories, mainly short ones, have a special name—

rugalice, mocking tales. These relate to some general traits attributed to the people of a given region or ethnic group. They deride naïveté, laziness, and miserliness. The following is an example:

The inhabitants of an island in the Adriatic heard there was wisdom and brains for sale in Venice, so they sent some of their people there to buy it and bring some back for them. The clever Venetians sold them a mouse closed in a barrel and told them that they must not open the barrel before they landed on their island. When they returned and opened the barrel, the mouse escaped and swam to an islet not far away from the shores of their island. The islanders then took ropes to draw the islet closer to their island in order to have wisdom close by.

Many jocular stories are based, however, on the conflicts between the exploiters and the exploited. In the southeastern parts the exploiters are Turks; in the north, Hungarians; in the west, Venetians and Italians; in the northwest, Austrians. Thus actual milieu and the persons are different, but all these stories share a common element: derision and mockery of those who hold power. Many features of nations or folk heroes, otherwise negative, are shown as positive because they help harm the masters.

An illustration of this is the story known under the title ''Ero from the Other World'':

Ero manages to convince a Turkish woman that he has arrived from the Other World where he saw her dead son living poorly. The woman gives him money to take along when he returns to the Other World. Ero succeeds not only in cheating her, but also her husband who wants to catch Ero and make him return the money; instead, he is eventually persuaded to give Ero a horse.

This is one of the best-known humorous folktales. The composer Jakov Gotovac of Zagreb used the story and expanded it for the plot of his opera of the same title. The opera has been performed in several opera houses in Europe and overseas.

The means used to express humor in folktales can be caricature, as, indeed, is most commonly the case in mocking verse. It can be a play on words (most frequently found in deriding foreigners, who as a rule are invaders or masters) or the use of different meanings of the same word. For instance,

While crossing a river in a boat, all of the passengers, among whom was a priest, fell into the water. As the priest could not swim, they stretched out their arms to pull him out, shouting ''Give us your hand.'' The priest, however, did not give his hand and was drowned. When they told his wife what had happened, she told them they ought to have shouted ''Here's the hand,'' because he had not learned to give but only to take.

Telling lies and competing in lying sometimes pass into the realm of the fantastic. The lies may consist of inventing unreal things and events; for instance, that somebody was born before his father, that a plant grew as high as the sky, or that somebody walked around headless. Such stories easily become fantastic, like the story of a man whose horse had a wound from the saddle:

Somebody suggested that he should sprinkle the wound with beaten walnuts. When he did that, a walnut-tree grew out of the horse's back. The man then threw a lump of earth against the tree to get some walnuts down. A field formed from the particles of the earth that had remained in the top of the tree. The man then took his plough and oxen, ploughed the field and sowed wheat.

Pranks are also quite frequent, usually in the relationship between servant and master, where the servant, of course, plays a practical joke on the master. However, the prank for prank's sake is also common. For instance,

Ero was keeping a Turk's cattle, among which there was also one of Ero's cows. It so happened that one of the Turk's cows and Ero's cow attacked each other and Ero's cow killed the Turk's cow. Ero reported the event to the Turk as follows:
Ero: One of your cows stabbed mine.
The Turk: Is anybody to blame for it, did anybody make her do it?
Ero: No, nobody, they stabbed each other for no reason.
The Turk: Well, nothing doing, there's no court for cattle.
Ero: But my cow stabbed yours, too.
The Turk: Ah, let me see what the law says.
Ero: No you won't, if there's no law for my cow, there is none for yours.

Here is another illustration:

A peasant came to his master the Turk and brought him something as a present.
The Turk: Is that all you've brought me?
Peasant: I wanted to bring you something else, but my wife wouldn't let me.
The Turk: One shouldn't obey one's wife; he who does is worse than she.
The next time the peasant brought a present to his master, the latter again asked if he had anything else to give him.
Peasant: My wife was giving me something else, but I wouldn't listen to her, as you told me not to, last time.

One of the commonest means of expressing humor is unexpectedness, and here the unusual, unnatural, impossible, or illogical is the vehicle, but in such a way that in the end it proves to be psychologically justifiable and possible. For instance,

The Gipsies are saying: if we had butter, and then if we had flour, we would borrow a pan in the village and make a pittah, and then we'd take it to someone to have it baked in the oven. One of the little boys among them begins to imitate gestures as if he were eating and says he would then eat it like this. His father smacks him on the face saying: "Steady there, you can't have it all and leave nothing for us."

Although some basic themes are common throughout the whole territory of the Yugoslav peoples, the influence of foreigners exercised in the southwestern, northeastern, and western parts is obvious. The eastern and southeastern parts of the country were mostly influenced by the Turks, the northern by Hungarians, and the northwestern parts by Gemans and Austrians, in the west the dominating force was the Italians. This variety can also be recognized in the heroes of humorous folktales.

There are a few figures who appear in funny stories as the main characters, as jokers. In the eastern and southeastern parts, one of the most frequent is Nasraddin Hodja, brought to our folklore through Turkish influence. He is a wiseacre, usually outwitting others, but sometimes he is outwitted himself. Here are two stories:

A wiseacre hears about Nasraddin Hodja and starts off for his village to meet and outwit him. He gets there and sees a man leaning against a wall so that it won't fall over, and he asks him if he knows Nasraddin Hodja and where he lives. This one tells him that he knows Nasraddin Hodja and that he will go and bring him, if the other will support the wall so it won't collapse. So he supports the wall and many hours later another man comes by and tells the one who has been supporting the wall that the one he met first was Nasraddin Hodja himself.

In the middle of the night Nasraddin Hodja hears a din in front of his house. He gets up, covers himself with a blanket and goes out to see what is going on. When he sees that there are two men quarreling, he approaches them trying to calm them down. These two, however, get angry with him, take his blanket and get away. So he goes back into his house and tells his wife that there were two men quarreling. She wants to know what they were quarreling about, and Nasraddin answers: "About my blanket, it seems."

Petrica Kerempuh (Petritsa Kherempookh), a figure greatly resembling Till Eulenspiegel, is very popular in northwestern Croatia.

In addition to those, some of the figures featured by folktales are autochtonous. In the area of the Serbo-Croatian language these are Ero, Ćoso, Raja, Vuk Dojčević, in Slovenia Peter Klepec, and in Macedonia Iter Pejo. Many funny stories are told at their expense, but mainly they figure as folk heroes, folk wiseacres, who by their resourcefulness outwit those who wield power. More recently the main characters of jokes are stereotypes from the different regions, such as the people of Lika, Zagorje, Srijem, and Bosnia. Such a figure can be a positive hero in one joke (he has outwitted others) and the subject of mockery in another, owing to his stupidity, ignorance, simplicity, or some other less attractive traits (miserliness, avarice).

Here are some illustrations showing how a simple man outwits the man in a privileged position. This common man may be nameless, a peasant or shepherd, or perhaps one of the figures mentioned earlier. Stories of this type can be found all over Yugoslavia.

A peasant has borrowed a kettle for the distillation of brandy for a sum of money fixed by a tradesman. A few days later the peasant brings the tradesman a very small kettle explaining that this was the offspring of the kettle he had borrowed, and which gave birth to the small kettle; he would return the big one when it recovered from delivery. The tradesman accepts the small kettle. A few days later the peasant comes again with the tidings that the big kettle died of the consequences of the delivery. When the tradesman protests, the peasant explains: whatever can give birth can die.

A traveler happens to get to a house to stay overnight. The landlady does not offer him anything to eat explaining that she has nothing to give him. He then asks for some water and a nail to make dinner for himself. He puts the nail into the pot with water and puts it on the fire. When the water is boiling, he asks for a little flour, then for just a little salt, then for just a few onions, etc., until he has made the usual dish—a broth.

The emperor (Turkish or any other) asks for an answer to three questions. If no one can answer all three questions he will punish the whole population. The questions are of the type: How far is it from the earth to the sky? Where is the middle of the earth?, etc. There are variations on these questions depending on the region where the story originated. Nobody can answer those questions except one man coming from among the people; the answers consist of witticisms or pranks, for instance, the question of how far it is from the earth to the sky, the folk wise answers by giving the emperor a large ball of thread (or something similar) and tells him that the distance is exactly equal to the length of the thread; if the emperor does not believe him, he should check for himself.

Quite a few funny stories have animals as the main characters, which probably shows that they are adapted from fables. An illustration of this type is the following:

The wolf has sworn not to slaughter and not to eat meat any more and has gone to the desert to become a saint. Passing a flock of geese on his way, he hears a gander hiss at him. The wolf jumps and devours him. In the court the wolf is asked why he did it if he has sworn not to slaughter any more. The wolf answers: Why did the gander hiss at a saint!

Funny folk stories can be erotic, but until ten years ago they were not published. As an example we shall retell one which found its place in collections published earlier, obviously in a milder form.

A group of young men, talking about girls, divided girls into the coy part—from the waist downwards—and the pretty part—from the waist upwards. Each of the young men said which three things from the pretty part of a girl's body he would like best. One said he would like the throat, teeth and cheeks. Another said he liked the eyes, hair and eyebrows, and so on. When it was the last boy's turn, he said: Since there is nothing left for me, I'll go to the nether part.

Only recently have collections of erotic folk poetry, where sex is the exclusive subject matter, been published. Furthermore, the rich and varied folk expressions concerning sex are occasionally used in literary fiction.

The verses in folk poetry are usually short and rhyming; they were recorded with other folklore but have been kept in archives until the present day. The verses are generally considered humorous, although it may be difficult to discern in many cases whether the verses are really witty or whether they elicit laughter because they speak about sex in an unrestrained manner.

Other forms of humor are perhaps even commoner than humorous folk poetry and folktales, especially in recent times. These forms may be better suited to their content because they are shorter: anecdotes, witticisms, jocular proverbs, humorous toasts, funny riddles, and jokes. People who can tell funny things have always been highly esteemed and welcome, especially in nonurbanized areas, where people gather on various occasions maintaining their local customs. Jokes are told whenever people get together, for harvests, fairs, in maize threshing, and the like. Especially convenient are various occasions during the winter when people gather to pick feathers and perform other chores. Here everybody is expected to joke, and if possible a joker should be present to lead in the jokes and prompt others to tell jokes and be merry.

Jocular verbal content can be associated with simple stage expressions, as is the case during carnival and in wedding customs. In the western parts of the country and above all in the coastal regions, most likely under Roman or Italian influence, carnival customs have been maintained for several centuries (records go back to the thirteenth century), when jokes and merrymaking were expressed mainly in a standard way. In recent times (since the beginning of this century) the celebration of Carnival Time has spread to other parts of Yugoslavia.

The greatest portion of wedding rites (except the formal act of wedding performed by a priest or by civilian authorities) aims at merrymaking, both verbal and scenic. Even at the beginning of the ritual, when the bridegroom comes to the bride's house to take her away, there are various jokes relating to wealth or the size of the dowry, or they may hint at sex; the parents, for instance, will bring an old woman instead of the bride. During the feast a person is appointed—there is a name for such a person, Čauš,—who must see to it that guests are merry. He does that by producing funny toasts, prompting the guests to eat and drink; making jokes at the expense of the bridegroom's, the bride's, and the bestman's parents; and not forgetting to include the young couple's sexual relations. It is not unusual to perform short sketches, mainly extemporized, on such occasions.

There is the shadow theatre and the folk puppet show, also produced on the occasions mentioned, namely, weddings, carnivals, winter gatherings, and the like. Here is an illustration of a puppet show:

The puppeteer is lying under a bench covered with a sheet. He puts up his hands with a puppet in each on either side of the bench. His voice changes for each puppet. The puppets' names are Casper and Melko; they are quarrelling about the land after their father's death. Location: northwestern Croatia.

CASPER: (gets up on the bench first) Melko! Melko!

MELKO: (coming up slowly) What is it?

CASPER: Our old folks are gone. We must divide the land. Father told me that the landmark should be here (he hits the bench with his hand).

MELKO: No, Casper, he told me that it must be here (hits the bench with his hand on the other side).

CASPER: No, he said here (hitting the other side).

MELKO: No, here (hitting again at his side).

They go on hitting until they come to grips and fall to the ground each at his end of the bench. Now Melko comes up first:

MELKO: Casper! Casper!

CASPER: (appearing slowly) What do you want, brother?

MELKO: Our old folks are gone. We must divide the land. Father told *me* that the landmark should be here.

So it goes on as long as the audience laughs.

Humor in the Literary and Performing Arts

The beginnings of theatre comedy on Yugoslav soil are associated with the name Marin Držić (born in Dubrovnik around 1508, died in Venice in 1567). Between 1548 and 1551 Dubrovnik saw the performance of his comedies *Pomet*, *The Story of Stanac*, and *Dundo Maroje*. At that time, as well as later on, in Dubrovnik and other towns on the coast there were nonprofessional theatre groups, which performed plays in real theatres (such a theatre in Hvar dates back to 1612). Držić's best-known comedies are *The Miser* and *Dundo Maroje*, both of them still performed. Their special feature is the lively vernacular of Dubrovnik. Themes inspired by Plautus dominate in Držić's comedies, but his characters are local people very plastically portrayed.

Some seventeenth and eighteenth century comedies by anonymous authors have also been preserved; they were performed during the carnival. These are situation comedies and comedies of character, written under a marked Italian influence; still, the people, the way of life, and the cities where the comedies are set are well presented.

In the eighteenth century a playwright from Zagreb, Tituš Brezovački wrote a few comedies, which have been played until today. The comedy called *Matijaš Grabancijaš Dijak* (The Sorcerer Student Mathias) has didactic tendencies and was written for carnival performances. In a series of scenes Brezovački condemns and punishes the vices and faults of his fellow citizens, denouncing behavior typical not only of the Zagreb milieu and society but of others as well. Brezovački makes ample use of battery to elicit laughter. His comedy *Diogeneš* is based on the idea of two lost brothers who cannot find each other, and the main aim is again the eradication of evil.

The best-known author of comedies in the nineteenth century is beyond any doubt Jovan Sterija Popović, who featured types such as the miser or snob characteristic of Voyvodina middle-class society of his time. The dominant influence in his numerous comedies is that of Molière.

An outstanding and original author of the second half of the nineteenth and the first half of the twentieth century is Branislav Nušić. He created his own style in numerous comedies to such an extent that we can talk of Nušićian humor. His themes are conditions prevailing in Belgrade at the turn of the century. By means of witty turns of phrase and skillful plots he ridicules nouveaux riches, careerists, snobs, and the like. He also wrote satirical prose. His humorous novel *Autobiography* is very popular; it is a general satire on the Serbian society of his time.

Humor in the Visual Arts

The notion of visual arts humor generally means cartoons. As far as we know, the first political cartoon in this country appeared in 1827 during the visit of the Hungarian Archduke to Croatia. A little later political cartoon came into being in Serbia. In other parts of present-day Yugoslavia it dates back to the end of the nineteenth and the beginning of the twentieth century. Caricatures have appeared in the so-called serious newspapers as well, but the majority were featured in specialized papers. Generally speaking, political and social cartoons were dominant in the nineteenth and the early twentieth century, because at those times cartoons commented on the struggle of the Yugoslav people against foreign rulers. If they were not political in character, their main role was enlightenment.

DEVELOPMENT OF HUMOR IN THE TWENTIETH CENTURY

Popular Forms

As we said previously, folk humor survives in its traditional forms in less urbanized areas and milieus, and is practiced mainly at weddings, carnivals, and similar events. Funny folk stories seem to have been transformed nowadays into the most widespread kind of humoristic expression, namely, the telling of jokes. In this country jokes are told on literally every occasion and are prompted by any situation. Traditional humor appears mostly (in a relatively unchanged form) in folk songs such as *bećarac* and *gange* and to a certain extent in the lyrics of songs composed to folk tunes.

Humor in the Literary and Performing Arts

The majority of older Yugoslav writers, especially those from the nineteenth century, wrote satirical poetry and prose. This is particularly true of Croatian, Slovene, and Serbian writers. Their satire concerned society and political life,

an instance of which is the satirical poetry of the time of the Illyrian Movement
of National Revival in Croatia at the beginning of the nineteenth century.

We should make some brief remarks on the major satirists of the last and
present centuries.

Stevan Sremac (1855–1906) sought and found inspiration for a humorist picture of the Serbian petty-bourgeois life and mentality of his time in lesser and
not very significant human experiences and events. Sremac's stories do not have
a main hero, nor a particular action; he places humor and laughter above all,
and his figures and action are subordinated to this comic atmosphere. Sremac
builds his work on anecdote, expanded by a series of other anecdotes, episodes,
and details.

Radoje Domanović (1873–1908) wrote political allegories and satires directed
against the regime of Serbia of his time. In addition, he made impressive descriptions of Serbian villages and a few sketches portraying the petty bourgeoisie.
His humor is not malicious, and he was at his best in noticing what was funny
in people: their mechanical habits, their playing of social roles for which they
were not fitted.

Zmaj Jovan Jovanović (1835–1904) is best known as a children's poet, for
whom he wrote patriotic, instructive, cheerful, and jocular verse. He was also
the editor of a few satirical papers. His work includes satirical poems exhorting
the Croatian and Serbian peoples to free themselves from foreign rule.

Antun Gustav Matoš (1873–1914) was a writer of stories, notes, feuilletons,
essays, travelogues, and poems, as well as a critic of literature, music, art, and
theatre. His satirical polemics earned him great popularity. Characteristic features
of the prose of Matoš, who worked and lived in Zagreb and Belgrade, are irony,
sarcasm, the comic, and the grotesque.

Miroslav Krleža (1875–1981), poet, novelist, short story writer, playwright,
and essayist, is one of the greatest Yugoslav men of letters. His entire work is
imbued with a specific humor; he excels in irony of a general human significance.
His best-known work is a collection of poems in Kaikavian dialect, the *Ballads
of Petritsa Kherempookh*, where he made use of this folk hero to picture the
destiny of the people in a derisive way by means of black humor at his own
expense. The *Ballads* are considered one of the best achievements of Croatian
literature as a whole. As they are written in dialect, a translation would necessarily
impair the general impression. An illustration of Krleža's humor, or rather irony,
is offered here in a translation by Mirjana Krizmanić of a poem written in standard
Serbo-Croatian dating from 1934.

A DIALOGUE IN JERUSALEM

—So? From Nazareth he comes?

—Sure, the vegetable women on the corner are his very aunts!

—But I've heard that he is an illegitimate chile' and that his father is cleaning
   the streets for a while.

—He was born in a stall, that is for certain.

Anyway his parentage is muddy and uncertain.
With some old man his mother runs around,
but who could know those scandals every round?
—Ah, well. Does he have some schooling?
Did he pass his maturity exam?
—Nothing of the sort. You must be joking, ma'm.
The other day, in the middle of the street
he kissed a fallen girl he just happen'd to meet!
He drinks with vagabonds and is followed
by beggars, fishermen and those whose eyes are hollowed,
and he could always be found in their midst
and now he's even started corrupting our kids.
Already complaints about him are arriving to the police boss,
just you watch it, my lady, this boy will end on the cross!

Slávko Kolar (1891–1963) in his stories written before World War II portrays peasants and rural and petty-bourgeois intelligentsia: lawyers, would-be politicians, lower civil servants, and careerists. With his specific sense of humor he managed to pinpoint the mentality of the middle class who, in fact, are "disguised peasants." A satirical short story stemming from the time of the occupation of the country ridicules the quisling armed forces backing the invaders.

Humor in the Visual Arts

Political and social caricatures are found daily or at least regularly in Sunday issues of practically all newspapers and magazines. Although they often present foreign authors and cartoonists, the majority are produced by domestic artists. Cartoons are widespread in Yugoslavia, and we could list at least a score of outstanding cartoonists, among whom a few have gained an international reputation. Their themes are political or social, of a greater or lesser significance, and recently ecology has become a popular theme. Only two are mentioned here; they are probably the best-known Yugoslav cartoonists.

Pjer Križanić (1890–1962), one of the best-known figures of Yugoslav cartoons, worked in Zagreb and Belgrade. In addition to caricatures regularly published in newspapers and magazines, he has three albums of cartoons: *Naše muke* (Our Troubles, 1923), *Kuku Todore* (Woe Is Thee, O Todor, 1926), and *Protiv fašizma* (Against Fascism, 1948). These albums prove that not a single area of social life could escape his sharp eye. His cartoons show the artist's firm hand in drawing and his awareness of political and social conditions. Križanić went far beyond the level of everyday newspaper illustration, and many of his caricatures are of a lasting value.

Otto Reisinger (born in 1927) lives and works in Zagreb. He published his first caricatures while he was a student of architecture, immediately after World War II. Although he eventually got his architect's diploma, he continued to work as a cartoonist and is today our most widely known humorist, not only in

Yugoslavia but in some European countries too. His best-known figure, Pero (Peter), drawn in a very characteristic and recognizable way, has appeared daily in Zagreb's most important nenwspaper, *Vjesnik*, for more than 25 years. Pero's comments are always very acute, and there is no shortage, social change, or event without an immediate comment from Pero.

The field of visual humor, however, is wider. Some of the works by noted painters should be included here, because they share many features with the cartoon. Caricature can be expressed in sculpture as well, and caricatures carved in stone dating from the twelfth century have been found. Visual humor includes carnival masks, which can present a great variety of facial expressions. Today masks serve exclusively for entertainment and amusement, and have completely lost, at least in Europe, the magic part they used to have at the time of their creation.

Contemporary visual humor includes cartoon strips and animated film. Unfortunately, systematic data and information have not been gathered, even though cartoon strips have been a popular way of expressing humor in this country since the early thirties. Animated film has achieved a high standard in Yugoslavia, and the Zagreb School of Cartoon Film has gained international recognition.

Yugoslav film production, which is not large (some twenty films a year), regularly presents film comedies beside other genres. The greatest number of comedies are made by film producers from Serbia.

Public or Specialized Places for Humorous Expression

Nowadays humor is cultivated—at least in town milieus all over the country—in specialized theatres and on radio and television. In Zagreb, for instance, there are three theatres specially intended for comedies, but comedies are occasionally performed in all the other theatre houses too. Productions of classical comedies, contemporary comedies, and plays by foreign and Yugoslav playwrights are staged in them. Among local authors of comedies written for stage performance, Fadil Hadžić is the best known. He has written a great number of comedies which, in addition to the classical gags and humor, present social satire. Hadžić writes not only for the stage but also humorous newspaper articles on current topics and contemporary figures. He has been director and screenwriter of a dozen pictures.

Humor in the Mass Media

Newspapers and periodicals specializing in humor and satire started, to the best of our knowledge, around the 1860s. Even before that time, however, occasional publications of that genre were issued during the carnival in some places on the Adriatic Coast.

The number of humorous newspapers published until World War I must have amounted to several dozens. Most of them were comparatively short-lived because the authorities banned them either directly or indirectly by hampering their means of finance. The main purpose of those papers becomes obvious from their names: *Bič* (The Whip), *Brico* (The Barber), *Trn* (The Thorn), *Jež* (The Hedgehog), *Satir* (Satyr), *Koprive* (The Nettles), *Komarac* (The Mosquito), *Osa* (The Wasp), *Bockalo* (The Punch), *Stršen* (The Hornet), *Muha* (The Fly), and *Domišljan* (The Resourceful). In addition to satire, those papers supplied room for the so-called folk humor and had significant enlightening aims.

After World War I the most popular satirical papers in the Kingdom of Serbs, Croats and Slovenes were *Koprive* (The Nettles), published in Zagreb from 1901 until 1936, and *Ošišani jež* (The Trimmed Hedgehog), published in Belgrade from 1935 till 1940. Their main topics were political and social satire. *Crveni smeh* (Red Laughter) was published in Belgrade for a very short time, from May 5 till July 4, 1920. It was a communist satirical weekly which, albeit for a short time, played an important role in the resistance to the establishment.

The most popular papers appearing regularly since the end of World War II are *Jež* (The Hedgehog) in Belgrade, *Pavliha* (a common name, Paul) in Ljubljana, and *Osten* (The Punch) in Skopje. In addition to these, other papers are issued on special occasions, e.g., for carnival, all over Yugoslavia; they are mainly of local interest. *Jež* also has a regular output of paperback collections of cartoons and verbal jokes, mostly taken from foreign periodicals, and to a lesser degree from the Yugoslav press. Such collections of jokes of a variety of types are from time to time offered by other publishers as well.

Jež is certainly the most popular humorous paper in Yugoslavia, and there is hardly any Yugoslav humorist that has not written for it. *Jež* is a continuation of the *Ošišani jež* (The Trimmed Hedgehog), whose publication was stopped after the occupation of the country in 1941. However, a paper called *Logorski jež* (Camp Hedgehog) appeared in the prisoner-of-war camp at Osnabrück in 1944. After the liberation of the country in 1945 *Jež* has been regularly published.

On Yugoslav radio there has been a Sunday night program running for over 30 years—''The Jolly Evening''—which deals with current events in Yugoslavia and abroad from a humorous point of view.

For several years some broadcasts by Radio Belgrade featured Dušan Radovič, who is also a children's writer. His wit and humor attracted large audiences all over Yugoslavia. In his very witty, sometimes sarcastic way, and yet at times poetic, he touched on all topics and all areas of individual and public life. Here is an example from one of his three books of jokes written for Radio Belgrade:

Let unemployed girls bear children. This is the only thing other people are willing to do for them.

Yugoslav Television regularly includes humorous broadcasts, and more recently (for some fifteen years now) humorous series, which are probably the most popular programs in Yugoslavia. The most avidly watched among them came from Belgrade Television; their author is Radivoje Lola Djukič, who was able to combine a folk sense of humor with social satire. Comedian-actors featured in these programs have become very popular (Mija Aleksič, Mjodrag Petrovič Čkalja). Similar programs were presented, with lesser or greater success in Ljubljana, Zagreb, Sarajevo, and Skopje.

CONTEMPORARY HUMOR AND TRENDS

There is not much to add about contemporary humor in Yugoslavia, because it follows the general trends established through the postwar years. There is still a division between the rural and township areas, with the former nursing the popular and traditional folk forms of humor, and the latter being open to some experimenting with domestic themes and current topics as well as imported ones.

Humor has found its place in all the mass media. Almost all newspapers and magazines for the wider reading public have special humor sections with contents mostly produced by domestic authors. Especially popular are comic aphorisms with social and political content.

On the radio there are regular humoristic broadcasts, mostly based on current issues and written by authors from all over Yugoslavia.

Yugoslav Television recently began broadcasting once a week the "Humor-Club," a half-hour presentation of sketches and songs referring to all important happenings in the country in a comical and satirical way. The program of the Yugoslav Television regularly includes some imported comedies and comic series, as well as short inserts by known artists like Dave Allen and Bob Hope. It could be said that, with some variations in time and place, all mass media publish and broadcast more local and national humor than imported humor. For the most part, probably because of the actuality of it, national humorous products are also more popular.

UNIVERSAL FUNCTIONS OF HUMOR AND THE NATIONAL MANIFESTATIONS

Aggressive and Social Humor

Yugoslav humor, or more precisely, the humor of the peoples of Yugoslavia, besides all its diversity originating from the variety of national mentalities on the one hand and the variety of foreign influence on the other, does have some characteristics in common. It is a kind of humor produced by small communities surrounded by an enemy, threats, hardships, and the forces of nature. Fighting for centuries against various enemies and invaders, the Yugoslav nations and nationalities tried above all to survive and to create and preserve their own identity. In such conditions the original and most important role of humor was, and still is, its social function, boosting the morale of the community and emphasizing and asserting the community's experience and behavior while ridiculing and refusing everything foreign and strange. The function of humor is in the first place social; it is also aggressive, however, because it derides anything or anybody that does not belong to the narrow community in which one lives. The objects of ridicule are invaders, strangers, high dignitaries, and all representatives of authority and power, both civilian and clerical. Dialects are often employed, as they emphasize the affiliation to a given community and at the same time exclude all those not belonging to it. The forms of this type of folk humor are uncouth; they include direct derision of a stranger's speech or the clothes of a nobleman. Nevertheless, they can be rather sophisticated and express aggression in a disguised manner or even through animal figures. The social function of humor is characteristic of literary humor as well; while it is true that the first comedies that appeared in this country were inspired by foreign influence, they always included the actual local situation and problems. In fact, we can state that there is practically no Yugoslav author who does not use humor in its social function.

Sexual Humor

Along with social humor, sexual humor appears not infrequently in folk creation. This is cheerful, frivolous wit, abounding in ''naughty'' words, its main purpose being to express sexual and life vitality and prompting gaiety and an appropriate, sexually charged atmosphere. Sexual humor finds expression in stories and jokes spread by word of mouth; it is also quite productive, and rhymes are produced ad hoc according to the occasion and situation. Interestingly enough, folk humor is expressed even in curses, often rather peculiar and very funny, although they naturally use rather ''strong'' phrases. It can be said that in folk humor, still existing in rural areas, sexual humor is employed within groups and communities, while social humor operates in the relationships between various groups and communities.

Humor as Defense Mechanism

During the War of the National Liberation, in which all layers of society took part, ranging from peasants and workers to intellectuals, there was an abundance of anecdotes and jokes, whose function was both social and aggressive as well as defensive. The troops made jokes at their own expense and at the expense of the much stronger and better-equipped enemy. Here is an illustration:

In 1942 Demonja and Jerković (two outstanding Partisani leaders) met and talked about the fights in which they were engaged at the time, about the enemy and its strength. At one point in the course of their conversation Jercović asked Demonja quite seriously: You've got enough experience by now. Who is the most dangerous to your troops? Says Demonja: The girls, comrade, the girls! When they attack my proletarians there's no way of resisting.

During the hard times of the fight against invaders and frequent shortages of food, clothing, and medicines, Partisani fighters told jokes to boost the morale of their group, to diminish the fear of wounds and death, and to create at least some gaiety in otherwise dire circumstances. Jokes dating from those days have been gathered in special collections. During the War of the National Liberation numerous theatrical groups consisting of actor-fighters were active, performing short sketches or comedies in the breaks between battles or in the areas already liberated. These shows were made up specially for such occasions; they mocked the enemy and ridiculed their traits and behavior.

Black humor, or *Galgenhumor*, appears mainly in urban circles, where it is associated with periods of crisis. Characteristic of urban milieus is the appearance of jokes inspired by any changes, crises, or shortages. Almost immediately black jokes start circulating, spreading so rapidly that the same joke crops up in different places and can be heard from different people. The jokes are triggered by local, national, and international events. Thus, for instance, a campaign to help the starving population of Africa was immediately followed by this joke:

Two friends are conversing and one of them says:
Have you heard that all the drugs sent to Ethiopia were returned?
  Why? says the other.
  The first answers: Well, because of the instructions written on every bottle: Take three times a day after every meal.

Jokes appear also as explanations of new or existing acronyms. Thus, for instance, jokes about the Yugoslav airlines are quite popular: the name of JAT (Yugoslav Aero-Transport) was interpreted as "Joke about time" or "Just any time."

Intellectual Humor

Intellectual humor, whether in the form of incongruous or absurd jokes, is not too frequent in this country, and it appears exclusively among students and intellectuals and in some cartoon films.

Since Yugoslavia is still a developing society, international crises are reflected in conditions at home. Crises of energy as well as others cause difficulties and shortages here. Jokes on the subject are invented immediately and spread at a very great speed. Very popular are the "chocolate" jokes, so called because chocolate can *arrest* the bowel movement and the joke may lead to *arrest* of the teller. The subject of those jokes is politics, and the objects are political figures; their target, however, as is the case with true satire, is a variety of social phenomena and faults. The popularity of those jokes can be seen in TV comedies relating to such subjects, which in the sixties were so well liked that city streets were empty when those were broadcast. Short satirical sketches are often shown during political programs presented by the republics and autonomous provinces every week in turn.

It is obvious that social humor is dominant in this country even today, with aggressive and black humor added to it to a greater or lesser extent.

Judging by the great number of jokes which always keep circulating, as well as by the widespread habit of telling and exchanging jokes on every possible occasion, both formal and informal, we must conclude that a sense of humor is considered a great personal asset. We would even claim that practically any Yugoslav would be offended if told that he or she did not have a sense of humor, while expressing doubts about the Yugoslav's brains or abilities would be less offensive. Nevertheless, self-disparaging jokes are rarely told by individuals but are comparatively common in wider social contexts when we laugh at our own national traits or typical behavior.

We may conclude by saying that generally Yugoslavs laugh most at gags and jokes relating to various current problems, especially if they are spiced with racy words, so that these mechanisms of expressing humor are employed by all popular humorists and show-people.

REFERENCES

Balog, Z. (1975) Selection and Foreword to *Od doseljenja Hrvata do najnovijih debata. Humor u hrvatskom pjesnistvu*, vol. 3 (From the coming of the Croats until the latest debates, vol. 3).

Bonifacic Rozin, N. (1963) Selection and Foreword to *Narodne drame, poslovice i zagonetke* (Folk dramas, proverbs and riddles). Pet stoljeca hrvatske knjizevnosti (Five Centuries of Croatian Literature). Zagreb: Zora-Matica hrvatska.

Boskovic-Stulli, M. (1964) Selection and Foreword to *Narodne epske pjesme II* (Epic folk poems II). Pet stoljeca hrvatske knjizevnosti (Five Centuries of Croatian Literature). Zagreb: Zora-Matica hrvatska.

———. (1975) *Usmena kjizevnost kao umjetnost rijeci* (Spoken literature as the art of words). Zagreb: Mladost.

Boskovic-Stulli, M., and Zecevic, D. (1978) *Usmena i pucka knjizevnost* (Oral and folk literature). Povijest hrvatske knjizevnosti, knjiga 1 (The History of Croatian Literature, Book 1). Zagreb: Liber-Mladost.

Cubelic, T. (1965) *Epske narodne pjesme* (Epic folk poems). Zagreb: Skolska knjiga.

———. (1975) *Usmene narodne poslovice, pitalice, zagonetke* (Spoken folk proverbs, queries and riddles). Zagreb: Liber.

Delorko, O. (1964) Selection and Foreword to *Narodne epske pjesme I* (Epic folk poems 1). Pet stoljeca hrvatske knjizevnosti (Five Centuries of Croatian Literature). Zagreb: Zora-Matica hrvatska.

Donat, B. (1973) Selection and Foreword to "Nasmijani udesi. Humor u hrvatskoj prozi" (Smiling destinies. Humor in Croatian prose). *Antologi ja hrvatskog humora, Knjika, 1 & 2* (Anthology of Croatian Humor, vols. 1 and 2). Zagreb.

Duric, V. (1969) Selection and Foreword to *Antologija narodnih pripovedaka* (An anthology of folk tales). Srpska knjizevnost u sto knjiga (Serbian literature in a hundred books). Belgrade: Matica srpska—Srpska knjizevna zadruga.

Enciklopedija Jogoslavije (1960) (Yugoslav encyclopedia). Zagreb: Jugoslavenski leksikografski zavod.

———. (1980) (Yugoslav encyclopedia). Zagreb: Jugoslavenski leksikografski zavod.

Fotez, M., ed. (1967) *Komedije XVII i XVIII Stoljeca* (Comedies of the seventeenth and eighteenth centuries). Pet stoljeca hrvatske knjizevnosti (Five Centuries of Croatian Literature). Zagreb: Zora-Matica hrvatska.

Hecimovic, B. (1973) Selection and Foreword to *Pometova druzba. Komediografija od Naljeskovica do danas*, Knjiga 3 (Pomet's company. Comedy from Naljeskovic until the present day, vol. 3). Zagreb: Antolgija hrvatskog humora (Anthology of Croatian Humor). Zagreb.

———. (1973) *Tito Brezovacki, Dramska djela, pjesme* (T. Berzovacki. Dramas and poems). Pet stoljeca hrvatske knjizevnosti (Five Centuries of Croatian Humor). Zagreb. Zora-Matica hrvatska.

Horvatic, D. (1975) Selection and Foreword to *Ples Smrti. Antologija hrvatskog likovnog humora*, Knija 5 (The death dance, an anthology of visual Croatian humor, vol. 5). Antologija hrvatskog humora (Anthology of Croatian Humor). Zagreb.

Ilic, M. (1934) "O saljivcima nasih narodnih pripovedaka" (On the jokers in Yugoslav folk tales). *Knjizevni sever* (The literate North): 201–205.

Jemersic, P. "Narodne humoristicke gatalice i varalice" (Humorous folk riddles). *Zbornik za narodni zivot i obicaje* (Collection of Popular Life and Costumes). 9, no. 2: 511–34.

Kekez, J. (1973) *Bibliografija poslovica i zagonetaka* (A bibliography of proverbs and riddles). Matica srpska, prestampano iz Zbornika za slavistiku br. 5.

———. (1983) "Usmena knjizevnost" (Oral Literature). In *Uvod u Knjizevnost* (Introduction to literature). Ed. Z. Skreb and A. Stamac. Zagreb: Graficki zavod Hrvatske.

Knezevic, V. M. (1972) Selection and Foreword to *Antologija govornih narodnih umotvorina* (Anthology of spoken folklore). Srpska knjizevnost u sto knjiga (Serbian literature in a hundred books). Belgrade: Matica srpska—Srpska knjizevna zadruga.

Mijatovic, A. (1973) Selection and Foreword to *Ganga* (The Ganga). Duvno.

Mrduljas, I. (1980) Selection and Foreword to *Kudilja i vreteno. Erotske narodne pjesme* (The tow and the spindle—Erotic folk poems). Zagreb: Znanje.

Mujicic, K. (1975) Selection and Foreword to *Protivnici, rugaci i zabavjaci. Polemika i pamfleti*, Knija 6 (Rivals, mockers and entertainers, polemics and pamphlets, vol. 6). Zagreb: Antologija hrvatskog humora.

Pasaric, J. (1923) Selection and Foreword to *Hrvatska narodna sala* (Croatian folk jokes). Zagreb.

Pavlica, D. (1979) *Anegdote NOB* (Anecdotes from the National War of Liberation). Slavonska Požega.

Pesic, R., and Milosevic-Dordevic, N. (1984) *Narodna knjizevnost* (Folk literature). Belgrade: Vuk Karadzic.

Prcic, I. (1971) *Bunjevacke narodne pisme* (The Bunjevci folk poems). Subotica: Osvit.

Prokic, D. (1934) "Smesno u nasoj narodnoj prozi" (Humor in Yugoslav folk prose). *Knjizevni sever* (The Literate North): 205–208.

Ratkovic, M., ed. (1964) *Marin Drzic*. Pet stoljeca hrvatske knjizevnosti, Zora-Matica hrvatska (Five Centuries of Croatian Literature). Zagreb.

Skreb, Z., and Stamac, A. (1983) *Uvod y knjizevnost* (Introduction to literature). Zagreb: Graficki zavod Hrvatske.

Spoljar, K. (Selection) and Simic, S. (Foreword) (1962) *Smijeh i rane. Hrvatska satiricna poezija* (Laughter and wounds. Croatian satirical poetry). Zagreb: Lykos.

Stojanovic, M. (1866) Selection and Foreword to *Sbirka narodnih poslovicah, riecih i izrazah* (A collection of folk proverbs, sayings and expressions). Zagreb.

————. (1879) Selection and Foreword to *Sala i zbilja* (Joke and reality). Senj.

Tokin, M., ed. (1970) *Jovan Sterija Popovic. Komedije* (Jovan Sterije Popovic, comedies). Srpska knjizevnost u sto knjiga (Serbian Literature in a hundred books). Belgrade: Matica srpska—Srpska knjizevna zadruga.

"Vrste nasa narodne proze." (1934) (Types of Yugoslav folk prose) *Knjizevni sever* (The Literate North): 219–40.

APPENDIX A

Academic Approaches to Humor

Experimental and systematic research on humor was first published in the 1950s. Psychologists initiated this approach, most formulating their working hypotheses based on Freud. Research on humor was, and still is, published in different professional journals as there is no specialized publication dealing with the topic.

The first bibliography of published experimental articles in humor research appeared in 1972 in the United States (Goldstein and McGhee, 1972). It included 389 articles from over 100 journals published in English between 1900 and 1971, demonstrating a steady growth in the output of empirical research on humor. In a more recent book, edited by the same authors (McGhee and Goldstein, 1983), they wrote that such a bibliography at that point would contain several thousand items.

The most important impetus for research on humor, disseminating knowledge about humor and creating interdisciplinary and cross-cultural exchanges, has come from the International Conferences on Humor. These conferences created, in addition, a worldwide community of academics interested in humor. A short history of these conferences follows.

INTERNATIONAL CONFERENCES ON HUMOR

The first International Conference on Humor was held in 1976 in Cardiff, Wales, under the auspices of the Welsh Branch of the British Psychological Society. The conference organizers and chairmen were two psychologists, Anthony Chapman and Hugh Foot. Ninety-one papers were presented by academics from 11 countries. A volume containing all papers presented at the conference was published by Pergamon Press in 1977 (Chapman and Foot, 1977). This volume also presented an extensive bibliography on humor in English, including 1052 items.

The second International Conference took place in 1979 in Los Angeles and was sponsored by Antioch University. It was also chaired by two psychologists, Harvey Mindess and Joy Turek. Sixty papers were presented and a book of abstracts was prepared.

The third conference, held in 1982 in Washington, D.C., was sponsored by Montgomery College, the Workshop Library on World Humor, and the American Humor Studies Association. The chairman of the conference was the late Rufus C. Browning. One hundred and sixteen papers were presented, and Larry Mintz, one of the organizers of the conference, edited the book of abstracts.

The fourth International Conference was the first one held in a non–English-speaking country. It was held in Tel Aviv, under the auspices of Tel Aviv University and chaired by Avner Ziv. One hundred and two papers were presented by humor scholars from ten countries. A book of abstracts of the papers presented was published. Following this conference, the first International Conference on Jewish Humor was held in Tel Aviv, where 46 papers were presented. In addition to the books of abstracts, a book including the best papers was published in English and Hebrew (Ziv, 1986).

The fifth International Conference was held in Cork, Ireland, in 1985, chaired by Des MacHale, the first nonpsychologist to chair such a conference. MacHale is a mathematician who also writes humorous books. Cork University, which co-sponsored the conference with the Workshop Library of Humor, inaugurated during the conference the Humor Collection Library, probably one of the richest collections of humor books in the world. One day at the conference was dedicated to presentation of papers on Irish humor. A book of abstracts was prepared, in which the 114 papers presented were summarized.

The second International Conference on Jewish Humor was held in New York in 1986, under the auspices of Tel Aviv University and hosted by the New School of Social Research. Fifty-six papers were presented and a book of abstracts prepared. A book based on the best papers presented at the conference is to be published by Greenwood Press.

The sixth International Conference on Humor was held in Tempe, Arizona, under the auspices of the State University of Arizona in 1987 and chaired by Alleen and Don Nilsen. Scholars from thirty-eight countries participated and 611 papers were presented (including editors' panel and panel of foreign visitors). A book of abstracts is in preparation, planned to appear in April 1988.

In addition to these International Conferences, some national ones are also organized.

NATIONAL CONFERENCES

Since 1981 Don and Alleen Nilsen from Arizona State University have organized at their university campus five National Humor Conferences. The proceedings have been published each year in *World Humor and Irony Membership Serial Yearbook* (*WHIMSY*). The titles of the volumes, edited by the Nilsens, are

The Language of Humor/The Humor of Language (1982)

Metaphors Be with You: Humor and Metaphor (1983)

Contemporary Humor (1984)

Humor across the Disciplines (1985)

American Humor (1986)

Bulgaria has a House of Humor and Satire in Gobrovo hosting a humor festival every odd year. The fifteenth festival was held in 1985. A journal, *A propos*, is edited in Gobrovo by Stephan Fortunov, the director of the House of Humor and Satire.

In France a conference on Humor and Translation was held in 1986 at the University of Paris. It was chaired by Anne Marie Laurian, and the proceedings were published in *Contrastes*.

In Hyderabad, India, a conference on Indian humor was held in 1984. The proceedings were published in a book by the conference organizers (Luther, Raju, and Khandmiri, 1985).

These conferences, combined with the growing number of books and articles dealing with the scientific investigation of humor, are conducive to a better understanding of humor's contribution to human life.

REFERENCES

Chapman, A. J., and Foot, H. C., eds. (1977) *It's a Funny Thing, Humor*. Oxford: Pergamon Press.

Goldstein, J., and McGhee, P., eds. (1972) *The Psychology of Humor*. New York: Academic Press.

Luther, N., Raju, P. A. G., and Khandmiri, T., eds. (1985) *A Manifesto for Laughter*. Bombay: Bhadrachalum.

McGhee, P., and Goldstein, J., eds. (1983) *Handbook of Humor Research*. New York: Springer-Verlag.

Ziv, A., ed. (1986) *Jewish Humor*. Tel Aviv: Papyrus.

APPENDIX B

Thematic Bibliography

This appendix will be divided into three parts. The first presents the main academic references on the study of humor written in English. Only books will be included since the number of articles published exceeds 3000. The second part presents the list of the main edited volumes published on humor theory and research. Works about the relations between humor and diverse areas of arts and sciences are included in the third part. Since the greatest number of books on humor were written from a psychological point of view (and they are included in the first part of this appendix), only specialized areas of psychology will appear in the third part.

BOOKS ON HUMOR

Bergler, E. (1952) *Laughter and the Sense of Humor*. New York: Intercontinental Medical Book Corporation.

Bergson, H. (1921) *Laughter: an Essay on the Meaning of the Comic*. London: MacMillan. (Originally published in 1911).

Bloom, E. A. and Bloom, L. D. (1979) *Satire's Persuasive Voice*. Ithaca, New York: Cornell University Press.

Eastman, M. (1921) *The Sense of Humor*. New York: Scribner.

———. (1936) *Enjoyment of Laughter*. New York: Simon and Schuster.

Elliott, R. C. (1960) *The Power of Satire*. Princeton: Princeton University Press.

Esar, E. (1952) *The Humor of Humor*. New York: Horizon.

Freud, S. (1960) *Jokes and Their Relation to the Unconscious*. New York: Norton. (Originally published in 1905).

Fry, W. (1963) *Sweet Madness*. Palo Alto, Ca.: Pacific Books.

Greig, J. Y. T. (1923) *The Psychology of Laughter and Comedy*. New York: Dodd Mead.

Grotjahn, M. (1957) *Beyond Laughter*. New York: McGraw Hill.

Gruner, C. R. (1978) *Understanding Humor: The Working of Wit and Humor*. Chicago: Nelson-Hall.

Helitzer, M. (1984) *Comedy Techniques for Writers and Performers: The "Hearts" Theory of Humor and Writing*. Athens, Ohio: Lawhead Press.

Hertzler, J. O. (1970) *Laughter: A Socio-scientific Analysis*. New York: Exposition Press.

Highet, G. (1962) *The Anatomy of Satire*. Princeton: Princeton University Press.

Hill, H. and Blair, W. *America's Humor*. New York: Oxford University Press.

Holland, N. N. (1982) *Laughing: A Psychology of Humor*. Ithaca, N.Y.: Cornell University Press.

Inge, M. T. (1982) *American Humor*. New York: AMS Press.

Killey, F. and Shuttleworth, J. M. (1971) *Satire: From Aesop to Buchwald*. New York: Odyssey.

Legman, S. (1982) *Rationale of the Dirty Joke*. New York: Grove Press.

Leonard, F. M. (1981) *Laughter in the Courts of Love: Comedy in Allegory: From Chaucer to Spencer*. Norman, Ok.: Pilgrim Books.

Mindess, H. (1971) *Laughter and Liberation*. Los Angeles: Nash.

Mindess, H., Miller, C., Turek, J., Bender, A., and Corbin, S. (1985) *The Antioch Humor Test: Making Sense of Humor*. New York: Avon.

Moreall, J. (1981) *Laughter and Humor*. Evanston, Ill.: Northwestern University Press.

———. (1983) *Taking Laughter Seriously*. Albany: State University of New York Press.

Oring, E. (1984) *The Jokes of Sigmund Freud*. Philadelphia: University of Pennsylvania Press.

Pepicello, W. and Green, T. A. (1984) *The Language of Riddles: New Perspectives*. Columbus: Ohio State University Press.

Piddington, R. (1963) *The Psychology of Laughter: A Study in Social Adaptation*. New York: Gamut Press.

Rapp, A. (1951) *The Origin of Wit and Humor*. New York: Dutton.

Reik, T. (1962) *Jewish Humor*. New York: Gamut Press.

Robinson, J. (1974) *The Comic: An Illustrated History of Comic Strip Art*. New York: G.P. Putnam's Sons.

Schmitz, N. (1983) *Of Huck and Alice: Humorous Writing in American Literature*. Minneapolis: University of Minneapolis Press.

Shibles, W. (1978) *Humor: A Critical Analysis for Young People*. Whitewater, Wi.: The Language Press.

Sidis, B. (1933) *The Psychology of Laughter*. New York: Appleton.

Sully, J. (1909) *Essay on Laughter*. New York: Longman.

Willeford, W. (1969) *The Fool and His Scepter: A Study in Clowns and Jesters and Their Audience*. Evanston, Ill.: Northwestern University Press.

Wilson, C. P. (1979) *Jokes: Form, Content, Use and Function*. New York: Academic Press.

EDITED BOOKS

Chapman, A. J. and Foot, H. C. (1976) *Humor and Laughter: Theory, Research and Applications*. Chichester: Wiley.
————. (1977) *It's a Funny Thing, Humor*. Oxford: Pergamon Press.
Cohen, S. B., ed. (1978) *Comic Relief: Humor in Contemporary American Literature*. Chicago: University of Illinois Press.
Goldstein, J. H. and McGhee, P. E. (1972) *The Psychology of Humor*. New York: Academic Press.
Keller, C. (1981) *Growing up Laughing: Humorists Look at American Youth*. Englewood Cliffs, N.J.: Prentice Hall.
Levine, J. (1969) *Motivation in Humor*. New York: Atherton Press.
McGhee, P. and Chapman, A. D. (1980) *Children's Humor*. Chichester: Wiley.
McGhee, P. E. and Goldstein, J. H. (1983) *Handbook of Humor Research*. New York: Springer Verlag.
Mendel, W. (1970) *A Celebration of Humor*. Los Angeles: Mara Books.
Nahemow, L., McCluskey, K., and McGhee, P. E. (1985) *Humor and Aging*. New York: Academic Press.
Oring, E. (1984) *Humor and the Individual*. Los Angeles: California Folklore Society.
Sypher, W. (1956) *Comedy*. Garden City, NY: Doubleday.

HUMOR AND SPECIALIZED FIELDS

In some areas of sciences and arts, humor is studied as a way to better understand different aspects of these disciplines. The following books study humor as related to sciences and arts:

Anthropology

Apte, M. (1985) *Humor and Laughter: An Anthropological Perspective*. Bloomington: Indiana University Press.

Cinema

Mast, G. (1979) *The Comic Mind: Comedy and the Movies*. Chicago: University of Chicago Press.

Developmental Psychology

McDowell, J. H. (1979) *Children's Riddling*. Bloomingdale, In.: Indiana University Press.
McGhee, P. E. (1979) *Humor: Its Origin and Development*. San Francisco: Freeman.
Wolfenstein, M. (1954) *Children's Humor: A Psychological Analysis*. Glencoe, Ill.: Free Press.

Education

Kelly, B. (1985) *Learning with Laughter*. Portland, Me.: J. W. Walsh.

Linguistics

Nilsen, D. L and Nilsen, A. P. (1978) *Laughing Play: An Introduction to Linguistics*. Rowley, Mass.: Newbury House.
Raskin, V. (1985) *Semantic Mechanisms of Humor*. Boston: D. Reidel.
Kirshenblatt–Gimblett, B. (1976) *Speech Play: Research and Resources for Linguistic Creativity*. Philadelphia: University of Pennsylvania Press.

Literature

Hazlitt, W. (1819) *Lectures on English Comic Writers*. London: Taylor & Hessey.
Leonard, F. M. *Laughter in the Courts of Love: Comedy in Allegory*. Norman, Ok.: Pilgrim Books.
Schmitz, N. (1983) *Of Huck and Alice: Humorous Writing in American Literature*. Minneapolis: University of Minnesota Press.
Tittler, J. (1984) *Narrative Irony in the Contemporary Spanish-American Novel*. Ithaca: Cornell University Press.

Mathematics

Paulos, J. A. (1980) *Mathematics and Humor*. Chicago: University of Chicago Press.

Medicine

Moody, R. A. (1978) *Laugh after Laugh: The Healing Power of Humor*. Jacksonville, Fla.: Headwaters Press.
Cousins, N. (1979) *Anatomy of an Illness*. New York: W. H. Norton.

Nursing

Robinson, W. M. (1977) *Humor and the Health Professions*. Thorofare, N.J.: Charles B. Slack.

Philosophy

Paulos, J. A. (1985) *I Think, Therefore I Laugh: An Alternative Approach to Philosophy*. New York: Columbia University Press.

Politics

Shutz, C. E. (1977) *Political Humor*. Cranbury, NJ: Associated University Press.

Psychology of Personality

Fry, W. and Allen, M. *Make 'em Laugh: Life Study of Comedy Writers*. Palo Alto, Ca.:
     Science and Behavior Books.
Fisher, S. and Fisher, R. (1981) *Pretend the World Is Funny and Forever: A Psychological
     Analysis of Comedians, Clowns and Actors*. Hillside, NJ: Lawrence Erlbaum.
Ziv, A. (1984) *Personality and Sense of Humor*. New York: Springer.

Psychotherapy

Kuhlman, T. L. (1984) *Humor and Psychotherapy*. Homewood, Ill.: Dow Jones-Irwin.

Religion

Hyers, C. (1981) *The Comic Vision and the Christian Faith*. New York: Pilgrim Press.
Samra, C. (1985) *Jesus Put on a Happy Face*. Kalamazoo, Mi.: Rosejoy.

Sociology

Koller, M. (1985) *Humor: A Sociological Perspective*. Houston: Cap and Gown Press.

Subject Index

Aborigines, 5

Absurd, 42, 55, 60, 65, 67, 72–75, 79, 87, 109, 114, 128–130, 141, 144, 145, 150, 152, 154, 206

Actors. *See names of specific actors*

Adultery, 38, 53, 80, 152. *See also* Cuckolds; Jokes

Advertising, humor, 49, 175, 178

Aggressive humor: in Australia, 2, 20, 22, 23–24; in Belgium, 37, 40, 45–47; demographic conditions causing, 2, 3; in France, 62, 80; in Great Britain, 100–101, 108–109; in Israel, 115, 125, 129–130; in Italy, 143, 151–152; in United States, 175–176, 178–179; in Yugoslavia, 193, 204–205. *See also* Weapon, humor as

Amusement, 37, 38, 57, 59, 150, 202. *See also* Behavior; Carnivals

Anecdotes, 8, 24, 38, 60, 72, 197, 200, 205

Animals, in humorous creations, 33, 56, 66–68, 78, 89, 98, 138, 164, 169, 196, 205. *See also* Art; Cartoons/Caricatures

Antiheroes, 79, 118

April Fool's Day, 21, 57, 88, 135

Art, humorous: in Australia, 7, 10; in Belgium, 34, 36, 38, 39, 42; in France, 65–68, 73, 74, 76; in Israel, 121; in Italy, 138, 142, 150; in United States, 164, 169, 183; in Yugoslavia, 202

Associations connected to humor, 17, 27, 44

Audience: appreciation, 99, 106; engaging, in humorous dialogues, 79, 101,

Name Index

About the Editor and Contributors

FRANÇOISE BARIAUD is a research fellow at the French National Research Institute, and teaches psychology at Paris University. She is the author of *Children's Humor Development* and *Adolescents' Time Perspectives*.

HENRI BAUDIN is Professor at Grenoble University and founder of the Center for Study of Humor and Communication. He is author of *Boris Vian—Humorist* and *The Metamorphosis of the Comic and the Renewal of the French Theatre from Jarry to Giraudoux*, and is editor of *Journal du Comique and Communication*.

PAOLO CONSIGLI is a medical doctor and humor scholar, interested in the development of humor in arts and literature. In addition to his professional work he has written articles on Italian humor, and is a regular contributor to the Italian magazine *Humor Graphic*.

PETER CROFTS is a stand-up comedian and writer. He is the founder of Comedy and Laughter League and his book, *Super Humor*, is now in preparation.

HYRAM DAVIS is an actor and writer. He wrote the filmscript for *Yatungka and Warri—An Aboriginal Love Story* and the play *Hard Act to Follow*. He presented papers at the First and Second International Conference on Jewish Humor.

KEN DONELSON is a Professor of English at Arizona State University. He has written extensively on media, English education, and censorship.

NELLY FEUERHAHN is a psychologist and research fellow at the French National Research Institute. She has written articles in developmental psychology, and has presented papers at International Conferences on Humor.

VLADIMIR KOLESARIĆ is Professor of Experimental Psychology at the University of Zagreb. His main interests are in psychophysics, perception, and humor.

MIRJANA KRIZMANIĆ is Professor of Clinical Psychology at the University of Zagreb. Her research interests include stress and health problems, personality, and humor.

ALLEEN PACE NILSEN is a Professor of Education and Assistant Dean of the Graduate College at Arizona State University. She is the author of *Dust in Our Desks: Territory Days to the Present in Arizona Schools* and *Presenting M. E. Kerr*. With Ken Donelson, she edited *English Journal* from 1980–1987.

DON L. F. NILSEN is a Professor of English Linguistics at Arizona State University. He is the author of *Toward a Semantic Specification of Deep Case* and *English Adverbial*. With his wife, Alleen Pace Nilsen, he chairs the annual conferences of the *World Humor and Irony Membership Serial Yearbook* (WHIMSY). Together they have published *Language Play: An Introduction to Linguistics*.

J.- P. VAN NOPPEN is Chairman of the Department of Linguistics and a Lecturer at the Vrije Universiteit Brussel. He is the author of *Spatial Theography: A Linguistic Analysis of Expression and Communication in British Popular Theology*.

JERRY PALMER is Senior Lecturer in the Arts at the London Polytechnic. He has published two books on popular culture, *Thrillers: Genesis and Structure of a Popular Genre* and *The Logic of the Absurd: On Film and Television Comedy*.

ANTUN ROHAČEK was Associate Professor of Comparative Psychology at the University of Zagreb, and worked mainly in the areas of psychophysics and humor.

JUDITH STORA-SENDOR teaches Comparative Literature at Paris University. She is the author of *Jewish Humor in Literature from Job to Woody Allen*.

H.-W. D. AM ZEHNHOFF is a Lecturer and Head of the German Department at the Brussel College of Administration and Economics. Author of *The Parody in the Satirical Writings of Kurt Tucholsky*, he has also written articles in comparative literature, parody, and humor.

AVNER ZIV is a Professor of Educational Psychology at Tel Aviv University where he was chairman of the Department of Educational Sciences for four years. As author of twelve books translated into six languages, he has written on humor in education (*L'houmor en Education: approche psychologique*, Paris, 1979), and is also the author of *Humor and Personality* (Springer, New York, 1984) and *Psychology of Humor* (Yahdav, 1981). He was chairman of the Fourth International Conference on Humor and of the First and Second International Conferences on Jewish Humor.